This Side of Silence

Pennsylvania Studies in Human Rights

Bert B. Lockwood, Jr., Series Editor

A complete list of books in the series is available from the publisher.

This Side of Silence

Human Rights, Torture, and the Recognition of Cruelty

Tobias Kelly

PENN

UNIVERSITY OF PENNSYLVANIA PRESS

PHILADELPHIA

Published by
University of Pennsylvania Press
Philadelphia, Pennsylvania 19104-4112
www.upenn.edu/pennpress

Printed in the United States of America on acid-free paper
10 9 8 7 6 5 4 3 2 1

Library of Congress Cataloging-in-Publication Data

Kelly, Tobias.
    This side of silence : human rights, torture, and the recognition of cruelty / Tobias Kelly. — 1st ed.
        p. cm. — (Pennsylvania studies in human rights)
    Includes bibliographical references and index.
    ISBN 978-0-8122-4373-4 (hardcover : alk. paper)
    1. Torture—Moral and ethical aspects—Great Britain.   2. Political prisoners—Abuse of—Great Britain.   3. Political prisoners—Legal status, laws, etc.—Great Britain.
4. Suffering—Political aspects—Great Britain.   5. Human rights—Great Britain.   I. Title.
II. Series: Pennsylvania studies in human rights.
HV8599.G8K45   2012
364.6′7—dc23
                                                                    2011023289

For Faye and Matilda

The great maxim of all civilized legal systems, that the burden of proof must always rest with the accuser, sprang from the insight that only guilt can be irrefutably proved. Innocence, on the contrary, to the extent that it is more than "not guilty," cannot be proved but must be accepted on oath, whereby the trouble is that this faith cannot be supported by the given word, which can be a lie.

—Hannah Arendt, *On Revolution*

If we had a keen vision and feeling of all ordinary human life, it would be like hearing the grass grow and the squirrel's heart beat, and we should die of that roar which lies on the other side of silence.

—George Eliot, *Middlemarch*

Contents

Introduction

In late April 2002 Binyam Mohamed was turned over to the US authorities after being arrested by Pakistani police at Karachi Airport. Mohamed was born in Ethiopia but in the mid-1990s had claimed asylum in the United Kingdom. He had converted to Islam in 2001, and later the same year traveled to Afghanistan and then Pakistan. Following Mohamed's detention in Pakistan, he was interviewed by Federal Bureau of Investigation (FBI) agents and flown to Morocco, where he was imprisoned for eighteen months. Mohamed was then sent to a detention center run by the Central Intelligence Agency (CIA) in Afghanistan, and finally, in September 2004, he was sent to Guantanamo Bay. The US military alleged that Mohamed had been trained in Kabul to make "dirty bombs" and was planning to carry out an attack on US soil. The charges against him were eventually dropped, and he was released and returned to the United Kingdom in early 2009.

While Mohamed was in Guantanamo Bay, he made allegations that he had been tortured when he was in Pakistan, Morocco, and Afghanistan. A US court later ruled that Mohamed's "trauma lasted for 2 long years. During that time, he was physically and psychologically tortured. His genitals were mutilated. He was deprived of sleep and food. He was summarily transported from one foreign prison to another. Captors held him in stress positions for days at a time."[1] Back in the United Kingdom, Mohamed's lawyers filed a petition in the courts demanding that the Foreign Office turn over all the evidence they had about his abuse. In the summer of 2008, English judges ruled that any documents held by British authorities should be given to Mohamed's lawyers but not made public, on the grounds that their full disclosure could harm the intelligence relationship between the United Kingdom and the United States. The judges also found that British agents had "facilitated" Mohamed's interviews by the Pakistani and American security services.[2] Two years later, English Appeal Court judges ruled that if it "had been administered on behalf of the United Kingdom," the treatment inflicted on Mohamed by US officials "would clearly have been in breach of the undertakings given by the United Kingdom."[3] They also ruled that all evidence about Mohamed's ill-treatment must be released.[4]

Alan Johnson, the British home secretary at the time, responded to the judicial rulings and newspaper headlines that followed by saying that allegations of British complicity in torture were a "gross and offensive misrepresentation of the truth" (Naughton and O'Neil 2010). The Metropolitan Police Service, however, announced that it was launching a criminal investigation into the involvement of the British security services in Mohamed's ill-treatment. In addition, Mohamed's lawyers launched a claim for civil damages, suing the Foreign Office, the Home Office, and the Attorney General, as well as MI6 and MI5, for their complicity in his unlawful detention and ill-treatment. In 2010, the newly elected Conservative-Liberal coalition government declared that once criminal and civil proceedings had come to an end, it would launch a judicial inquiry to "look at whether Britain was implicated in the improper treatment of detainees, held by other countries, that may have occurred in the aftermath of 9/11."[5] By the autumn of the same year, Kenneth Clarke, the new minister of justice, told parliament that an out-of-court settlement had been reached. He argued that if the case had continued, "Our reputation as a country that believes in human rights, justice, fairness and the rule of law . . . risks being tarnished."[6] Clarke added that no admission of liability had been made and that the details of the settlement were to remain confidential. The following day, the director of public prosecutions announced that the MI5 officer investigated for complicity with Mohamed's ill-treatment in Pakistan and Morocco would not be prosecuted.

Since 2001, images of tortured bodies and the claims and counter-claims they generate have shaped much international politics. Binyam Mohamed's case was just one among many. Probably the most infamous incident involved the release of pictures of American troops mistreating Iraqi detainees in Abu Ghraib prison. After the release of these photographs, there were further revelations about ill-treatment by the US military in Guantanamo and Bagram, as well as the use of secret detention centers and "extraordinary rendition" to places where torture was, in effect, outsourced. In the United Kingdom, the photographs from Abu Ghraib have also been overlaid by several subsequent events. Six months after the invasion of Iraq, British soldiers used stress positions and beatings on Iraqi detainees, resulting in the death of one man and the hospitalization of others. A few years later, photographs were released showing British soldiers forcing Iraqi detainees to simulate oral and anal sex. In another story, which was later revealed to be a hoax, a British newspaper published photographs apparently showing soldiers carrying out mock executions of Iraqi detainees.[7] As well as the claims made by Binyam Mohamed, other allegations were made about the complicity of MI5 and MI6 in torture carried out by Pakistan and Egypt, among other countries. Further controversies arose over the use of British airspace in the "extraordinary rendition" of detainees to places outside the protection of the law. The list of examples could go on.

Torture is a word with immense ethical, political, and cultural power, seeming to encompass all that is wrong with arbitrary and excessive power. It has become seen as close to the very worst thing that can happen to someone or that one person can do to another. One respected commentator has even argued that it is worse than all forms of killing (Shue 2004). Many people would concur. Some may disagree over the definition of torture, but in doing so they are not challenging the privileged status of torture as a form of suffering and cruelty above nearly all others. To be sure, the moral objection to torture is not universal. However, torture is still not something that many people will openly admit to doing. Perpetrators will dress up their acts in euphemisms, deny that what they have done counts as torture, or dance around the edge of definitional debates. Torture remains beyond the pale, in words if not in deeds. It is not a term that is going to be given a positive spin any time soon. Even those who would condone the use of torture in very specific circumstances say they do so with heavy hearts (see, for example, Elshtain 2004). From this perspective, torture is still very wrong but just not quite as wrong as other things.

Current debates about torture are saturated with law. In the United States, lawyers were involved in writing memos that justified nearly every aspect of military and CIA interrogation programs. Since the memos were made public, there have been numerous court cases concerning the treatment of detainees. In the United Kingdom, the meanings and implications of torture have been thrashed out in a number of legal and quasi-legal forums. The extensive litigation around Binyam Mohamed was just one of several cases. Conflicts have ranged over the protections owed to torture survivors, the responsibilities of those complicit in the perpetration of torture, and the United Kingdom's international human rights obligations. These disputes have taken place in court-martials, judicial inquiries, immigration cases, reports before UN monitoring mechanisms, appearances before the European Court of Human Rights, and in domestic civil litigation, among others. Legal forums have entered deep into the political arena, as judges have been asked to adjudicate on some of the most contentious contemporary concerns. Not only have judges become heavily politicized in this process, but politics has become judicialized.

We are increasingly accustomed to thinking about responses to cruelty and violence in terms of the legal category of torture. However, this has not always been the case. It is only since the late twentieth century that torture has been associated with precise legal definitions and thought of as a specific human rights violation above nearly all others. Over the last three hundred years, the meanings ascribed to torture have changed from a legitimate judicial procedure to elicit the truth, to be seen as the very worst infraction of the physical, psychological and moral integrity of human beings. Our current understandings of torture are a product of ongoing struggles between nongovernmental organizations (NGOs), governments, and international organizations, as concerns over post cold war armed conflict, medical notions of trauma, and concerns about immigration have all come together.

To stress the historical contingency of the legal category of torture is not to say that people do not act cruelly, and that people do not suffer. Rather, it is to ask why this person's suffering and not that of the next is taken into account, why this form of pain and not another is deemed significant, and why this action and not another is recognized as torture. The point is not to trivialize the suffering of torture survivors nor to denigrate the effort of all those who work against torture. Neither is it to relativize torture or to deconstruct it into thin air. At its heart, the concept of torture contains a crucial ethical concept: People should not be treated cruelly and the deliberate infliction of pain is something that should be avoided at (nearly) all costs. It is also important to recognize that the fight against torture can serve as an important "tool in the demand for justice" (Fassin and Rechtman 2009, 279). The struggle to prohibit torture has made a real difference to people's lives around the world. However, it is important to note that our concepts of torture do not include all possible harms and that legal processes do more than neutrally recognize when torture takes place. They determine what acts count as torture and how we should respond.

This book asks what can be seen and said, and what has to be ignored, when we understand suffering and cruelty through the legal category of torture. In doing so, it treats torture as, above all, a problem of recognition. One of the dominant cultural images of the torture survivor is a body wracked by pain, crying out in anguish, unable to express what has happened to him or her (Scarry 1988). However, the problem of recognition is not caused by the inability of the survivor to communicate. Binyam Mohamed, for example, could give long, articulate statements about his treatment in detention.[8] The issue is, instead, one of our ability to listen, to see, to name, and to take responsibility for what is in front of us. The key question is therefore what types of victim and perpetrator, what forms of innocence and guilt, do legal understandings of torture allow us to acknowledge?

Whereas most recent books on torture have focused on why it happens, the ethics of the prohibition of torture, or the effects of torture on its victims, I will examine empirically how real or supposed instances of torture are constructed, debated, questioned, and brought into focus. Much analytical ink has been spilled in trying to define the ethical and legal boundaries of what does and does not count as torture.[9] The topic was given an added urgency by the attempts of the George W. Bush administration to redefine where the line between acceptable and unacceptable treatment of detainees lay. But torture is not simply an abstract category to be debated in terms of broad principles. The issue is not merely about choosing between competing legal or ethical norms but about deciding how and whether those norms apply to any given situation. It is not simply about setting out the rules clearly but about making a judgment about how and whether those rules apply in specific contexts (compare Anderson 2011). It is therefore important to examine the concrete dilemmas and difficulties involved in documenting and recognizing when torture has taken place. If, as Stanford Levinson has argued, "Torture as a term is a place holder—an abstract word made concrete by the imagination of the reader" (2004, 27), it is through the everyday practices of the lawyers, judges, doctors, psychologists, and bureaucrats charged with documentation and recognition that the implications of what is and what is not torture are produced.

The central argument of this book is that although the legal category of torture appears to prioritize individual suffering and cruelty, the turn to law can make it very difficult to recognize specific survivors and perpetrators. In part, this is because torture can be inflicted in ways that produce few identifiable traces. As Darius Rejali has shown, the twentieth century saw the development of coercive interrogation techniques specially designed to leave behind no evidence (2009). However, the issue is broader than simply the techniques through which torture is perpetrated. Although the prohibition of torture may be absolute in principle, in practice it becomes slippery and indeterminate when applied to concrete cases, making demands for forms of proof that are often unobtainable. Legal processes can therefore give with one hand, promising to protect and prosecute, and take away with another, by setting conditions that are very hard to meet. In this context, legal discussions of torture tend to break down into arguments about due process and the rule of law. The suffering of specific individuals and the intentions of particular perpetrators melt into the background. We are left with broad ethical injunctions and general procedural guidelines.

Focusing on the United Kingdom in a book about torture may at first glance appear a little peculiar. There is an implicit bias in many social science studies of human rights toward states that are seen as being unstable, authoritarian, and illiberal. However, in this process not only are the often-contradictory ways in which human rights are embedded within established liberal democracies ignored but, perhaps more important, it is often assumed that human rights are only a real problem for non-Western states. Britain's role as a junior partner in the "war on terror" has disturbed many of these assumptions. Even before this, anyone with a cursory acquaintance with the history of British involvement in Ireland, Cyprus, Kenya, or Aden; France in Algeria; or the United States in the Philippines or Vietnam would know that torture has not been practiced only by rogue states. Furthermore, although much of the critical focus in the last ten years has been on the decisions made by the Bush administration, this has had the effect of narrowing the discussion and ignoring the greater historical depth and wider import of debates about what does and what does not count as torture. Torture, as a category, is often used to draw a line between the civilized and the uncivilized, the compassionate and the barbarous. Focusing on the United Kingdom, rather than on, say, Iraq, might help us rethink where those boundaries lie.

Torture has been a key trope through which Britain has related to the rest of the world, caught between the self-imposed duty to "save" distant others from suffering, and the desire to "protect" its own citizens from seemingly threatening outsiders. In the United Kingdom, a history of colonial expansion and retraction has given the word *torture* its very own political and ethical connotations. In the early twenty-first century, as the concept of torture moves between the laws of war and asylum, the tension within Britain's international relationships are laid bare. These contradictions can be seen most clearly in its relationship with the citizens and states of the broad arc from North Africa to Central Asia. On the one hand, the human rights and refugee principles to which the British government has committed promise to save people fleeing from torture in Iraq, Algeria, Afghanistan, and elsewhere. On the other hand, British security policy toward many of those same states can sit uneasily with ethical injunctions against any involvement in torture. Binyam Mohamed, for example, had come to the United Kingdom claiming protection but ended up suing the British state for its complicity in his torture.

At this stage, it is important to make it clear what I am *not* trying to do. I am not investigating the complicity of UK officials in torture. Although the issue is important, an anthropologist is probably not the best person to carry out such a project. I am also not exploring the different definitions of torture. Again, such a project is best left to a philosopher or lawyer, and there are numerous impressive examples.[10] Furthermore, I am not attempting to examine whether torture can ever be justified. Once more, not only is an anthropologist not the best person for this job, but there is already a vast literature on this issue.[11] Finally, I am not attempting to examine the impact of torture on survivors. I am neither a doctor nor a psychologist and am not in any way qualified to make such an evaluation. Rather, I am investigating the ways in which legal processes classify, sort, and prioritize different forms of suffering and cruelty, in order to bring the processes they label "torture" into view.

Understanding Torture

What do we talk about when we talk about torture? We might take it for granted that lawyers have a special place in the conversation, but this is far from inevitable. In this section, I will outline five different but related ways of understanding torture—the ethical, the political, the therapeutic, the sentimental, and the legal—before explaining why this book focuses on the last. The distinctions are not hard and fast, and the different understandings play an important role in informing one another. However, the distinctions can serve as a useful heuristic device, as they highlight the ways in which different types of intervention create alternative notions of victim, perpetrator and remedy.

The ethical objection to torture rests on two legs: suffering and cruelty. It is an abhorrence of the deliberate infliction of pain, in a direct infringement of another person's dignity, which lies at the heart of the objection to torture. As philosopher Henry Shue has argued, torture is inflicted on the defenseless, forced on those who cannot fight back (2004). Equally important, the objection to torture is based on an abhorrence of the particular intent of the perpetrator. As Judith Shklar has implied, torture is the worst form of cruelty (1984). It was, for example, the fact that the photographs from Abu Ghraib showed the soldiers enjoying their brutality that was particularly disturbing.

Along with such ethical claims, the argument against torture can also take a political shape. In the eighteenth and nineteenth centuries, the campaign against torture was used to mark opposition to the ancien régime in the name of the values of enlightened liberalism (Peters 1996, 75). Voltaire, for example, turned the judicial torture of Jean Calas, a French Protestant convicted of killing his son, into a cause célèbre, standing for all that was wrong about intolerance, arbitrariness, and unnecessary cruelty (1764). Similarly, the Italian philosopher and politician Cesare Beccaria's polemic *On Crime and Punishment* became a central text in campaigns for penal reform from the late eighteenth century (1778). In his short book, Beccaria condemns torture, as well as the death penalty, as historical anachronisms. As a utilitarian philosopher, Beccaria's principle objection to torture was not simply that it caused suffering, but rather that it was outdated and inefficient. He wrote, for example, that "by this method the robust will escape and the feeble be condemned" (1778, 64). For Beccaria, torture was above all an issue of due process. In late eighteenth-century Europe, campaigns against judicial torture therefore brought into focus a wider critique of the legal and political regime.

In the twentieth century, an aversion to torture was used to mark opposition to totalitarian forms of government, from both left and right. Torture was seen as standing in absolute opposition to liberal democracy, and its presence was a key, and often problematic, marker of distinction between modern democracy and authoritarianism. Amnesty International, for example, wrote, "Torture has by all indication increased over the last few years . . . [I]ncreasing perpetration is accounted for by states who use torture as a means of governing. Torture in those countries plays an integral role in the political system itself" (1973, 17). Furthermore, in 1970s North America and Western Europe, as the numbers of refugees from totalitarian regimes in Eastern and Southern Europe, as well as in South America, grew, opposition to torture became a way of expressing solidarity with political exiles. Crucially, as both eighteenth- and twentieth-century political understandings of torture were aimed at reforming the state, emphasis was placed on state officials as perpetrators, significantly narrowing the ethical objection to torture as an infringement on human dignity. It is this emphasis on state officials that has run through the human rights campaigns of the late twentieth and early twenty-first centuries.

A third way of understanding torture treats it as a particular type of trauma, and therefore an issue of therapy. Although a focus on suffering may grow out of an ethical objection to torture, for the eighteenth-century anti-torture polemicists torture was not a distinct experience; rather, it was part of a broader process of irrational punishment. Indeed, much of Beccaria's concern was with the coarsening effects of torture on those who witnessed it rather than on the victims themselves. However, from the mid- to late twentieth century, there was growing emphasis on the unique nature of the pain and suffering experienced by torture victims. The presence of large-scale refugee populations in Europe and the United States, with their own vulnerabilities and health needs, also saw an increasing emphasis on torture as a physical and psychological problem (Pupavac 2008). Medical doctors, psychologists, psychiatrists, and psychoanalysts became central figures in the production of knowledge about torture. In many places, the anti-torture movement became a torture rehabilitation movement, focused on providing therapeutic services—rather than political or legal reform—to those in need. There was also therefore a potential, although not always fulfilled, move away from an emphasis on state officials as perpetrators. If torture is a unique and specific form of suffering, it can seem irrelevant if the perpetrator is a police officer or a former boyfriend.

Along with ethical, political, and therapeutic notions of torture lies what might be called a "sentimental" understanding (Peters 1996; Rorty 1993). In the early twenty-first century, the word *torture* is widely used to describe intolerable and objectionable forms of pain and cruelty inflicted on people. In 2009, when two boys aged eleven and ten beat two other boys to death in northern England, the ordeal was widely described as "torture" (Walker and Wainwright 2010). That same year, a mother who killed her disabled son by injecting him with heroin told the court before she was sentenced that his life was "torture" (Rojas 2010). The term can also be used in everyday language to describe unpleasant experiences, such as the morning commute, a particularly difficult exam, or a visit with one's in-laws. The sense of intense suffering found in the ethical or trauma-based understandings of torture are used to signify displeasure and dislike of relatively mundane events.

In expanding the notion of who can be responsible for torture, as well as the forms of pain and suffering that it involves, there is a danger of diluting the meaning of torture. The risk exists of spreading the idea of torture too thin and of applying the notion to any sort of discomfort, robbing the word of ethical or political force. Legal practices have historically given torture its greatest definitional coherence, albeit often drawing on broader ethical objections and forms of knowledge that come from clinical practice and political activism. More specifically, the concept of torture has its origins in legal practices concerned with the correct procedures for interrogations and the provision of evidence. John Langbein has argued that the growth of judicial torture in medieval Europe was not simply the product of an arbitrary and a capricious politics but rather a desire to create legally reliable evidence (2006). It is from this particular judicial history that we get the sense that torture is the deliberate infliction of pain by state officials in order to collect information.

Despite this judicial history, by the end of the nineteenth century, torture was widely considered a primarily ethical and political category that was used to critique practices felt to be uncivilized, irrational, and inefficient (Peters 1996, 75). It was only after World War II and late into the twentieth century that the concept of torture began to regain greater legal precision, as principles of due process, criminal law, and international human rights came together, often in contradictory ways. In 1948, the Universal Declaration of Human Rights (UDHR) stated that no one should be subjected to torture or other forms of ill-treatment. However, the following years saw a realization among human rights campaigners that without the power of enforcement, the UDHR would remain solely aspirational. As a result, NGOs, some governments, and many people within the United Nations lobbied for the increasing codification of human rights and the creation of legal mechanisms of enforcement.

Because torture was a crime perpetrated by state officials, the anti-torture movement sought to appeal to a higher authority, above and beyond the state, and therefore turned to international law. The meanings and implications of torture have therefore been shaped by international institutions, such as the United Nations, and NGOs, such as Amnesty International. As such, to talk about torture is to always bring into play wider international politics. By the start of the twenty-first century, the prohibition of torture could be found in numerous international conventions, protocols, and agreements, including the Geneva Conventions, the Universal Declaration of Human Rights, the UN Convention Against Torture, and the European Convention on Human Rights.[12]

This legalization of the definition of torture does not mean that wider ethical, political, therapeutic, or sentimental definitions of torture are not widely used. Nor does it mean that legal dominance of understandings of torture is uncontested. The torture rehabilitation movement, in particular, has played an important role in current understandings of torture, pushing the boundaries of legal claims. Clinicians and political activists can often be exasperated with the narrow formalism of legal approaches to torture, pushing at its edges to include wider forms of suffering and more varied responses. Furthermore, and perhaps most important, legal understandings of torture are not self-enclosed. Legal processes can often draw on other forms of expertise—medicine in particular—to provide evidence about pain and suffering. In addition, there are significant tensions within legal attempts to define what counts as torture. Specifically, there are disagreements about the level of pain and suffering necessary to be considered an act of torture, the nature of intention, and the relative balance between the level of pain and intention in distinguishing torture from other forms of ill-treatment.

Nevertheless, legal forums remain the central place where the precise meanings of torture are debated and recognized. Furthermore, political and clinical movements often refer to international conventions when defining what they do. It is legal forums that decide on the criminal prosecutions, civil damages, and grants of residency, among other things, that do or do not follow from claims of torture. As Samuel Moyn has argued, law has become our "privileged instrument for moral improvement" (2010, 211). It is therefore of crucial importance to ask what are the implications of entering the legal realm for the ways we seek to allocate responsibility, redress and the promise of protection.

Issues of Recognition

In early 2004, I was approached by a British immigration lawyer to write a report to support the claim of one of her clients for asylum in the United Kingdom. I had previously carried out research in Israel and Palestine, and I am therefore often called on to provide evidence in refugee cases involving people originating in that area. The client, whom I shall call Hassan Ahmed, was a Palestinian from the West Bank. He claimed to be a former activist in the Popular Front for the Liberation of Palestine. Ahmed had told his lawyer that on several occasions throughout the 1990s he had been detained by the Israeli military. During these detentions, he had been beaten, had been forced to crouch in a sitting position in a cold cell for hours on end, and had his hands forcibly tied behind his back and yanked upward. He was never charged with any offense but was kept for several different three-month periods in administrative detention. He had also been detained by the Palestinian Authority *mukhabarat* (secret police), who had dealt with him in a similar way. Ahmed eventually decided to leave the West Bank and had found his way to the United Kingdom overland, traveling through Syria, Turkey, Bulgaria, Romania, and onward in the back of a lorry.

Ahmed's lawyer was now trying to collect enough evidence to support his case for asylum. The witness statement that Ahmed had produced was full of intricate and precise details about what the Israelis and the Palestinians had done to him. However, it was also rambling and at times confused. Ahmed had long-standing mental health issues, some of which seemed to predate his detention, making his memories often erratic. A medical doctor had examined Ahmed and found no scars on his body that he could document and also said that it would be difficult to say, with any certainty, to what extent Ahmed's forgetfulness and occasional delusions were the result of his mistreatment in the West Bank. The lawyer had turned to me to try to corroborate his case. Amnesty International, Human Rights Watch, and even the US State Department have all documented the use of torture and other forms of ill-treatment by the Israelis and the Palestinians.[13] However, although I could document the situation regarding the general treatment of detainees, I could not write a report that said there was specific evidence that Ahmed had been tortured. Without this, it was open to the immigration authorities to say, "Yes, torture happens, but we do not think it happened in this case." Ahmed was therefore forced to rely heavily on his own witness statement. His lawyer was concerned that his account would not be believed. She was right to be worried. Ahmed's case for asylum was denied. His account was deemed by the immigration authorities not to be credible.

How can we recognize when torture has taken place? Elaine Scarry has argued that the distinctive nature of torture lies in its ability to destroy the capacity to communicate (1988). For Scarry, the pain of torture can produce silence, as victims turn in on themselves. However, the idea that the pain of torture is a fundamentally private experience denies the ways in which pain is itself a social relationship. As Veena Das argues, the statement "I am in pain" is a declarative statement that does not seek to describe a state, but to voice a complaint (1997). Ahmed was able to articulate his experiences; the problem he faced was that people did not believe him. The issue is therefore not so much that victims cannot voice their suffering, but that lawyers, doctors, and other practitioners find it difficult to know when and where legally significant cruelty has taken place. This is not to say that the pain of the victim of torture can be directly experienced by another. There is always an "irreproducible excess in pain" (Asad 2003, 85; Lyotard 1989). All attempts to grapple with the meanings and implications of any horrific form of suffering, not just torture, can seem to fail to do them justice. However, pain and suffering are not all about incommensurability. The experience of pain is always at least partly constituted by social interaction. As such, the problem of torture is not one of the failure of language but of the failure of recognition. It is not the survivor's inability to speak; rather, it is our inability to listen.

The issue here is not the ability of the law to grasp and represent the full experience of suffering and cruelty in its entirety, for what would be the point of that? To grasp pain in its fullness would only be to reproduce it (Perrin 2004). Rather than addressing profound questions about experience, legal forms of recognition are above all pragmatic—they are about the granting of residency rights, passing prison sentences, and allocating compensation—and as such they seek to recognize pain and suffering in very particular ways. As Andrew Williams argues, what counts as a wrong, as far as legal processes are concerned, is not suffering in and of itself, but the breach of a legal norm. To count as a legal harm, suffering therefore has to be framed according to the correct legal categories and standards of evidence (2007). To be a legal violation, there must be a victim, a perpetrator, and a remedy. To be accepted, a claim must adhere to procedural rules and evidentiary tests. Many claims about suffering and cruelty simply will not meet these standards (Veitch 2007). The legal recognition of torture is therefore not about sharing intimate experiences, making deep claims about the nature of being, or acknowledging the other with all their differences and similarities (see, for example, Honneth 1996; Povinelli 2002). Legal recognition is instead instrumental, concerned with the distribution of rights and the acceptance of obligations, and the meeting of the conditions necessary to make those decisions.

Yet, the legal recognition of torture is never a neat process. Behind the façade of certainty found in legal definitions, the concrete recognition of torture is itself shot through with disjunctures and fissures. It is marked as much by gaps that have to be continually jumped over, as it is by internal coherence. In this context, the task is not to examine how the processes of recognizing torture bleach out and thin down subjective experiences but rather to explore how the legal recognition of torture produces multilayered and often contradictory forms of knowledge about suffering and cruelty.

Recognition has its twin in the form of denial. Given the special stigma attached to torture, denial is often the immediate response in the face of an accusation. As the direct or indirect involvement of a public official is one of the key components of torture, the full resources of a state can be put into denying that torture took place. Denial is rarely just the act of an individual but is publicly sanctioned. There are a range of reasons for refusing to acknowledge torture. As Stanley Cohen has argued, these reasons can include the simple calculus of realpolitik or compassion fatigue, among other things (2000). The mechanism through which denial takes place can include individuals turning a blind eye, a bureaucratic deferral of responsibility, or simply the renaming of an atrocity as something else. As Cohen has also argued, denial is not the opposite of knowledge (2000). To say that someone is in denial, you must also be able to say that at some level, the person knows what is happening. There is no simple opposition between a truth and a lie or between knowledge and ignorance, but instead, both sides of the coin can be bound to one another in complex ways, forming "public secrets" or "unknown knowns" (Taussig 1999; Zizek 2004). The forms of denial involved in legal processes are very particular. Legal processes can know about events but deem them, legally, irrelevant. The relationship between legal denial and recognition is therefore not simply about the inability to speak truth to power. Such an argument would assume that the legal category of torture exists as an ahistorical or a metaphysical category. Rather, sorting among all the forms of violence that are inflicted on a daily basis, legal processes seek to make a series of historically contingent distinctions between legitimate and illegitimate force, in the full knowledge that they are producing a limited picture of suffering and cruelty.

Evidence of Torture

The legal recognition of torture is a problem of evidence. Talal Asad has argued that at the heart of the concept of torture is the notion of a universally comparable form of suffering, the precise levels of which can be calculated (2003, 117). However, in practice, torture resists easy measurement. Under most definitions, for an act to be considered torture, along with the direct or indirect involvement of a public official, it must contain at least two further elements: a severe level of pain in the victim and the intention of the perpetrator. However, although pain may be a universal and an inherently social experience, it has famously resisted attempts at replicable measurement. Far from creating an easily replicable standard, the emphasis on pain generates questions about the very subjective nature of the experience. Intention also raises its own often awkward evidentiary issues, as it implies a particular state of mind and therefore requires inferences about private thoughts and beliefs.

In assessing evidence, legal processes rarely treat the individual claims of torture survivors as self-evident. Survivors often face a general skepticism that their claims are fabricated. Writing about France, Fassin and d'Halluin argue that as doubts are cast about individual narratives, the body and mind become the places from which attempts are made to read the truth of particular claims (2007). They write, "Scars, both physical and psychological, are the tangible sign that torture did indeed take place and that violent acts were perpetrated" (2007, 599). In a context where the claims of survivors are doubted, medical doctors, psychologists, and social scientists, among others, are called on to provide further evidence about torture. Past suffering becomes accessible only through legal and diagnostic criteria, rather than through direct testimony (Antze and Lambek 1996, xxiv). Claims about torture are therefore often filtered through specific forms of expert knowledge, with their particular understandings of causation and subjectivity. However, courts and other forums often express as much skepticism about professional forms of expertise as they do about the claimants appearing before them. Ahmed, the Palestinian asylum seeker, and his lawyers had tried to collect as much evidence as possible to support his claim, calling on doctors, anthropologists, and the reports of human rights organizations to support his claims after his testimony was deemed not to stand alone.

Yet, even this evidence was limited and questioned by the judges hearing his case. All claims, expert or not, are open to second-guessing. By entering the legal realm, claims of torture must come up against standards of proof which they often cannot meet.

It is important to remember though that the forms of proof demanded by legal processes do not exhaust the ways in which it is possible to talk about torture. When I was carrying out fieldwork in the Occupied West Bank at the height of the second intifada, my Palestinian next-door neighbor, a police officer with the Palestinian Authority, was detained by the Israeli military. Several weeks later, he returned to the village in obvious physical pain and was unable to walk without difficulty. His account of torture (*ta'dhib*) by the Israelis was accepted by everyone in the village without any demand for further evidence or debate about what was or was not torture. In a very different context, as part of the research for this book, I spent time at the offices of the Medical Foundation for the Care of Victims of Torture in London and Glasgow. Among other things, the Medical Foundation provides therapeutic care to survivors of torture, mainly refugees or asylum seekers. The remit of the Medical Foundation focuses on torture, so potential clients are assessed before being accepted. The evaluation of claims in this process, though, is very different from that found in a court of law because it is based on therapeutic practices. Doctors, activists, survivors, and perpetrators can all demand very different forms of proof from legal forums. As legal regimes face different ways of knowing, built on different methodological assumptions, theoretical foundations, and political commitments, there can be a clash of epistemologies. In legal forums, though, it is legal actors who come out on top.

Researching Torture

To explore how, when, and where legal processes make torture visible, and what happens when this occurs, I carried out anthropological fieldwork with lawyers, with human rights groups, at the United Nations, and in British (English and Scottish) courts between early 2004 and the end of 2010.[14] The fieldwork was led by a sense of following the issues, rather than a focus on a particularly bounded location or group of people. I tracked attempts at the legal recognition of torture through different jurisdictions and forms of expertise. In particular, I carried out ethnographic fieldwork at an anti-torture NGO in London and Glasgow over a period of one year. In addition, I followed thirty-five immigration cases from start to finish. I also sat in on British immigration tribunals and criminal court hearings. I made three separate trips to the UN Committee Against Torture (CAT) in Geneva. The research also involved more than 140 interviews with lawyers, judges, police officers, doctors, psychologists, therapists, government officials, human rights activists, and politicians. The questions focused on the problems, dilemmas, and potentials they felt when carrying out their work. This has been supplemented with extensive archival work in London and Geneva and the analysis of domestic case law and international conventions.

Crucial to the nature of the arguments I am making here is the fact that I did not speak to torture survivors, for two reasons. The first was ethical. It would be presumptuous to assume that someone who has been through experiences of immense suffering and pain would necessarily want to recount these experiences to an academic who could offer no obvious or immediate practical help. Although in some cases talking may be cathartic, I am not the right person to undertake such a role. Torture survivors in the United Kingdom, in many cases, are already forced to recount their experiences to a vast array of people, including immigration officials, lawyers, judges, and doctors, and it seemed unnecessary to add to that number. The second reason has to do with the analytical thrust of my arguments: the key issue in cases of torture is one of recognition, of being able to acknowledge when and where torture has taken place. As a result, the focus is on the doctors, lawyers, and officials who are charged with documenting and recognizing incidents of torture. It is their dilemmas and conundrums that I examine. There is of course a real risk here of a double silencing of survivors, by writing them out of the account. However, I am not making any claim to be able to speak in their name. Rather, I am trying to examine how the myriad professionals that they encounter try to understand and document what has happened to them.

There are limitations but also opportunities in carrying out fieldwork in such a context. Many of the issues I examine are highly confidential. They not only involve secret evidence presented behind closed doors but also private patient or client information. Some sources of information, while not confidential, were not obtainable through traditional methods of participant observation. Policy documents, case law, medical reports, and UN conventions, to name just a few, all play a crucial role in shaping the terrain. Although such texts always have to be placed in their historical context, if as anthropologists we want to limit our claims to evidence that can be obtained through participant observation, we are, I believe, unnecessarily limiting what we can say. I believe also that there is something central to anthropology that lies between participant observation and high theory. This is a desire to interrogate our key political and social categories and to explore their implications, histories, and trajectories. It involves a commitment to understanding how these categories are used and understood on the ground, rather than simply examining their abstract or normative properties. Crucially, this skepticism toward categories is not a form of relativism. It is not cynical about torture as a category, but it seeks to look at torture from different angles, based on a desire not to take it for granted.

A Critique of a Focus on Torture?

At this point, I want to examine some of the criticisms that might be made of any attempt to understand cruelty and suffering through the legal category of torture, before setting out why such critiques fail to hit home. Many of these arguments can also be made of much of the broader human rights project, but they are brought into particular focus by the example of the attempt to prohibit torture.

One criticism of a focus on the legal prohibition of torture, is that it unhelpfully narrows the scope of the vision. As John Parry has argued, an emphasis on torture separates it from the wider forms of state violence of which it is a part, drawing an arbitrary line through a wider spectrum of practices (2010). The definition of torture in the UN Convention Against Torture, for example, excludes pain or suffering arising from "lawful sanction," but it is not clear why pain inflicted for legal reasons is any better than other forms of deliberately inflicted suffering. By focusing on the abhorrent and the seemingly abnormal practice of torture there is an obvious danger of implicitly legitimizing other forms of violence perpetrated by the state. Bracketing off torture invites states to play games over where the line lies, rather than dealing with the issue of ill-treatment more broadly.

A second and linked potential criticism is that placing an emphasis on torture reduces politics to an attempt to eradicate pain, rather than economic or political redistribution (compare Berlant 2003; Ticktin 2006a, 2006b). As Wendy Brown puts it, writing more generally, but in terms that could apply directly to torture: "When social 'hurt' is conveyed to the law for resolution, political ground is ceded to moral and juridical ground" (1995, 27). In this process, there is a stress on victimhood, of the suffering of a passive individual who needs to be rescued, rather than an engagement with the broader political and economic processes that produce the infliction of violence.

A third related criticism is the claim that the legalized category of torture is simply inadequate to get to grips with the experience of torture. As Kirsten Hastrup argues, by translating thick moral and political problems into thin legal representations, vast areas of conduct are cut off from acknowledgment (2003). From this perspective, the language of human rights simplifies complex and ambiguous situations, erasing important differences among both victims and perpetrators (Kennedy

2004, 14; Wilson 1996). The multiple experiences of torture cannot be reduced to the dry formal language of universal human rights or legal judgments. The causes and consequences of the ill-treatment of detainees in Guantanamo Bay, Republican prisoners in Northern Ireland, leftist guerrillas in Latin America, dissidents in China, or even child soldiers in Uganda are squeezed into the limited meanings of one word.

The implicit assumption in all three arguments above is that the dominance of the legal notion of torture as a way of understanding suffering and cruelty makes other emancipatory strategies less available. As David Kennedy argues, "As a dominant and fashionable vocabulary for thinking about emancipation, human rights crowds out other ways of understanding harm and recompense" (2002, 108). Attempts to legally recognize when torture has taken place attract resources and energies that might go elsewhere.

Several immediate responses can be made to these points. First, whether or not the categories of law, human rights, and torture blot out other ways of looking at the world is an empirical question; no answer can be given once and for all. Victims, perpetrators, witnesses, and prosecutors can all pursue their own, often complex and contradictory, agendas within the spaces opened up by human rights mechanisms. The word *torture* can be understood in many different ways by all those involved. The legal recognition of individual suffering may be just one goal among many, one way in which people may try to mobilize politically. Wider ethical and political concerns can remain.

Perhaps more important, the simplifications caused by the categories of human rights and torture are not necessarily a problem in and of themselves. Reduction can create new possibilities for action (Law and Mol 2002). Although the use of the word *torture* may gloss over important differences between, say, the acts of the Greek colonels and the Egyptian secret service, it nevertheless provides a useful rallying cry through which global campaigns against state violence can be articulated. The word *torture* has immense force, as a great ethical taboo; therefore, to accuse someone of torture can get people's attention.

Finally, legalization does not necessarily result in depoliticization. To argue as much would be to assume a problematic and crude distinction between law and politics. It would be unfair to assume that no one involved in the litigation around accusations of the complicity of MI5 and MI6 in torture thinks that the issue is not inherently political. The same could be said of the court-martial of British troops in Afghanistan, or decisions over whether the United Kingdom can deport a "terror suspect" to a place where he or she might face torture. Rather than make general statements about whether this is "political" or "legal," one must ask the crucial questions "Who is authorized to speak?" "What are they allowed to say?" and "What types of claims count as persuasive?" It is only by doing so that we can begin to understand how the claimed universal prohibition of torture is made and unmade, again and again, in distinct local contexts.

A criticism that comes from a slightly different angle from those already discussed above, and that has different implications, is that by focusing on violence perpetrated by those acting in the name of the state in particular, the legal category of torture creates discriminatory distinctions between legitimate and illegitimate forms of violence. This has important implications for survivors of domestic violence, for example. From this perspective, the intentions of the perpetrator and the experience of the victim in cases of prisoner and domestic abuse may be similar, and it is therefore arbitrary to distinguish between the two cases simply because one is carried out by someone acting in the name of the state and the other is not (Edwards 2006; McGlynn 2009). The criticism here is not so much that a focus on torture is a problem, but that the way it is defined is limiting. The argument therefore is for a broadening of the notion of torture to include nonstate actors. In partial response, it may be argued that although the classic human rights position may be that only states can be held accountable for human rights abuses, other areas of law, most notably international criminal law, have no such requirements (Burchard 2008). At the same time though, it is important to point out that simply expanding the definition of torture will not inherently expand the scope of protection it offers. The key issue is the conditions of entry into the legal realm. Formal protections are not enough unless we can expand the ground on which people can claim those entitlements.

British Understandings of Torture

The idea that torture happens elsewhere and that Britain has a responsibility to save other people from these horrors is historically ubiquitous, even if not always supported by events, resulting in a number of legal and political contortions. In the spring of 2007, fourteen British marines were detained after the Iranian navy claimed they had strayed into Iran's territorial waters. The British press reacted by implying that the captured marines were most probably being tortured (see, for example, Beeston and Bone 2007). However, after twelve days the marines were released and the worst they had to complain about was being asked to wear some ill-fitting and outdated suits for their handover. A year later, the British army issued an internal report in response to the brutal treatment and unlawful killing of Iraqi citizens by British soldiers in Basra

(Aitken 2008). Des Browne, the minister of defence, issued a statement that said, the "British public should be reassured that such behaviour is not representative of our thoroughly professional and disciplined armed forces" (Ministry of Defence 2008). For the minister of defence, torture was not something that British soldiers did. In contrast, torture was expected of the Iranians.

Judges have not been immune from such assumptions. In 2004, ten men from across North Africa and the Middle East appealed the decision of the British government to certify them as terrorists and effectively detain them without trial. The case before the Court of Appeal was largely based on the argument that much of the evidence used against them had been obtained through torture in their home countries. The Court of Appeal ruled that evidence that might have been obtained through torture was admissible, as long as British officials had not been complicit.[15] The logic of the decision was that as long as British hands were clean, everything was fine. Although the courts could not use evidence collected through torture by British officials, the law did not rule out the use of torture by people in other countries. The decision was later overturned on appeal to the House of Lords. In this decision, Lord Bingham argued, "English common law has regarded torture and its fruits with abhorrence for over 500 years, and that abhorrence is now shared by over 140 countries which have acceded to the Torture Convention."[16] Bingham seemed to be claiming that the international prohibition of torture has its origins in English principles. The House of Lords decision, however, still did not explicitly rule out the use of evidence obtained under torture in intelligence operations, as long as it was not collected with the complicity of British agents.[17]

English legal actors have long had a self-understanding that torture was somehow alien to the principles of its common law. During the eighteenth-century European campaigns to abolish torture in continental Europe, English commentaries were widely self-congratulatory about their own relative rejection of torture. In his treatise on the history of the common law, English judge and academic William Blackstone argued, "It seems astonishing that this usage of administering the torture should be said to arise from a tenderness for the lives of men; and yet this is the reason given for its introduction into the civil law, and its subsequent adoption by the French and other foreign nations" (1829, 325). He also praised the system "in England, where our crown-law is with justice supposed to be more nearly advanced to perfection; where crimes are more accurately defined, and penalties less uncertain and arbitrary; where all our accusations are public, and our trials in the face of the world; where torture is unknown" (1829, 3). For Blackstone, torture was something that happened on the other side of the English Channel.

It is important to note that the English judicial system did not need to torture, as it could convict with virtually no evidence (Langbein 2006, 78). Furthermore, torture had actually continued under special warrant until 1640 (2006, 81). As such, rather than torture being prohibited, it is perhaps more accurate to say that the use of torture was never regularized within English criminal law as a form of interrogation. The English objection to torture was largely because of concerns about its reliability as a source of evidence rather than for humanitarian concerns. As Blackstone argued, it was absurd to be "rating a man's virtue by the hardiness of his constitution, and his guilt by the sensibility of his nerves!" (1829, 329). However, seemingly cruel punishments were still used in the United Kingdom throughout the eighteenth and nineteenth centuries. Executing traitors by drawing and quartering continued in the United Kingdom until 1814 and beheadings were not abolished until 1870.

A key part of Britain's nineteenth-century colonial civilizing mission was the abolition of torture in distant places. In the 1850s, for example, reports reached the United Kingdom of the use of torture as a policing method in the Madras Presidency, in what is now southern India. The official report into the incidents, however, placed the primary blame on native police. It argued that "the whole cry of the people . . . is to save them from the cruelties of their fellow natives, not from the effects of unkindness or indifference on the part of the European officers of Government" (Commissioners for the Investigation of Alleged Cases of Torture in the Madras Presidency 1855, 35). The British colonial presence was not seen as a cause of these abuses but as necessary to prevent them from taking place. The charge of torture was also often levied against the Ottoman Empire, as one way of demonstrating that the regime was corrupt and decaying. As one member of parliament put it, "Statements . . . have been received of tortures such as it must be a shock to anyone in the civilised world."[18] British intervention was then demanded in order to protect the Christian inhabitants of the Middle East.

The sense that the United Kingdom has a unique duty to save the rest of the world from torture continued into the late twentieth century. When the Labour government came to power in 1997, it soon announced what it said was going to be an "ethical foreign policy." Looking for something on which to apply this, it latched onto the Optional Protocol for the UN Convention Against Torture, which would allow UN teams to inspect places of detention directly. The assumption was that this would bring little change domestically, but that British diplomats should be asked to lobby for other states to ratify the protocol. The Foreign Office also pumped large amounts of money into the Swiss-based Association for the Prevention of Torture, which had been central in the campaign for the new protocol. All this took place before the launch of the war on terror. Although the photographs from Abu Ghraib initially disturbed the sense that torture was something that only happened in places like Iraq and was perpetrated by people like those in the Ba'ath Party, there was still a strong feeling that this was an American problem and that British troops had a far more civilized way of behaving (see, for example, Bishop 2004; Raymont 2006). Subsequent events proved that this was largely wishful thinking.

Much of the worry about allegations of abuse during the beginning of the twenty-first century has been about the damage they might do to the reputation of the United Kingdom abroad, rather than about the suffering of the detainees. Prime Minister David Cameron called allegations of torture a "stain on Britain's reputation" (Cobain 2010). Such sentiments are not confined to the United Kingdom. Senator John McCain told the US Senate, in response to allegations of American involvement in abuse, "This is about who we are. These are the values that distinguish us from our enemies" (2005). As John Parry argues, debates about torture are often debates about identity (2010). Talking about torture can therefore be a proxy for talking about how one perceives his or her nation-state and its commitments.

The sense that torture is simply not something that the British (or Americans) do, can have pernicious implications. It is arguably, for example, behind the use of extraordinary renditions and the outsourcing of coercive interrogation to other regimes. British security officials may not have directly tortured Binyam Mohamed, but they seem to have been involved indirectly. Allowing someone to be sent to Morocco or Afghanistan is an attempt to maintain the claim of British innocence.

In writing about the often-contradictory relationship between self-perception, policy, and practice, the point is not to highlight obvious double standards. To do so would be to ignore the often genuine ways in which torture is abhorred and opposed by state and nonstate actors. Rather, the aim is to examine the ways in which a focus on torture can lead to blind spots and predilections. People acting in the name of the British state have been involved both in acts of cruelty and in acts of compassion, sometimes at the same time. Focusing on attempts to recognize torture allows us to explore how a "differentiated geography of harm and redress," compassion, and indignation is formed in the political imagination of the British state, its officials, and its citizens (Das 2007, 333).

Structure of This Book

The roots of our contemporary notions of torture include three common origin stories. The first is to see the category of torture as an inevitable response to cruelty and suffering. The second is to understand a concern with torture as growing out of the increasing humanitarian sentiments born of the Enlightenment. The third is to argue that modern notions of torture have to be understood as a response to the horrors of World War II. However, in Chapter 1, I argue that torture did not gain its particular prominence as a harm above all others until the 1970s. It was at this point that Cold War politics, medical practice, refugee flows, and international human rights activists came together to lead to a focus on individual trauma and precise legal definition.

Torture involves distinct notions of victims and perpetrators, innocence and guilt. To count as a legally recognized survivor of torture, or to be found legally culpable as a perpetrator, one must pass a series of evidentiary and conceptual hurdles. Chapters 2, 3, and 4 examine how a focus on torture leads to the recognition of particular types of victims and survivors. The vast majority of claims for recognition as torture survivors in the United Kingdom involve immigration claims, and it is therefore on these that I focus. In Chapter 2, I examine the issues raised by attempts to recognize torture survivors in immigration claims. Using the example of one particular Iranian male, I argue that given the inherently problematic nature of much of the evidence presented, the recognition of torture survivors is an inevitably erratic process. In Chapter 3, I explore the dilemmas involved in the production of medicolegal reports about torture survivors. These reports are used by lawyers as evidence to corroborate a claim—made as part of an asylum application—that someone has been tortured. The clinicians writing these reports face the problem that torture is far from being a straightforward clinical category, and they are forced to read their clients' minds and bodies for often highly ambiguous signs.

In immigration cases involving claims of torture, the key issue is not past incidents but events that have not yet taken place. The question asked by judges is not simply whether someone has been tortured in the past, but whether that person might be tortured in the future. In Chapter 4, therefore, I examine attempts to protect people from future acts of torture. I do so by exploring the efforts of the British government to deport a number of terror suspects to Algeria and the claims by their lawyers that they will be tortured on return to that country. I argue that the ways in which the courts attempt to speculate about the future leads to a focus on formal structures rather than on the often contingent and political causes of violence. An absolute prohibition is made much more ambiguous when it is projected into the future.

The other half of the definition of torture is the specific intent of the perpetrator. If torture is widely understood as a crime so horrific that it transcends boundaries, what type of person can be found guilty of torture? In Chapter 5, I explore the successful prosecution in 2005 of an Afghan "warlord," the first person ever to be charged with torture in the United Kingdom. Given the events of the last ten years, as well as Britain's record in its struggles against anticolonial insurgency, this seems a little surprising. The trial of the Afghan "warlord" is therefore compared to the largely unsuccessful prosecution of British soldiers for the abuse and beating to death of detainees after the invasion of Iraq. I argue that there is a structural prejudice, inherent in the law, to seeing torture as a crime committed by other people in other places.

Torture is understood as a uniquely international issue, subject to international conventions and monitored by international organizations. In Chapter 6, I shift focus again to examine the international human rights monitoring mechanisms that oversee the United Kingdom's compliance with the human rights obligation to prohibit torture. In particular, I focus on the use of internationalized shame as a device to prevent torture. I argue that, as a result of the technical ways in which obligations are interpreted, the shame of torture is dispersed into arguments about procedure. By the end, there seems little to be ashamed of.

The internationally recognized legal prohibition of torture has brought many things with it. The focus on individual suffering has meant that the experience of victims cannot be totally forgotten, either politically or legally. The creation of international conventions means that there is a new language by which states can be held accountable for their actions. More precise definitions have created the possibility, still largely unfulfilled, of criminal prosecution for perpetrators. However, the political, legal, and ethical priority given to torture also raises its own questions. Torture is not simply a neutral category but inevitably favors some and disadvantages others, and it obscures particular political relationships while revealing alternatives. By stressing the contingencies and contradictions in the use of the legal category, I seek to tread a path between dismissing human rights claims as a veil that hides other forms of domination and treating those claims as a product of a transcendent moral realm, which no social or political inquiry "can hope to illuminate" (Haskell 2000, 236).[19] The aim is to examine how one of the most powerful elements of our contemporary moral economy has been made possible and how it creates particular distributions of sympathy, indignation, and entitlement.

Chapter 1

Talking about Torture after the Human Rights Revolution

In May 1936, British troops rounded up the male residents of the Palestinian village of Halhoul and held them at gunpoint in the open air. The soldiers, from the Black Watch Regiment, were looking for weapons after Palestinians had attacked British positions nearby. An armed revolt against British rule had broken out three years earlier, after the British had initially arrived nearly twenty years before that, claiming to free the Arab residents from Ottoman despotism (Norris 2008; Hughes 2009). The men in Halhoul were told that they would not be released until the guns were handed over. It was not clear what they were to do if they did not have guns. Over the next few days, the detainees were held in full sunlight without food or water, during unusually hot weather. In order to get a drink, one man claimed that he knew where weapons were held at the bottom of a well. When he climbed back up from the well without a gun, he was reportedly pushed back down and drowned. During their detention, between eight and twelve men died from dehydration. Although the Arabic-language newspapers were closed at the time by the British army, news of the event made it to the European press. British diplomats were particularly concerned about the propaganda potential, as Italy and Germany tried to increase their support among the Arab population.[1] Several petitions were also written by Palestinian groups to the League of Nations, demanding intervention.[2] British actions in Palestine were condemned in London by the Howard League for Penal Reform and the National Council for Civil Liberties, as well as by the Tel Aviv–based League for the Rights of Man.[3] In response, a few hundred pounds was paid to the family of each dead man by the British high commissioner, and, although internal disciplinary action seems to have been taken by the British army, no criminal convictions were made.[4]

Nearly seventy years later, in September 2003, British soldiers from the Queen's Lancashire Regiment (QLR) raided a hotel in Basra looking for weapons used in the growing insurgency against the British and American occupation of Iraq. During these raids, nine Iraqis were detained and taken to the British base. A few months previously, a captain of the QLR, who had just taken over from the Black Watch in the area, had been killed by a roadside bomb in Basra. Over the next day and a half, the detained men were hooded with hessian sandbags, placed in stress positions, prevented from sleeping, and subjected to loud noises.[5] They were given only limited food and water as temperatures reached 60 degrees Celsius (140 degrees Fahrenheit), and they were kicked and punched over and over again. One man, a hotel receptionist called Baha Mousa, died after reportedly trying to escape. The case was eventually picked up by the British and international press. Human rights groups, such as Liberty, the successor to the National Council for Civil Liberties, as well as Amnesty International and Human Rights Watch, condemned the actions, making presentations to the United Nations calling for a full investigation and prosecutions (Amnesty International 2008b; Human Rights Watch 2006; Liberty 2008). The British army reportedly initially offered the family of the dead man $3,000 in compensation (Fisk 2004). However, after a case was taken to the UK courts, this was increased to £2.83 million (US$4.5 million), split between ten Iraqis who had been abused by British soldiers.[6] A court-martial eventually resulted in the dismissal of all charges against six soldiers. A single corporal pleaded guilty to "inhumane treatment" but not the killing of Baha Mousa, and received a one-year jail term. After the court-martial, the head of the British army, General Sir Richard Dannatt said that "everyone inside and outside the Army should recognise the harm that is caused to our hard earned reputation and, potentially, to our operational effectiveness when anyone commits serious breaches of our values" (Ministry of Defence 2007). A public inquiry was established in 2009 that would look into the causes of Mousa's death and would make relevant policy recommendations but could not form the basis of criminal prosecutions.[7]

There are many similarities in the moral and political responses to the events in Iraq and Palestine. In both cases, the British military offered to pay financial compensation to the families of the dead. In both cases, the British government was primarily worried about the ways in which news of the events could be used to damage the reputation of the United Kingdom. In both cases, it was argued that such actions were simply not "the British way." In addition, questions were asked in the House of Commons, protests were made within the British army and civil service, and human rights organizations condemned the acts and demanded redress. Finally, the affected communities also sent reports demanding justice to international organizations.

What is most striking about the response to the two events, however, is the different ways in which the violence is described. In the case of Mandate Palestine, words and phrases such as "atrocity,"[8] "brutality and cruelty,"[9] "torture,"[10] "inhuman," "unnecessary and quite indiscriminate roughness,"[11] "ill-treatment,"[12] and "beatings"[13] were used. However, in the case of occupied Iraq, although the military and the British government described the events as "mistreatment" and "abuse," nearly everyone else, including newspapers, human rights groups, and members of parliament referred to the incidents as "torture." In the seventy years between the Arab Revolt in Palestine and the Anglo-American occupation of Iraq, torture has gone from just one of many ways of describing the deliberate infliction of violence to becoming almost the default term used to describe such acts. The differences in the words used to describe both events cannot simply be dismissed as an inevitably different reaction to the different nature of the events, distinct as they are. Nor is it simply that people in 1930s Britain were too coy to use the word *torture*. There has instead been a widespread shift in the words we use to describe deliberately inflicted violence. *Torture* has only relatively recently been given the ethical priority as close to the worst thing that the British army can do.

This chapter explores how the category of torture has gained its public prominence as a universal wrong and what we now mean when we talk about torture. It may be tempting to think of the growth of the abhorrence of torture as a product of the increasing sensitivity to the pain of others (see, for example, Hunt 2004). Yet, humanitarian sentiments do not require that we think of cruelty and suffering in terms of the very specific category of torture (Moyn 2007). The classic eighteenth-century tracts, on which it is often assumed our contemporary abhorrence of torture rests, thought about torture very differently from the way we do today. Voltaire and Beccaria, for example, did not object solely or specifically to torture but to much wider forms of cruelty (Beccaria 1778; Voltaire 1764). Furthermore, at the heart of their critique was the idea that torture simply did not work as a means of eliciting truth and was therefore irrational. It was the needless pain they objected to, rather than pain itself. Their fundamental concern was with due process.

The two events—in Mandate Palestine and in contemporary Iraq—described earlier, are separated by World War II. It has been popular to think of the late twentieth-century concern with torture as being born, at least in part, of the horrors of Occupied Europe (see, for example, Morsink 1999). However, the deliberate infliction of pain to intimidate or to collect information seems fairly low on the list of the horrors of Nazi Germany. Furthermore, in the late 1940s, the word *torture* was by no means the self-evident term used to describe such brutality. When that word was used, it was used to signify a broader opposition to totalitarian politics rather than specific concern with a unique and precise form of suffering.

Instead, our particular understanding of torture has a much more recent genealogy in the 1970s and early 1980s, as law, medicine, the Cold War, international refugee flows, and international human rights organizations, came together to make the image of the suffering body a key currency in international politics, and torture an archetypal international crime.

Torture and the Universal Declaration of Human Rights

Most accounts of the international prohibition of torture now start with Article 5 of the Universal Declaration of Human Rights (UDHR), which states that no one shall be subjected to "torture or to cruel, inhuman or degrading treatment or punishment." It is important to make three points here: First, torture is not defined by the UDHR but is left self-evident; second, torture is not singled out as a particularly heinous act, above all others, but is merely one form of violence and humiliation; and, third, torture might not have been included in the UDHR at all.

In 1945, the Austrian émigré and Cambridge academic Sir Hersch Lauterpacht published what is widely taken to be the first systematic legal examination of an international system for the protection of human rights (1945). The book, *An International Bill of the Rights of Man*, makes no mention of torture. Instead it speaks of the right to personal liberty and freedom from slavery. Similarly, the influential draft of the *International Bill of Rights* produced by the American Law Institute contains no reference to torture, but it has articles instead providing freedom from wrongful interference and arbitrary detention (Lewis 1945). At one point, it was suggested that the American Law Institute draft be adopted by the United Nations (Simpson 2001, 322). The initial drafts submitted to the United Nations by France, the United Kingdom, and the United States also made no mention of torture, but they talked about the rights to life, to freedom from arbitrary arrest, to freedom from slavery, and to a fair trial.[14]

When the word *torture* was eventually added to a draft of the declaration, it was grouped together with the previously proposed passages on physical integrity and cruel punishments, to create an entirely new article.[15] It is worth remembering here that by the 1940s, the word *torture* had long since lost its precise meaning of judicially monitored interrogation and had become used as a general term of moral approbation. As such, René Cassin, the French representative at the negotiations, veteran of the League of Nations, and later winner of the Nobel Peace Prize, expressed a concern that the word was too vague. Charles Malik, a Lebanese philosophy professor thought by many to be the intellectual heavyweight in the drafting committee, wondered whether torture might include "forced labour, unemployment or dental pain."[16] The Soviet representative asked whether there was any link at all between torture, physical integrity, and cruel punishment.[17] There was also some debate over whether torture was primarily a right that related to the integrity of the person or was linked to principles of due process.[18] In the various drafts, the meaning of the word moved between being next to the right to life, on the one hand, and the right to a fair trial, on the other.[19]

The wording of what would become Article 5 was eventually agreed to as "No one shall be subjected to torture or to cruel, inhuman or degrading treatment or punishment." The UK delegate, Lord Dukeston, a former Labour MP and Trade Union leader, was anxious that the inclusion of the word *punishment* would prohibit forms of corporal punishment practiced in British prisons and schools.[20] He was reassured, however, by Cassin that the phrase "cruel and inhuman" would mean that these forms of punishment would still be allowed. This was not enough, though, and the United Kingdom abstained from the initial vote on the article.[21] The Cubans attempted at the last moment to replace the entire article with the phrase: "Every human being has the right to life, liberty, and integrity of person," but they were voted down.[22]

The meaning of the word *torture* was left deliberately vague in the declaration, so as to be as inclusive as possible. The words *cruel*, *inhuman*, and *degrading* were also left undefined. As Charles Malik argued, it was "better to be on the side of vagueness than on the side of legal accuracy."[23] For Malik, this meant that Article 5 could act as a general moral statement that explained "in an international instrument that the conscience of mankind, had been shocked by inhuman acts in Nazi Germany."[24] For others, however, this vagueness was worrisome. A proposal that "no one shall be subjected to any form of physical mutilation or medical or scientific experimentation against his will" was vetoed by the United States, for fear that it might exclude compulsory vaccination and medical experiments on the insane.[25] The association of torture with judicial interrogation and punishment was almost certainly heavily in the minds of many of the delegates, and several proposed that torture should be prohibited "even when guilty of a crime."[26]

Torture was also missing from the early drafts of the European Convention on Human Rights (Simpson 2001, 654–72). The final draft took Article 5 of the UDHR almost word for word, only omitting the word *cruel.* During the drafting process, Frederick Cocks, a Labour Party MP and prominent antiwar campaigner, gave an impassioned speech calling for the prohibition of "any form of mutilation or sterilization, or of any form of torture or beating," as well as "imprisonment with such an excess of light, darkness, noise or silence as to cause mental suffering."[27] Given later events in Northern Ireland, the condemnation of sensory deprivation seems somewhat ironic. Cocks expressed confidence that "Europe, clad in the shining robe of civilisation, treading under her feet this unclean and loathsome serpent, will not only live but will lead the world towards a higher future and a nobler destiny."[28] Although not taking issue with Cocks's sentiment, the other delegates found a certain amount of disquiet in his speech. The Scandinavians pointed out that sterilization was a widespread policy in their countries.[29] Another British delegate was worried, yet again, that Cocks's suggestion might see the prohibition of corporal punishment.[30] A third British delegate thought the focus on such brutalities could "over balance" the convention away from its core objectives. As a result, the simpler and shorter formulation, based on the UDHR, was eventually decided on.

From the late 1940s, the prohibition of torture and other forms of ill-treatment found its way into several international agreements. Article 7 of the International Covenant on Civil and Political Rights (ICCPR) mirrors the UDHR, with the addition of the prohibition on anyone being "subjected without his free consent to medical or scientific experimentation." which had been left out of the Universal Declaration of Human Rights. The prohibition of torture was also included in what is known as Common Article 3 of the Geneva Conventions, which seek to regulate the conduct of armed conflict and the treatment of prisoners of war. However, torture is not singled out for particular attention by the Geneva Conventions; it is included along with a list of other prohibited acts, such as "violence to life and person . . . mutilation, cruel treatment, torture . . . [and] outrages upon personal dignity."[31]

The British approach to the signing of all these instruments was based on the assumption that they reflected the status quo of domestic law and practice. As legal historian A. W. Brian Simpson describes in his magisterial history of British involvement in the drafting of the UDHR and the European Convention on Human Rights (ECHR), the implicit assumption was that the "traditions of liberty" that human rights sought to express had their strongest rooting in English history (2001). It is ironic that the language of human rights was largely alien to the common law, to the extent that the first British diplomat sent to oversee the negotiations for the UDHR had never heard the term before (Simpson 2001, 38). Human rights, though, were still understood in terms of Britain exporting its traditions to the rest of the world.

The Wars of Decolonization

The impact of the international human rights agreements that the United Kingdom ratified in the late 1940s and early 1950s was minimal domestically, with very few people taking notice of what was essentially seen as a foreign policy issue. It is important to note that the ECHR could be applied to the British colonies, if they agreed to the extension. Many, if not all, did so. Much of the colonial world would have been amused by claims that the prohibition of torture or other forms of ill-treatment was an integral part of British policy and practice. As Britain's anticolonial wars erupted in Kenya, Malaya, and Aden, interrogation, mass arrest, and detention without trial were widely used.

In 1950s Kenya, for example, the Mau Mau rebellion against British colonial rule was met with tactics that included forced confessions, shoot to kill, mass executions, and large-scale internment (Anderson 2005). For much of the colonial administration, and a great deal of British public opinion, this was simply what was necessary to preserve the Empire and put down a brutal uprising. There was some opposition, not least from the Kenyans themselves but also from the British-appointed judiciary, missionaries, and a few MPs. By and large, the language of torture was rare, and very few references were made to international human rights agreements.[32] Instead, the dominant image was that of the gulag or concentration camp (Anderson 2005). Common references were made to "extreme pressure," "maltreatment," "serious beatings," and the "third degree."[33] When the International Committee of the Red Cross visited the Kenyan detention camps in 1957, it noted the use of corporal punishment and "drew attention to its severity."[34] Following specific allegations of the "beating up of prisoners" and the offering of financial rewards for the killing of Mau Mau, Captain G. S. L. Griffiths was convicted in 1954 of "disgraceful conduct of a cruel kind" after he threatened detainees with mutilation.[35] Although some perpetrators were brought to trial for and convicted of crimes such as murder or assault, torture was not a crime or even a civil offense under either Kenyan or English law at the time.

At the same time as the Mau Mau uprising, the British colonial authorities were dealing with growing unrest in Cyprus. The counterinsurgency methods of the British were challenged by the Greek government in 1956. As the ECHR applied to Cyprus, the Greeks lodged allegations of atrocities with the European Commission of Human Rights (see Simpson 2001, 924–1052). In lodging their case, the Greeks argued that the "case of the Cypriots differs from that of other peoples of the world still fighting for their freedom in that the Cypriots are Europeans nourished on Western civilization" (Simpson 2001, 929). The applications alleged

"many cases of torture, degrading punishment and inhuman treatment," as well as collective punishments; detention without trial; deportation; and violations of the rights of privacy, freedom of expression, and
assembly.[36] The initial reaction of the British government was shock and
surprise that the ECHR could actually apply to its actions in Cyprus
(Simpson 2001, 13). The British government also objected to the protest
about whipping, with one senior diplomat arguing that it was commonly
used in public schools and "is a mild and humane treatment. . . . If anyone can think of a more humane and effective treatment . . . H.M.G
[Her Majesty's Government] would be glad to hear of it."[37] The European Commission of Human Rights never issued any public findings on
the case, however. The case was quietly dropped when, in early 1959, the
Zurich Agreement paved the way for the independence of Cyprus.

Internment and Northern Ireland

Trouble, when it came, came much closer to home. Following the outbreak of civil unrest in the late 1960s and a bombing campaign by the
Irish Republican Army (IRA), internment without trial was introduced
in Northern Ireland on 9 August 1971. More than 340 arrests of Republi-
cans were made on the first day alone. By the end of the week, allegations of brutality had made their way into the British press (*Sunday Times*
1971). In response to the allegations, the British Conservative government, led by Edward Heath, set up a Committee of Enquiry in late
August 1971. The committee was chaired by Sir Edmund Compton, a
former civil servant and a man who, according to former Labour Prime
Minister Harold Wilson, was "one of the shrewdest, cleverest, and nicest,
men in Whitehall" (Dalyell 1994). The committee's mandate was to
"investigate allegations by those arrested . . . of physical brutality"
(Compton 1971, 1). However, almost all the internees refused to cooperate, fearing reprisals from the British security forces. The British army
did not contest the use of four interrogation techniques—wall-standing,
hooding, noise, and a bread-and-water diet—but argued they were an
essential part of the security operations. There was an initial denial that
sleep deprivation was used, but this denial was later dropped. The
Compton Committee reported in November 1971 and made the general
finding that what had become known as the "five techniques" were in
use, but the committee made few specific statements on individual cases
(Compton 1971). Most famously, the report concluded that the use of
the five interrogation techniques was justified given the circumstances
in Northern Ireland at the time.

Under continued pressure, the Heath government set up another
committee to look at the future of interrogation methods. The Parker

Report was led by Lord Parker of Waddington, formerly the most senior judge in England and Wales. It also included Lord Gardiner, who as Lord Chancellor had been the head of the English judiciary. Earlier in his career, Parker had been a supporter of corporal punishment, whereas Gardiner was one of the founders of Justice, the British branch of the International Commission of Jurists. The brief of the Parker Report was more specific than the Compton Report, namely to "consider whether, and if so, in what respect, the procedures currently authorized for the interrogation of persons suspected of terrorism . . . require amendment" (Compton 1971, iii). Looking at the medical risks posed by the five techniques, Lord Parker concluded that if the interrogations were conducted with care, the effects of the use of the five techniques were acceptable, as even under normal domestic circumstances it was reasonable for detainees to be subjected to some discomfort (Parker 1972, 40). He also argued that the techniques, if used correctly, could elicit useful information (1972, 5). As such, the report concluded that given the civil unrest in Northern Ireland, it was wrong to rule out use of the techniques on moral grounds (1972, 7). However, Lord Gardiner refused to let his name appear on the report and issued his own minority version. In his report, Gardiner was far more concerned about the physical and mental impacts of the use of the five techniques, quoting the medical evidence before the committee that it was impossible to set firm objective limits on the use of the techniques, as people had individual thresholds as to what they could endure (Gardiner 1972). He was also worried about the effect the use of the five techniques would have on Britain's international reputation, as they "marked a departure from world standards we have helped to create . . . (and) gravely damage our own hard won reputation" (1972, 21).

The Heath government was somewhat bemused by the uproar. Both the prime minister and his home secretary, Reginald Maudling, argued in Cabinet committee meetings that it "had to be remembered that the lives of British soldiers and of innocent civilians depended on intelligence. We were dealing with an enemy who had no scruples and we should not be unduly squeamish over methods of interrogation in these circumstances."[38] Heath expressed exasperation that the accusations against British troops amounted to the claim that "anyone not given three-star hotel facilities suffered hardship and ill-treatment."[39] There was also a feeling that similar techniques had been used elsewhere by the British army—in Palestine, Malaya, Kenya, Cyprus, Brunei, and Aden—without the same level of fuss. Indeed, a 1966 publicly available report by Roderic Bowen QC, a former deputy speaker of the House of Commons and Liberal MP, had implicitly cleared many of the same techniques for use against the counterinsurgency in Aden (1966).

Bowen had pointed out that soldiers were bound by the Geneva Conventions. At the same time, however, he made it clear that "permissible techniques" could be used to overcome resistance to interrogation.

The key distinction being made by the Heath government, as well as by the Compton and Parker reports was between "brutality" on the one hand and "ill-treatment" on the other. There is hardly any mention of torture. Even Gardiner in his minority report argues that words such as *torture* are vague and open to doubt, and therefore he does not use them (1972, 15). For Parker and Compton, the distinction between brutality and ill-treatment, which has no legal meaning, rests on the intention of the perpetrator. Brutality is a worse form of ill-treatment. Compton defined brutality as "an inhuman or savage form of cruelty, and that cruelty implies a disposition to inflict suffering, coupled with indifference to, or pleasure in, the victim's pain" (1971, 15). Compton's report found that British soldiers had been responsible for forms of ill-treatment but not brutality. What is noticeable here is the emphasis on morals rather than on legality, and for Compton the use of the five techniques was morally justifiable. The Parker Report was not explicitly mandated to look at the legality of the techniques, but given that it included two men who had been the most senior members of the English judiciary it is hardly surprising that it did. In its investigations the Parker Report revealed that the British army had never considered whether their interrogation techniques were legal under domestic law and had only made the vaguest references to the Geneva Conventions. The regulation of interrogation, such as it existed, had been primarily done for functional and disciplinary ends—to make sure it worked and was controlled. The majority Parker Report thought the techniques were morally justifiable but almost certainly illegal, and therefore the government should take further advice. Gardiner in his minority report argued that the use of the techniques was both immoral and illegal, and that the idea of legalizing the use of such techniques was abhorrent.

Although torture was widely referred to in the protests against the treatment of Republican detainees, it was far from the default term used to describe the techniques. The initial *Sunday Times* article that broke the story on mainland Britain referred only to "brutality," setting out the allegations of what it called "psychological pressuring . . . virtually unrelieved harassment and psychological intimidation" (Barry and Jacobsen 1971, 5). Amnesty International published a report of its own inquiry in early 1972 and did not use the word *torture* once in the main body of the text, instead referring to "ill-treatment" and "brutal treatment" (1972). One of the first written accounts of the treatment of internees was by Seamas O Tuathail, a Sinn Fein member and journalist, who was rounded up in mid-August 1971.[40] He accuses the British army of "brutality and torture." The same phrase is widely used in other publications.[41] "Torture" is used to describe the physical act, but brutality is the multiplier referring to both the cruelty of the perpetrator and the suffering of the victim. "Torture" here does not stand alone as a moral harm. There is also little direct reference to the law or human rights in general. Where O Tuathail makes reference to the ECHR, it is to the right to a fair trial and the prohibition of arbitrary arrest, rather than the prohibition of torture.

The Heath government was privately adamant that the techniques were morally justifiable and initially planned on publicly stating as much.[42] However, the government also recognized that, under the current laws in Northern Ireland and the rest of the United Kingdom, as well as in most other places in the world, the use of the techniques was illegal.[43] The law in question was that of assault, and mention was made only in passing of international obligations. After considering the possibility of passing legislation to legalize the techniques or to take a conscious decision to continue acting illegally and then passing a law to indemnify those involved, it was decided to simply state that the techniques would not be used in the foreseeable future. Heath therefore stood up in the House of Commons and declared, "The Government . . . have decided that the techniques . . . will not be used in future as an aid to interrogation. . . . If a Government did decide—on whatever grounds I would not like to foresee—that additional techniques were required for interrogation . . . they would probably have to come to the House and ask for the powers to do it."[44] There is no moral condemnation of the acts here, merely an indication that because of a change in the circumstances in Northern Ireland, the techniques would not be used again. Crucially, some space was left open for the use of the five techniques to be reintroduced but with the requirement of further parliamentary legislation.

Amnesty International and the International Campaign Against Torture

At least part of the story behind the current role that the prohibition of torture plays in the popular imagination cannot be told without reference to Amnesty International (see Clark 2001; Power 2001). Indeed Amnesty International played a central role in documenting the allegations of ill-treatment in Northern Ireland and increasing the pressure on the Heath government. More broadly, Amnesty International was very significant in putting the prohibition of torture on the international agenda. The organization was founded in the early 1960s to campaign for the release of prisoners of conscience. Torture was not within its original mandate, and was only included in 1966 after much internal debate about the dilution of expertise and resources (Amnesty International 1976).[45] The broadening of the mandate to include torture was given added impetus by a 1967 investigation into the treatment of political detainees in Greece, following the coup in April of the same year.[46] A two-man team was originally sent to Athens simply to record "who was detained, where they were held, and why they had been arrested" (Amnesty International 1968, 1). However, when the men arrived they found evidence of what seemed to be systematic and deliberate abuse. The report of the trip concluded that torture was "deliberately and officially used", and was a "widespread practice against Greek citizens suspected of active opposition" (1968, 3).

At the same time, an application had been brought against Greece in the European Commission of Human Rights by the three Scandinavian countries and the Netherlands, alleging widespread breaches of the European Convention on Human Rights. Torture was not originally included in the submission but was added after the release of the Amnesty International report. In 1969, the commission found Greece in breach of the European Convention, including Article 3 prohibiting torture or inhuman or degrading treatment or punishment. Crucially, although it did not impact the findings, the commission drew a distinction between the different parts of Article 3, describing torture as an "aggravated form of inhuman or degrading treatment."[47] For the first time, an intergovernmental organization had suggested that torture was of a higher degree of seriousness than the other forms of ill-treatment with which it had been associated since World War II.

Amnesty International was not the first organization to campaign against the use of torture. However, in the United Kingdom, at least, Amnesty International had the most popular appeal, and its methods of naming and shaming had the most impact on the general public. Important developments were also taking place in Latin America throughout the 1970s, and in many ways Amnesty International drew on this work. The Amnesty International campaign was given added impetus by the presence in Europe and North America of tens of thousands of articulate exiles from Latin America, Chile and Argentina in particular, who could give firsthand accounts of their treatment. Amnesty International's campaigns worked alongside the lobbying from groups such as the Mothers of the Plaza de Mayo and the Barcelona-based but Argentina-focused, COSOFAM (Commission of Solidarity with Relatives of the Disappeared) (Robben 2005, 306–10; Sikkink 1993). Literary representations, such as Jacobo Timerman's account of his abuse in an Argentinean jail, *Prisoner Without a Name, Cell Without a Number*, also added to the popular consciousness of widespread torture (1981). From the 1970s, Europe and North America were confronted with the systematic torture of people of European descent in a way that seem to remind them of Nazi Germany.

Amnesty International formally launched its Campaign Against Torture in December 1972, initially for one year. Until the early 1970s, Amnesty International employed no lawyers on its full-time staff, and its focus on torture was primarily moral in orientation. The first lawyer appointed on a full-time basis to Amnesty International, Nigel Rodley, would play a central role in the campaign. He would also add a new, stricter focus on international human rights law to Amnesty International's work. After leaving Amnesty International, he went on to become the UN Special Rapporteur on Torture and he sat on the UN Human Rights Committee. It is important to note that although the broadening of Amnesty International's mandate in the late 1960s referred to all of Article 5 of the UDHR, the campaign left out "cruel, inhuman or degrading treatment or punishment". Always quick to recognize the value of brevity and clarity, Amnesty International singled out torture for specific attention.

Torture was seen by Amnesty International as a singular and universal problem. It could therefore publish a *Report on Torture* between 1973 and 1975 and again in 1984, setting out the practice of torture from Albania to Zambia, via Chile, India, Israel, Morocco, Togo, Vietnam, and many others besides. Torture was the same thing wherever it took place and could be understood in the same terms. For Amnesty International, by 1973 "what for the last two or three hundred years has been no more than an historical curiosity, has suddenly developed a life of its own and become a social cancer" (1973, 7). Amnesty International sought to define torture as the "systematic and deliberate infliction of acute pain in any form by one person on another, or on a third person, in order to accomplish the purpose of the former against the will of the latter" (1973, 31). Torture here is organized rather than casual and includes the infliction of great suffering on the powerless by the powerful. Although not explicitly mentioned in this definition, the implicit assumption was that torture was carried out by the state, and all the examples documented refer to state torture. The possibility that torture might include domestic violence, for example, was simply not on the horizon.

Three features of this campaign warrant particular mention. The first is that Amnesty International did not simply work by lobbying politicians and officials but sought to mobilize grassroots public support through letter writing, petitions, and public meetings. Its arguments therefore took hold far away from the corridors of power. The second feature of the Campaign Against Torture is that the history of supporting individual prisoners of conscience meant that the experiences of individual torture survivors were given a prominent place. Perhaps deriving from the presence of broadly progressive and liberal Latin American exiles in Europe and North America, torture survivors were also seen as heroic and principled. The opening pages of the Amnesty International 1973 *Report on Torture*, for example, begin with first-person narratives detailing the suffering and pain experienced by torture survivors in Turkey, the Soviet Union, and Uruguay, in a style that is familiar from many Amnesty International documents. In this process, individual pain is highlighted as a cause of special horror.

From the early 1970s, medical groups were set up alongside most national Amnesty International sections. They were driven by a worry that doctors were participating in torture in many places around the world (Amnesty International 1977). Furthermore, and perhaps more important, was the need to provide evidence for allegations of torture (see Chapter 3; Amnesty International 1974). Later, attention would also turn to rehabilitation. Initially the focus was on the documentation of physical scars and other marks on bodies, as this was quickest and most practically feasible in contexts where doctors might only have a very short period of time to examine their patients. The Danish medical group, which in the early days was the largest and most influential, also focused on the neurological implications of torture, as many of its leading members were expert in this field. However, the language of psychological trauma also began to play a significant role, perhaps because of the increasing importance of the Latin American anti-torture movement, which was heavily influenced by psychoanalysis (Plotkin 2001). As such, the first publication by Amnesty International on the medical documentation of torture argued that "unquestionably the worst sequelae of torture were psychological and neurological" (1977, 12). In this work there was a profound sense that torture was unique in its levels of suffering, leading one Amnesty International publication to quote Jean Amery's claim that "torture is the most terrible event remaining in man's memory" (1973, 58). As such, torture was seen as leaving distinct wounds in the mind.

The third feature of the Amnesty International campaign was that, stemming from the success of the Greek case before the European Commission, the emphasis was on the norms of prohibition rather than on the political causes of torture. This was reflected in campaigns for declarations and conventions setting out the prohibition on torture at the United Nations. By the early 1970s, human rights had become caught up in Cold War politics, and many in the developing world and the Communist bloc were deeply suspicious of any criticism phrased in human rights terms. Indeed, many involved in the British and wider anti-torture movement saw the opposition to torture as a continuation of the opposition to Nazi Germany and totalitarian politics. However, the Campaign Against Torture had the benefit that some of its most important objects, such as Pinochet's Chile, were US allies, and it was therefore able to drive straight through the middle of Cold War rivalries. The United States and its allies were not going to oppose a broad declaration prohibiting state violence. For the Soviet bloc the condemnation of torture provided a useful stick with which to beat Western-aligned governments in South America and Southern Europe. Furthermore, the prohibition of torture did not seem to be like other human rights, like the right to freedom of opinion, gender equality, or education, about which it was possible to have a debate on their relative merits. No state was going to say it was pro-torture. Instead, the debate was over what counted as torture.

The UN General Assembly adopted a resolution on 9 December 1975 condemning the use of torture. Amnesty International's campaign was referred to many times during the debate over the resolution (Rodley 1987, 19). During the debate, several member states argued that if they were to lend their name to anything they would need to define what torture meant, otherwise it was far too vague (1987, 72). Therefore, although not legally binding, for the first time in any international instrument, the resolution provided a definition of torture as "any act by which severe pain or suffering, whether physical or mental, is intentionally inflicted by or at the instigation of a public official on a person for such purposes as obtaining from him or a third person information or confession, punishing him for an act he has committed or is suspected of having committed, or intimidating him or other persons. It does not include pain, or suffering arising only from, inherent in or incidental to, lawful sanctions."[48] Crucially, unlike the UDHR, ICCPR, or ECHR, but drawing on the European Commission's report on the Greek case in 1969, the resolution drew a distinction between "torture" and "cruel, degrading or inhuman treatment or punishment," arguing that torture was a particularly "aggravated and deliberate form of the latter."[49] Torture is therefore given particular and specific prominence. The intention of public officials and the level of pain and suffering of the victims are seen as singling it out for particular approbation.

The United Kingdom Stands Accused Before the European Court of Human Rights

Following the outbreak of unrest in Northern Ireland and the introduction of internment in the early 1970s, the government of the Irish Republic was under domestic pressure to do something about British counterinsurgency tactics in Northern Ireland. Unable to intervene militarily, it tried to place diplomatic pressure on the United Kingdom by protesting to the European Commission of Human Rights in late 1971.[50] Referring to the report from Amnesty International as well as to the Compton Report, the Irish government alleged that internment without trial was discriminatory and violated the right to liberty and security of the person. Although the Irish government did not make specific allegations of torture, it alleged a broader breach of the prohibition of torture or inhuman or degrading treatment under Article 3 of the ECHR.[51]

It took until mid-January 1978 for the European Court of Human Rights to come to a decision on the case. The British government did not contest the claim of a breach of Article 3 or the existence of the five techniques. However, one key issue in the case became how to characterize the techniques of sensory deprivation, such as hooding, and the use of white noise, the effects of which seemed primarily to be psychological. Although sensory deprivation was certainly not new, the incidents that had received most public attention through the late 1960s and early 1970s in Greece and Latin America had involved much more physical forms of violence.[52] In an earlier advisory opinion, the European Commission of Human Rights had argued that Republican detainees had "described feelings of anxiety and fear as well as disorientation and isolation during the time they were subjected to the techniques and after."[53] However, they also noted that psychiatrists were unable to agree as to the long-term impact of the use of such methods. Some doctors argued that the aftereffects could last for a considerable time. Others, in contrast, claimed that the "psychiatric symptoms developed . . . during interrogation had been minor and that their persistence was a result of everyday life in Northern Ireland."[54] The commission surmised that although it was unable to establish the exact degree of psychiatric aftereffects, the possibility of those aftereffects could not be excluded. The commission's conclusion was that "the systematic application of the techniques for the purposes of inducing a person to give information shows a clear resemblance to those methods of systematic torture which have been known over the ages."[55] Although the commission found that the psychological implications of the techniques could not be predicted with any accuracy, it argued that the mere possibility of severe psychological effects was enough to prohibit the use of those techniques.

The European Court of Human Rights looked at the same evidence as the commission and agreed with the implicit assumption that the level of suffering was the crucial factor. However, it drew the line at a different point, concluding, "Although the five techniques . . . undoubtedly amounted to inhuman and degrading treatment . . . they did not occasion suffering of the particular intensity and cruelty implied by the word *torture* as so understood."[56] The judgment insisted on the distinction between torture and inhuman or degrading treatment or punishment, arguing that torture "held a special stigma."[57] In making the distinction, the court cited the UN General Assembly resolution that defined torture as a particularly aggravated form of ill-treatment.[58] The judges were reportedly persuaded to make the distinction by Sir Gerald Fitzmaurice, the British judge at the court and a former legal adviser to the British Foreign Office.[59] However, Fitzmaurice also issued a dissenting opinion, which argued that it was impossible and undesirable to come up with a precise definition of torture, as it was an entirely subjective term.[60] He then went on to claim that although the five techniques were "certainly harsh," to call them inhuman or degrading was to "debase the currency of normal speech." For Fitzmaurice, in a clear allusion to George Orwell's *1984*, calling the five techniques "torture" left no room to describe acts such as "kicking a man in the groin, or placing him in a blacked-out cell in the company of a bevy of starving rats."[61] For Fitzmaurice, the court was setting the threshold of suffering too low.

It is important to note two things about the court's judgment. First, although the United Kingdom was found guilty of a breach of Article 3, the court was implicitly arguing that some breaches are worse than others. Torture was singled out for special censure. Second, the distinction that was being made here between torture and other forms of ill-treatment was in terms of the intensity of the suffering. However, the court offered no way to measure this pain, nor did it provide a sense of the level necessary to be considered "torture." If the British had wanted to argue that its interrogation techniques were not torture it could not rely on a distinction based on intention, as the five techniques were openly aimed at eliciting information through physical and psychological pressure. Back in the United Kingdom, the press widely reported the decision as a victory for the British government, ignoring the fact that the government had still been found in breach of the convention (see, for example, Walker 1978). There was, however, considerable criticism of the judgment elsewhere. Gerald Fitt, the leader of the Social Democratic and Labour Party, the largest nationalist party in Northern Ireland at the time, accused the court of "playing with words" (Seton 1978, 5). The Northern Ireland Civil Rights Association accused the court of "nitpicking," and Amnesty International announced it would continue to describe interrogation methods such as those used by the British in Northern Ireland as torture (Seton 1978, 5).

An International Torture Convention

The momentum gained by the Amnesty International Campaign Against Torture during the lobbying for the UN resolution against torture in 1975 continued with the drafting of a new Convention Against Torture (CAT) throughout the late 1970s and early 1980s. Originally, three drafts were reviewed, including one written by the International Penal Law Association, with heavy input from Amnesty International, and another by the Swiss-based Committee Against Torture. However, it was a draft prepared by the Swedish government that eventually formed the basis of negotiations. The new draft CAT built heavily on the 1975 Declaration Against Torture, using much the same definition, with its focus on the level of suffering and the intention of public officials.[62] The drafting committee had originally been mandated to prepare a Convention Against Torture and Other Cruel, Inhuman or Degrading Treatment or Punishment. However, although the name of the convention continued to include all forms of ill-treatment, in practice the final convention focused almost exclusively on torture. The aim of the convention was to set out specific legal obligations for states, such as the criminalization of ill-treatment within domestic law and the principle of universal jurisdiction, where states have the responsibility to prosecute perpetrators no matter where the act has been carried out. According to J. Herman Burgers, the Dutch chair of the drafting committee, and Hans Danelius, the Swedish diplomat who wrote the initial draft, many states were concerned that specific obligations such as these should not be tied to vague concepts like "cruel, inhuman or degrading treatment or punishment" (1988, 39). It is therefore only when we get to Article 16 that we hear mention of other forms of ill-treatment. The definition of torture differed from the jurisprudence of the European Court of Human Rights at the time, as it placed relatively greater weight on the intention of the perpetrator and less on the level of pain. Despite the arguments for precision, the definition of torture given in the convention is still not, according to probably the two most influential figures in its drafting, really a definition at all (Burgers and Danelius 1988, 122). Rather it is a description, including debatable terms such as "pain and suffering," intended as a guide for implementation.

Although there were considerable limitations placed on the obligations of states, the United Kingdom still remained nervous about many of the articles in the convention. In particular, it was concerned that universal jurisdiction would be unworkable in practice (Burgers and Danelius 1988, 40). The United Kingdom also insisted, successfully, that the principle of "non-refoulement," that no one should be returned to a state where they may face mistreatment, should be limited to situations of "substantial" rather than merely "reasonable" grounds for believing they may be subjected to torture (Burgers and Danelius 1988, 50). Against the background of the recent findings of the European Court of Human Rights with regard to Northern Ireland, the United Kingdom tried to persuade the drafting committee, unsuccessfully this time, to adopt a more restrictive definition of torture, as systematic and causing extreme pain, rather than simply intentional and causing severe pain (Burgers and Danelius 1988, 45). The United Kingdom, however, was more successful, again against the background of the European Court of Human Rights decision, in persuading the drafting committee to imply that cruel, inhuman, or degrading treatment were of lesser gravity than torture.[63] A separate Swiss and French proposal suggesting that torture included other forms of ill-treatment was rejected (Burgers and Danelius 1988, 42, 47). The final draft said that cruel, inhuman, or degrading treatment did "not amount to torture."[64]

On 10 December 1984, the UN Convention Against Torture and Other Cruel, Inhuman or Degrading Treatment or Punishment was unanimously adopted by the UN General Assembly. As a result of ratifying the convention, the United Kingdom made torture a specific criminal offense for the first time in English law.[65] In the debate to mark its ratification, most parliamentarians seemed to agree that it would make little difference to actual policy and practice in the United Kingdom but would serve to "reinforce the solidarity of the international community."[66] For domestic British politicians, as with the signing of the Universal Declaration and the European Convention on Human Rights, there was an assumption that the United Kingdom was already substantively, if not technically, compliant with the convention, and its signature was more of a call to the rest of the world.

Shortly after the election of Tony Blair in 1997, the Labour government announced that it would follow through on its preelection pledge to pass a Human Rights Act. The White Paper on the proposed law was entitled "bringing human rights home," echoing the sense that human rights are somehow inherently British. The new law was motivated in part by the large number of British cases being taken to the European Court of Human Rights and the extensive delays found there. The Human Rights Act 1998 makes a remedy for breach of a convention right available in English courts without the need to go to the European Court of Human Rights. This includes Article 3 and the prohibition of torture and inhuman, or degrading treatment or punishment. Space was therefore opened for specific human rights claims about torture in English courts for the first time.

Torture after the "War on Terror"

For a visitor acquainted with the protests against the actions of the British army in 1930s Palestine, many of the arguments regarding the brutal treatment of detainees during the "war on terror" would seem very familiar. The sense that torture and other forms of brutality are simply not the "British way" has lasted through the years. Whether it is the drafters of the UDHR or the ECHR, or the Heath and Blair governments, torture is seen as something that is done by other people, or at least by people in other places. Compared to 1930s Palestine, however, much of the way in which we talk about torture is unrecognizable. The frequency with which the word is used to describe forms of brutality has increased exponentially. A brief look at the records of the British House of Commons, for example, reveals that the word *torture* was mentioned relatively rarely throughout the late nineteenth and early twentieth centuries—and, if it was, it was mentioned mostly to condemn the Ottoman Empire. There was a rapid acceleration in the 1970s, when the word was used just over 600 times. However, from 2000 through 2010, *torture* is mentioned more than 1,600 times. Indeed, the word is used more times in the first decade of the twenty-first century than in the entire nineteenth century. Given the United Kingdom's record in its wars of colonization and decolonization, it seems there is an indirect relationship between the infliction of violence and the fixation on torture.

The current prohibition of torture is not simply an inevitable product of the Enlightenment or a reaction to World War II, as it did not take its particular shape until the late 1970s and early 1980s. The meeting of international diplomacy, human rights activists, refugee flows, medicine, and the Cold War has not simply clarified how we think about torture but has changed and shaped our understanding, both in its technical definition and in its ethical load. Torture is now also seen as a uniquely international offense, reflecting the spaces of international diplomacy within which its norms of prohibition took shape. The UN Convention Against Torture, for example, calls on states to prosecute people who torture, irrespective of whether they are citizens of the state, abuse the state's citizens, or carry out the act in an area under their jurisdiction. Torture is seen as transcending national boundaries. Above all though, to talk about torture is to talk about the law and forms of trauma.

The point is not that we did not sometimes talk about torture in terms of law and suffering beforehand, but in the wake of the ethical prioritization of torture, the two elements take on a new form. Discussions continue about the relative weight to be given to pain and suffering in marking out torture as distinct, but torture is now closely associated with particular forms of trauma. Furthermore, what is and what is not torture has become a matter of precise legal argument rather than broad ethical injunction. Until the late 1970s, the debate about brutality was primarily about ethical standards. Now those standards are shaped by reference to international human rights law. Although the torture rehabilitation movement has played a considerable role in how we think about torture (see Chapter 3), these concerns have been translated into legal terms. The intense legalism of the discussion means, for example, that when the British ambassador to Uzbekistan expresses concern about the use of intelligence information seemingly obtained under torture by third parties, he can be referred to the legal adviser at the Foreign & Commonwealth Office, who tells him that there is nothing in the UN Convention Against Torture that says this information cannot be used.[67] The focus on trauma has also meant that the United Kingdom could claim its interrogation techniques in Northern Ireland did not amount to torture, as they did not produce the required level of suffering. The US government can also argue that acts do not count as torture unless they produce pain equivalent to serious organ failure.[68] Such arguments have, of course, been widely dismissed, but nevertheless they take place within a much broader frame of reference that was not available before the 1970s at the earliest. In this process, room was created for new categories of victim and perpetrator, but as we shall see in subsequent chapters, there were also new opportunities for denial.

Chapter 2
The Legal Recognition of Torture Survivors

This chapter explores the conditions under which torture survivors gain legal recognition. In doing so, it examines the ways in which legal techniques prioritize and distinguish between different types of victim and the accounts they can give of themselves. Torture survivors are often, formally at least, singled out for specific attention, as deserving of particular respect for what they have suffered. The campaigns of the antitorture movement have been at least partially successful in having the protection for torture survivors codified into law. In the United States, people fleeing torture are granted protection under immigration laws, and the Torture Victim Protection Act of 1991 allows torture survivors to litigate for civil damages from perpetrators no matter where the torture occurred.[1] In the United Kingdom, there has been a long-standing attempt to pass similar legislation, in the form of the Torture Damages Bill. However, the vast majority of claims about torture in UK courts are made during asylum procedures. Although not singled out in the 1951 Refugee Convention, torture, with a few notable exceptions, will nearly always qualify as a form of persecution. Perhaps more important, the Human Rights Act 1998, by making the European Convention on Human Rights, and more specifically its Article 3, enforceable in English courts, explicitly extends protection to victims of torture.[2] The UK Border Agency has also given torture survivors special status in its assessment of claims for protection.[3]

The legal processes of recognition are seen by some critics as transforming fundamentally political issues into a form of passive victimhood. Wendy Brown, for example, has argued that rights "fix the identity of the injured . . . (and) codif[y] . . . the meanings of their actions against all possibilities of indeterminacy, ambiguity" (1995, 27). However, such arguments are in danger of creating too rigid, neat, and precise a picture, ignoring the ambiguity and indeterminacy of legal processes. They also ignore the ways in which victimhood is never taken for granted, and claims are always subject to second-guessing. Refugees in Europe and North America are widely said to face a "culture of disbelief." In the 1970s, refugees were largely portrayed as heroic figures fleeing from oppression in Chile, Argentina, or Southeast Asia; by the 1990s, however, the popular press and much political rhetoric has portrayed them as self-serving and duplicitous. As Didier Fassin and Estelle d'Halluin have argued, writing in the context of France, "feelings of solidarity and compassion gave way to suspicion often mixed with racist prejudices" (2007, 309–10).

The central argument of this chapter is that the legal recognition of torture survivors is not so much a technical process of codification but a series of unstable judgments played out on the boundary between fact and law. The processes of legal assessment mean that the recognition of torture survivors can be unpredictable and erratic. Despite their formal legal and administrative protections, the crucial issue for the vast majority of people claiming protection as torture survivors is not law but evidence. Most cases fall on issues of credibility. Put simply, torture survivors are not believed. Far from being treated as passive and fragile victims, those claiming protection are seen by immigration officials and judges as active agents who are always capable of manipulation.

In a context of generalized suspicion around people claiming asylum, legal processes provide a technique for assessing claims and thereby trying to move from uncertainty to a measure of certainty. In particular, attempts to produce legal certainty are filtered through rules of evidence. There is a relatively low standard of proof in asylum and human rights claims. In the United Kingdom, criminal claims have to be proved "beyond reasonable doubt" and civil cases on the "balance of probabilities," but claims for asylum and humanitarian protection are formally decided on a standard of "reasonable likelihood."[4] Furthermore, the United Nations High Commissioner for Refugees (UNHCR) *Handbook* says that applicants, "unless there are good reasons to the contrary, be given the benefit of the doubt" (1992, para 196). Yet, in practice, many lawyers argue that they actually find it hardest to prove an asylum claim and easiest to get a criminal conviction. There has been a *de facto*, if not officially recognized, increase in evidential requirements, and although no corroborative evidence is formally required, in practice tribunals are asking for ever higher levels of proof.

Claims for recognition as torture survivors take place in a context where evidence is inherently scarce. It is often very difficult for claimants to provide any evidence at all, apart from their own testimony. According to one Canadian immigration decision-maker, "We rarely even have as much information as I would consider necessary to choose a new appliance, much less make a decision about a person's future" (Maklin

2007, 1103). Lawyers must therefore present often-fragmented cases in a way that makes them seem credible and plausible. However, judges are well aware that all evidence is a human construct, and they are always looking for motivations behind the evidence. The lower standard of proof and relatively relaxed rules of evidence in asylum cases can make cases less predictable. Virtually anything can be submitted as evidence, but judges have no solid standards against which to assess it. Without firm rules of evidence, there is a constant switching between treating claims at face value and looking behind them for forms of dissimulation, a focus on formal legal proof and a wider concern with "what really happened." In all legal judgments, recognized uncertainty has to be transformed into practical certainty (Good 2007; Latour 2004). Yet, in the asylum process, the path from uncertainty to certainty is shot through with hesitations and doubts. There is, of course, always an element of chance in all legal proceedings, and no lawyer can predict with certainty which way a particular case will go. However, in asylum and human rights cases uncertainty over the facts is accentuated. It is not simply that judges are skeptical about claimants, but rather that they have no solid ground on which to decide to be skeptical.

This chapter focuses on a single claim by an Iranian male. It views the process from the perspective of the lawyers, bureaucrats, and judges who have to assess and process the claim. The chapter follows this individual case, from initial submission to final appeal, in order to examine the practical issues of evidence and legal argument involved in the recognition of torture. The case is reconstructed following interviews with the lawyers and attendance at the case hearing, as well as with analysis of the case documents. My research also included following an additional thirty-five claims from start to finish. Formally, assessments in refugee and human rights cases are about judgments of future risk. However, the first step to having a claim accepted is most often making a claim of past persecution or torture. This chapter will therefore focus on the attempt to prove past events. Judgments about future risk will be covered in Chapter 4.

Applying for Asylum

In the spring of 2009, Ali Khalili, a thirty-year-old Iranian male, arrived in the United Kingdom. Within three days, he had claimed asylum. Describing himself as a farmer and an atheist, Khalili said he had been accused in Iran of evangelizing Christianity, drinking alcohol, and insulting Islam. He told the British immigration official with whom he lodged the claim that he had been tortured by the Ettelaat, the Iranian intelligence service, before managing to escape to the United Kingdom.

Khalili was given a cursory screening interview when he made his initial claim, but he was not interviewed in depth until one month later, when he was questioned by a UK Border Agency official through a Farsi interpreter. The official went through a set of questions about what had happened to Khalili, why and how he had left Iran, and why he did not want to go back. The interview was led by the immigration official, focusing on the questions that he deemed important, giving little space for Khalili to explain what he thought was most relevant.

The British immigration official asked Khalili how he was arrested. Khalili explained that three months previously, the Ettelaat had come to his family home at night and searched his room before detaining him. The official then suddenly changed topic and asked Khalili if he had had previous problems with the Ettelaat. Khalili explained that two years prior, during the celebration for the festival of Ashura, he had been accused of laughing at a procession of self-flagellating men. He was detained by members of the Basij militia and beaten on his chest and legs. When the Ettelaat went to search his house, they found cans of beer as well as an illegal satellite dish. The next day, he was taken to the Ettelaat office, where he was beaten again. His left eye socket was broken by a particularly heavy blow. As he was blindfolded, he did not know whether it was a kick, a punch, or a strike with an object. He then went on to explain to the British official that after a few days he was taken to court and sentenced to twenty-four lashes for possessing alcohol and fined for having the satellite dish. After paying the fine and receiving the lashes, Khalili was released.

In the interview, the topic then turned to the conditions during Khalili's most recent detention. Khalili told the official that he was held in the Ettelaat office for about one week. He claimed to have been tortured during this time. When pushed to give more details, Khalili explained that he had been blindfolded and handcuffed. He had then been hung from the ceiling by his hands and spun around while being beaten. The soles of his feet were hit with sticks, and he was later wrapped up in a rug until he felt he would suffocate. The Ettelaat officials also sat heavily on his knees and punched him in the head until he bled. After one week, he was taken to the hospital because he had blood in his urine.

The immigration official then asked Khalili how he had managed to escape. Khalili explained that on the second night in the hospital his brother bribed one of the Ettelaat guards and he had managed to climb out a window and get into a waiting car. Khalili was questioned at length by the immigration official about the room he managed to escape from, and there was some confusion over whether Khalili climbed out the window of his room or of a nearby nurse's room. Khalili described how he stayed at his cousin's for two weeks, moving between his house and a shop. After a short break, the immigration official then turned to some apparent further inconsistencies in Khalili's account. He claimed that Khalili had said that he had been arrested three and a half months ago, which was before he had said he had talked to his friends about Christianity. Khalili said that he had difficulty remembering the precise dates because of his "psychological status."

The immigration official told Khalili that he found it hard to believe that, given the torture described, he had not received more injuries. Khalili explained that this was because the Ettelaat "do their job very well" and do not want to leave any marks. The immigration official then turned to the issue of Christianity. Although Khalili knew Jesus had been crucified, when questioned he could not name the disciple who betrayed Jesus, the names of Jesus' parents, or Jesus' birthday. Khalili again explained that his psychological state made it hard for him to remember these things. Finally, Khalili was asked if he had attended any Christian services while he was in the United Kingdom, and he replied that he had not had any time. The interview was drawn to a close and Khalili was told he would be informed of the decision in due course.

The Rejection

Khalili's case was being dealt with under a process within the UK immigration system, known as the New Asylum Model, which had been established in 2005 and was supposed to deal with cases in a faster and more efficient manner than previously. The UK Home Office boasted that this would lead not only to swifter decisions but also to faster removals (2006). Historically, cases had taken years to process, but under the new system some claims were being dealt with in a matter of weeks, although they could still take months or even years. One week after his interview, Khalili received a letter from the UK Border Agency signed by a different official from the one who had interviewed him. The letter quoted a report from the Danish immigration authorities that claimed "the consumption of alcohol in private homes is, in practice, not considered a crime any longer." The letter argued that therefore, "Your account of being arrested, charged and sentenced partially for alcohol consumption in your own home is not consistent with the above objective evidence." The letter went on to say, however, that even if this story were true, by Khalili's own account he was released and he was therefore not believed to be of any further interest to the Iranian authorities.

The letter then turned to Khalili's account of his religious interests. It pointed out that Khalili had failed to identify Jesus' birthday or the name of Jesus' parents. Although it was noted that he had been able to provide other information about Jesus, the letter argued that the information was in the public domain, and therefore they gave it little weight. It was therefore claimed that the level of knowledge of Christianity that Khalili showed was not consistent with his claim to have had conversations about Jesus with his friends. The letter went on to quote a previous Asylum and Immigration Tribunal decision, where it was ruled that "for the ordinary convert, who is neither a leader or ordained, nor a Pastor, nor a proselytiser or evangelist, the actual degree of risk of persecution or treatment breaching Article 3 is not sufficient to warrant the protection of either Convention."[5] The letter pointed out that by Khalili's own account he was none of the above, and therefore "according to the objective evidence" he would not be at risk on his return to Iran.

The issue of Khalili's second arrest was then addressed. The letter argued that numerous inconsistencies appeared in his claim, not least about the timing of events. It was also argued that the fact that Khalili claimed that the only significant long-term symptom he could show—blood in the urine—was inconsistent with his claims of repeated beatings. Quoting the Home Office's own Country of Origin Information Report, which claimed that Ettelaat was "one of the largest and most active intelligence agencies in the world," the letter argued that it was inconsistent that they were not able to find Khalili after he had escaped (COIS 2009). It was concluded that Khalili had given an "inconsistent and implausible account" of his experiences and therefore it was not accepted that he had ever been detained or was of interest to the Ettelaat. In short, the claim was not believed. As a result, the letter ended by saying that Khalili did not qualify for protection under the Refugee Convention or Article 3 and it was "therefore considered that your removal from the UK is appropriate."

Legal Representation

Shortly before his initial application, Khalili had found himself a law firm with a reputation for representing Iranian clients. The firm had been recommended by another Iranian who was staying in the same hostel as Khalili. The involvement of lawyers in initial claims is often limited. The appeals of most asylum applicants are publicly funded.[6] However, faced with growing bills and numbers of people claiming asylum, there is a constant squeeze on the cost of cases. Most lawyers can therefore only afford to spend a few hours on initial claims without losing money. The result is that only those who are politically dedicated, those who process cases at great speed, or those who subsidize the work with fees from more lucrative areas stay in asylum work.

Immigration lawyers run the spectrum from the dedicated, who share the concerns of their clients at a deep political level, to the solely pragmatic and instrumental.[7] Many lawyers entered the field in the 1990s, when immigration was a boom area for legal practice, and did so for entirely strategic reasons rather than a commitment to the area. They could equally be working in property or tort law. However, many others are profoundly committed to the cause of asylum and work in the area out of a sense of conviction. Whatever their motivations, all lawyers must negotiate a fine line in terms of dealing with the often slightly incoherent accounts that their clients might give them and of trying to present as persuasive a case as possible. In this sense, the area is little different from criminal or other areas of law. Lawyers are under a professional obligation not to mislead the court knowingly. However, they are aware that their clients will not always be telling the whole truth, and in immigration cases especially, might have very good reasons for not doing so, such as threats from people smugglers. The firm representing Khalili had a reputation among other practitioners for being both dedicated and efficient. However, they were still under immense time pressures, not least because of the faster processes introduced under the New Asylum Model. As a result, they tended to focus more on cases at appeal than on initial claims.

Very few applicants are accompanied by lawyers to their interviews with the UK Border Agency, as they cannot gain financial support for this, and even if they do attend, lawyers are not allowed to intervene during the interview. Furthermore, initial claims seldom set out the legal basis for the claim, hoping that the story will speak for itself. Following the initial rejection, Khalili's lawyer helped him appeal the decision. Appeals are very common. Of the more than 19,000 decisions made on initial asylum applications in 2008, more than 70 percent were refusals (Home Office 2009). Although not necessarily from the same cohort, as there would be a hangover from previous years, the tribunal received more than 10,000 appeals in the same year (Home Office 2009).

Torture and the Refugee Convention

Khalili's lawyer appealed under the Refugee Convention, as well as Article 3 of the European Convention on Human Rights. To qualify for protection under the Refugee Convention, a person must show that he or she has a "well-founded fear of being persecuted for reasons of race, religion, nationality, membership of a particular social group or political opinion."[8] Although it is not mentioned explicitly, torture can count as persecution as long as it is done for Refugee Convention reasons. However, there is no necessary relationship, and it is possible to envisage someone being tortured who would not qualify for refugee protection, as the person would have been tortured for non–Refugee Convention reasons.

The European Convention on Human Rights offers specific protection to victims of torture and related forms of ill-treatment. It is fair to say that its drafters never envisaged that Article 3 on the prohibition of torture and inhuman or degrading treatment or punishment would be used in immigration cases. However, case law now means that Article 3 is interpreted to mean that states cannot send people back to countries where they face a "real risk" of torture or other forms of ill-treatment.[9] In 1990, the then Conservative home secretary had tried to deport Karamjit Singh Chahal, a Sikh separatist activist, to India. The basis for the attempted deportation was that Chahal's "continued presence in the United Kingdom was unconducive to the public good for reasons of national security and other reasons of a political nature, namely the international fight against terrorism."[10] Chahal had twice been arrested by the British police under the Prevention of Terrorism Act and released without charge. The first arrest involved allegations that he was involved in a conspiracy to murder the Indian prime minister, Rajiv Gandhi; the second involved a claim that he had conspired to murder moderate Sikhs within the United Kingdom. Chahal's deportation order was fought all the way to the European Court of Human Rights. The court ruled that if there is a real risk of torture, deportation or expulsion is absolutely prohibited and "the activities of the individual in question, however undesirable or dangerous cannot be a material consideration."[11] The risk of torture was grounds for preventing deportation.

Prior to 1998, the prohibition on returning someone to a place where they face the risk of torture and other forms of ill-treatment was not directly enforceable in English courts. However, the incorporation of the European Convention into English law, through the Human Rights Act 1998, opened a new category of protection.[12] The UK Border Agency Guidance states that in order to count as an Article 3 violation, the risk must reach a "minimum level of severity and involve actual bodily injury or intense physical or mental suffering" (UKBA no date, 16). This is in contrast to the Refugee Convention, in which persecution does not need to entail actual injury or suffering. Acts must also go beyond the suffering produced by legitimate punishment, although this leaves open what counts as legitimate punishment. In one leading Iranian case, for example, it was ruled that an Article 3 breach does not involve "mere distress, or poor economic conditions, low level harassment or deprivation of social rights."[13] Crucially, Article 3 does not discriminate between torture and other forms of inhuman or degrading treatment.

All are equally prohibited. Furthermore, unlike the Refugee Convention, there is no requirement that torture be carried out for reasons of race, religion, nationality, membership in a particular social group, or political opinion.

Article 3 has been used in cases brought by citizens of Iran who seek protection from risks involving general prison conditions, punishment for adulterers, military punishments, and punishment of homosexuals.[14] In most cases, however, Article 3 and Refugee Convention arguments are run together, with little, if any focus on the specific nature of the article. Article 3 is tacked on, almost as an afterthought, to more detailed claims under the Refugee Convention. Recognition under the Refugee Convention provides marginally greater benefits, such as free-travel documents. Many lawyers admit, though, that where possible they will try to squeeze any claim under the Refugee Convention, as they fear that judges assume the Refugee Convention is so broad that if a claim does not stand under the convention, it has deep problems of its own. Even in a human rights claim, torture is rarely singled out, and the far broader category of Article 3 is used. Khalili was relatively unusual in making a claim of torture early in the process. Most claimants describe beatings and interrogations, but they do not necessarily describe them as torture.

Lawyers seem to be of two minds as to whether to use the word *torture* in their submissions. Some worry that it can appear too emotive or that it is too imprecise. As the task is to persuade judges over the facts, it is better to provide a vivid description than to use a general catchall word. Other lawyers argue that using the word *torture* can be useful, as it increases the severity of the potential risks faced on return.

Issues of Evidence: From the General to the Specific

To make a persuasive claim, applicants must demonstrate why they would be tortured, who would torture them, why they cannot move elsewhere in their own country, and why they cannot seek protection from the state. They must provide evidence that the state or other actors behave in this way, and that the individual applicant has been singled out for attention. There are both general and individual issues that need documenting (Thomas 2008). In theory a claim does not need corroborating evidence, but in practice most lawyers will worry that a claim left to stand for itself could be unpersuasive to a judge. For this reason, lawyers will try to collect as much evidence as possible in order to support the claim. Collecting evidence is often difficult at the initial claim stage because of pressures of time and money, so in practice most evidence is gathered at the appeal stage. However, the individualized evidence to back most asylum claims is sparse. There are very seldom eyewitnesses and little potential for close forensic examination. The perpetrator of the violence or persecution is also absent.

In contrast to events that occur in places like the Democratic Republic of the Congo or Somalia, events in Iran are relatively well documented. A host of human rights organizations and newspapers report on the country. Amnesty International and Human Rights Watch, among others, routinely report human rights violations, and torture in particular. Lawyers, as well as the UK Border Agency, also rely heavily on the annual human rights reports of the US State Department. Perhaps not surprisingly, given the condition of US–Iran relations, these reports are highly critical of Iran's human rights record. In 2008, they made the following claims: "Common methods of torture and abuse in prisons included prolonged solitary confinement with sensory deprivation, beatings, long confinement in contorted positions, kicking detainees with military boots, hanging detainees by the arms and legs, threats of execution, burning with cigarettes, sleep deprivation, and severe and repeated beatings with cables or other instruments on the back and on the soles of the feet" (US State Department 2008).

The UK Border Agency also compiles its own publicly available Country of Origin Information Service (COIS) reports on the main countries from which UK asylum seekers originate. These reports are based on a compilation of sources from human rights organizations and newspapers. The COI report for Iran in 2009 quotes Human Rights Watch as reporting "numerous reports of torture and mistreatment" and Amnesty International as claiming that "torture and other ill-treatment of detainees were common and committed with impunity" (COIS 2009). In all, there are more than forty mentions of torture in the COI report on Iran.

Asylum tribunals have also adopted a system known as country guidance cases, where it makes findings of fact with regard to the situation in specific countries. The focus here is on whether particular groups—rather than individuals—are at risk. The system was introduced following a concern that the tribunal was making widely varying decisions on the general situation in the same country. In Iranian cases, the tribunal often came to different conclusions as to whether Christian converts, for example, would be at risk of execution. By 2010, more than fifteen country guidance determinations had been made on Iran. In these decisions it is argued that the Iranian state is involved in "kidnapping and beatings, torture and killings" and that security forces and prison personnel "continue to torture detainees and prisoners."[15] Against this background, the UK Border Agency and the asylum tribunal accept that the

Iranian state tortures its citizens. However, the key issue is to prove that it has done so, or is likely to do so, in a particular case.

One of the most important forms of detailed, case-specific evidence is "country evidence reports," which are usually written by British or émigré academics and set out details in a particular country in relation to the specific claim. Khalili's lawyer, however, pointed out that she was not sure how much a specific country evidence report would add in this case. The key point here was to individualize Mr. Khalili's case and to provide evidence that he had been tortured. Given that he was not high profile and was unlikely to have been written about by a human rights organization or newspaper, it was unlikely that any country expert could provide this kind of supporting evidence.

Given the absence of much other evidence, the key document in a claim for protection is often the witness statement of the claimant. In many cases, lawyers will not submit a witness statement at the initial stage, as they are concerned that the UK Border Agency will simply use it to seek inconsistencies at the asylum interview. Even when a witness statement is taken earlier on, and some lawyers think it provides their clients with good practice for later UK Border Agency interviews, it will often be held back and only submitted at the appeal stage.

The writing of the witness statement is a negotiation between the lawyer and the client and a carefully crafted statement will iron out any contradictions and set out the account in a clear and concise manner. Following receipt of his rejection letter, Khalili composed a witness statement with his lawyer, through an interpreter, over a number of meetings. The statement was written in English and then read back to him in Farsi. In his statement, Khalili outlined his claim once more, and added some further details. He wrote that his father had been a local leader prior to the 1979 revolution and his family thereafter had a reputation of being antirevolutionary. He went on to claim that, as a result of his beatings during his first detention, part of his lip was numb and he could still feel the broken bone underneath his eye. It was also argued that the confusion over his manner of escape was the result of a translation error. He accepted that he was not Christian, merely someone who had been interested in talking about Christianity, but he argued that the authorities would still be interested in him because he came from a very isolated area and people are "small minded and insular." He added, finally, that he had spoken to his brother who had told him that a summons had been posted ordering him to attend the revolutionary court and that he was expecting this to be sent to him soon.

Medicolegal reports are also commonly used to support asylum claims by providing individualized evidence. They can be used to speak about physical scars as well as psychological trauma and therefore to corroborate claims of ill-treatment. The recognized leaders in the field are reports by the Medical Foundation for the Care of Victims of Torture; the UK Border Agency has historically had special arrangements to delay decisions if a Medical Foundation report is pending. However, the Medical Foundation can sometimes take more than six months to write a report and the tribunal will often refuse to adjourn cases in order for reports to be written. As a result, many lawyers will go directly to independent doctors and psychologists. Given that Khalili and his lawyer were not expecting the case to be heard for several months, Khalili's lawyer requested a report from the Medical Foundation.

The Medical Foundation doctor saw Khalili twice and wrote a report on the basis of his interview and examination. The doctor had written dozens of reports and over time had become known as something of a specialist in Iranian cases. In writing his report, the doctor used the language set out in the Istanbul Protocol (OHCHR 2004). The Istanbul Protocol, which has been adopted by the United Nations, is a set of guidelines for the assessment of claims of torture. The tribunal has required its use in the assessment of scars (see Chapter 3 for an extended discussion).[16] The doctor's report on Khalili said that the "scars on his ankles confirm that he was restrained in chains tightly bound around them for a prolonged period." He went on to say that although "he has no signs on his body of the beating and kicking he experienced, this does not mean that it did not occur, for in a man of this physique, recovery would be expected without residual marking." The doctor added that "there is evidence of facial nerve damage caused by a heavy blunt blow to his left maxillary arch. . . . This injury is the consequence of a blow to the area by blunt trauma and is consistent with the history [given by Mr. Khalili] . . . although it could have occurred in a number of other ways such as a blow to the face in a farming accident or in highly competitive physical sport such as rugby. Mr. Khalili does not nor has he previously played such sports." The report also concluded that it "is my opinion that Mr. Khalili has suffered from post traumatic stress disorder [PTSD] occasioned by his ill-treatment. Mr. Khalili's psychological distress pattern was consistent with the DSM criteria, as his ill-treatment was remembered in the form of flashbacks and nightmares, he has difficulty in concentrating and his sleep pattern is deranged by intrusive flashbacks." Although the doctor clearly felt that Khalili had been tortured, he could not say for sure what had caused Khalili's injuries and psychological states, but his clinical opinion was that they were entirely consistent with the account Khalili had given.

Having collected all the evidence, Khalili's lawyer told me that she thought Iranian cases were relatively easy to win compared to, say, cases from Afghanistan because politically there was a widespread acceptance that the Iranian regime was "nasty."[17] The key issue though would be moving from the general to the particular. The lawyer hoped that the medical report, by tying Khalili's account to particular injuries, would provide this individualized evidence. Although medicolegal reports in particular can provide persuasive individualized evidence, lawyers are not always entirely sure how useful expert reports are in their arguments. Some told me they commission them simply because they will be criticized if they do not. Others argued that it was their professional responsibility to prepare the case as thoroughly as possible, and this meant collecting as much evidence as possible, irrespective of its impact. Furthermore, they hoped that by putting in as much evidence as possible, it would open up the possibility of further appeal, if the judge makes an error of law and fails to treat the report adequately.

The Appeal

An appeal is a full rehearing of a case. It is formally adversarial. The UK Border Agency presents its reasons for refusing the claim, and the applicant's lawyer makes the argument that this is unlawful, with the judge deciding between the two claims. Khalili's appeal was heard four months after his initial refusal, on the fourth floor of a modern office block overlooking a superhighway. He was made to wait for several hours, until the previous case was finished. When his turn came, the UK Border Agency had not arrived; it was relying instead on the Reasons for Refusal letter that it had sent to Khalili in order to make its case. This is not unusual.

During the hearing, Khalili sat in the middle of the room, accompanied by an interpreter. His lawyer was reluctant to talk to him, as the interpreter had been appointed by the tribunal rather than supplied by her firm. Khalili was wearing a dark suit and white socks, which appeared to be covered in bloodstains. The judge began by asking Khalili for some clarifications. In the absence of the UK Border Agency, many judges are accused of taking on the immigration authority's role themselves, by asking inquisitorial-style questions, when judges are supposed to limit their questions to issues of clarification.[18] At Khalili's hearing, the judge asked how the Ettelaat knew that the beer and satellite television did not belong to his parents, and Khalili explained that he had confessed immediately that they were his. Khalili's lawyer confirmed that although the summons to the court was posted by his brother, it did not seem to have arrived. There were no questions at all about his torture, and his cross-examination ended after about fifteen minutes.

The hearing then moved on to legal arguments. At this point, the judge turned to Khalili and explained that the interpreter would do her best to give him the gist of what was being said, but they did not want to interrupt the flow in order to give him all the details. Khalili's lawyer turned directly to rebutting the Home Office Reasons for Refusal letter. In particular, she pointed out that the claims that Khalili did not know enough about Christianity were misplaced, as he had never claimed to be an expert on Christianity, merely someone involved in casual conversations among friends. She then pointed out that the immigration official did not have the medical expertise to say whether someone would be expected to have more scars than Khalili if that person had been treated in the way he claimed. Indeed, she argued that the medicolegal report explicitly says that Khalili would not, and that the doctor was of the opinion that he was suffering from PTSD. Khalili's lawyer ended her presentation by reminding the judge of the low standard of proof required in asylum hearings and that there was nothing implausible in anything that Khalili had said. Indeed the fact that he had not embellished his claims should be seen as an indicator of his honesty. With that, the hearing ended and the judge said he would give his decision in three weeks.

The decision was posted one month later. In the written judgment, the judge noted that the doctor had argued that the scars on Khalili's ankles were consistent with being tied by a chain, that there was evidence of facial nerve damage caused by a heavy blow, and that Khalili suffered from PTSD. However, the judge noted that on its own this did not establish that Khalili had been tortured or even detained, merely that he had been chained at some point and had suffered a blow to the face. He added that the medicolegal report's description of Khalili's psychological state did not particularly assist with the case, as the description provided to the doctor "could easily have been self-serving." Indeed, the judge noted that the doctor had written that Khalili gave the "outward appearance of being happy." The judge went on to say, however, that he was prepared to accept Khalili's account of his initial detention as credible, according to the lower standard of proof, but noted that Khalili did not experience any difficulties with the authorities between 2006 and 2009.

The judge wrote though that he had more problems with Khalili's account of the events in 2009. He noted that he found it of "great significance that the appellant did not know the circumstances of Jesus' birth or his parentage," which are "central to any understanding of Christianity." The judge went on to argue that "even making allowances" for Khalili's "psychological upset, it is difficult to determine that he has been anything other than vague in relation to the time line in relation to this part of the account." The judge also said he found it implausible that Khalili could walk from his cousin's house to the shop if he was in the condition he claimed, and that furthermore he would have not taken this risk if he was wanted by the Ettelaat. The judge's determination stated that he was "unable to accept that the appellant has given a credible account of the circumstances leading up to his claimed detention, torture and subsequent escape." He added that "there is no reason why the appellant should not be returned to Iran in safety and with no real risk of serious harm coming to him." Khalili's appeal was dismissed.

Inconsistent Decisions?

The major issue lawyers complain of is inconsistency in asylum decisions.[19] Khalili's lawyer had been fairly confident that Khalili would win the appeal, but had rightly refused to predict with any certainty whether this would happen. There is some sense of predictability when the specific judge who will hear the case is known. A few large law firms have potted profiles of judges, but by the time the judge is known it is usually too late to change the way the case is argued, although sometimes it is possible to argue for an adjournment on other grounds. There are also clearly some benefits in preparing a case well. Although the type of cases they take on is clearly an important factor, some lawyers report a success rate around 20 percent, whereas others report success rates of 70 percent. However, general success rates do not determine individual cases; they show only overall trends. One can never be sure where an individual case will fall on this broader spectrum. All cases therefore remain inherently unpredictable. One experienced asylum lawyer told me that more often than not he lost cases he had thought were certainties and won cases that he had thought were hopeless.[20] The best he could do, he said, was to prepare his case as thoroughly as possible, given the constraints on his time, and hope that if he had a negative decision he could launch an appeal. There is of course an element of unpredictability in all legal cases. If the outcome of litigation were 100 percent certain, then no rational person would go to court. However, the broad consensus among lawyers is that asylum cases are off the scale in terms of unpredictability.

For some lawyers, the particular unpredictability of asylum cases is put down to the relative expertise or prejudice of the judges. Asylum judges are relatively low on the judicial ladder, and in general the area has low status in the legal profession. Judges, like lawyers, cover the full range of political and legal background. Some are former high-profile immigration lawyers themselves. Others use the job as a first rung up the judicial ladder, coming from other areas of law. Some judges are thought of as especially cynical, but this does not necessarily map onto political background. Many of the toughest judges are former pro-asylum campaigners. However, whether they are viewed as prejudiced or not, judges are still widely seen as inconsistent in their decision making.

British immigration processes are not alone in being accused of producing inconsistent decisions. A wide-ranging analysis of American asylum decisions found that "there is remarkable variation in decision making from one official to the next, from one office to the next, from one region to the next, from one court of appeals to the next, and from one year to the next" (Ramji-Nogales, Schoenholtz, and Schrag 2009, 3). However, British lawyers complain that it is not just that decisions are inconsistent between judges or courts, but that individual judges can also seem to be inconsistent in their own decisions.

The widespread consensus, from both left and right, is that the practices through which asylum and human rights claims are processed are inadequate. Criticism of the asylum process in the United Kingdom focus on either its implicit discriminations and prejudices or its technical inadequacies. The UK Border Agency and judges are accused of bad faith, incompetence, or a desire to put efficiency targets ahead of the thorough assessment of claims (House of Commons Home Affairs Select Committee 2004; IAC 2008; National Audit Office 2004; Smith 2004; UNHCR 2005). There is an implicit assumption that as long as the right reforms are put in place, the correct training initiated, and the most suitable technical fixes rolled out, everything will be, if not perfect, at least considerably fairer and more just. However, such calls for reform are perhaps too optimistic about the potential for the legal assessment of claims. What I want to argue here is that inconsistency is a product of the very process of decision making in asylum cases.

The Standards of Proof

In large measure, the unpredictability of judges' decisions has to be seen in the context of the limitations of the evidence before them and the legal techniques available for assessing it. The lack of any rules of evidence produces a broad space of uncertainty at the heart of the asylum process.

The standard of proof in asylum claims is informally often said by practitioners to be the same as a one in ten chance.[21] Although the claimant bears the burden of proof, in that it is up to the claimant to substantiate the claim, the burden is relatively low. This means, for example, that the claimant is not formally required to produce any corroborative evidence, if he or she can show that the claim is in and of itself credible and plausible. Furthermore, any evidence that a claimant can muster does not have to go through the same legal tests as it would in civil and criminal cases to see whether it is admissible. The ordinary civil law rules of evidence do not apply, and judges do not have to decide whether to admit or not admit evidence, but rather they have to decide how much relative weight to give it.[22] As Lord Justice Sedley, one of the most famously liberal judges on the bench, said, "Some will be so unreliable as to be worthless; some will amount to no more than straws in the wind; some will be indicative but not, by itself, probative; some may be compelling but contra-indicated by other evidence. . . . No probabilistic cut-off operates here: everything capable of having a bearing has to be given the weight, great or little, due to it. . . . [This is not] a forum in which the improbable is magically endowed with the status of certainty, but as a unitary process of evaluation of evidential material of many kinds and qualities against the Convention's criteria of eligibility for asylum."[23] No evidence can be ruled out, no matter how apparently flimsy. All evidence must be considered in the round and in the light of the claim as a whole.

However, despite the lower formal standard of proof, it is hard to see how this relates to the ways in which decisions can be reached in practice. Indeed, this has been recognized by the courts, which have called the standard of proof a "pragmatic legal fiction."[24] The standards of "reasonable likelihood" and "benefit of the doubt" should mean that judges are comfortable with saying "I do not believe this claim, but nonetheless some of the evidence is plausible, however slight, and I am therefore allowing the appeal." This hardly ever happens, if at all. Indeed, if a judge wrote that in an appeal that was allowed, it would only invite a challenge by the Home Office. If we take the lower standard of proof as implying a one in ten chance of success, at a practical level it is not clear what it might mean to give probability a numerical value in asylum cases. Statistical probability applies only across a range of cases, and legal decisions are applied one at a time. Probability judgments are also always based on assumptions and are made in the light of the facts available (Eggleston 1978). In legal proceedings, assumptions are normally kept stable by rules of evidential procedure. Yet in asylum cases, these rules of evidence are deliberately loose; as a result, in these cases, it is not known what is known and what is unknown.

The lower evidential standards in asylum claims mean that all evidence is always in question. Writing about the French Conseil d'État, Bruno Latour has argued that legal decision making is a process of moving away from the facts as fast as possible (2004). Latour claims that once they are decided on, the facts are held static and in place, while the more important business of law moves forward. Although there are important particularities to French administrative law, the general argument is useful when examining the relationship between "fact" and "law" more generally. Broadly speaking, judges are not concerned with profound philosophical questions as to what "really happened," as much as assessing the evidence that is presented before them. Legal processes are pragmatic; they are aimed at getting something done, at coming to a decision, rather than making a statement about the world (Good 2007, 261–65). Legal facts are important not because they shed light on the cosmos but because they help judges come to a decision about a particular legal dispute. According to Latour, judges ask for "nothing more transcendent than a simple ending of the discussion" (2009, 239). If a fact cannot be proved according to the rules of legal evidence, it is considered not to have happened.

In common law systems the processes of moving from fact to law are governed by rules of evidence, which set out what can be allowed into the legal domain and what cannot. However, in asylum cases, the relative flexibility of the rules of evidence means that it is hard to move beyond the facts. The facts are nearly always all still in question. It is very difficult to reach that stable point where a judge can decide that, for the sake of legal argument, he or she is going to take it as read that a particular event has happened, and then move on. Having more precise and rigorous rules of evidence would force judges to rule out a great deal of the evidence that is presented to support asylum claims. Conversely, having no rules of evidence means that there are no solid standards through which evidence can be interpreted. As a result, all pieces of evidence presented in the course of asylum and human rights appeals can be assessed at face value or questioned in terms of the motives behind their production. The distinction between legal evidence and truth is a basic part of any introductory law course. Yet given the relaxed rules of evidence in asylum cases, this separation is hard, if not very hard, to make. In this context, on the one hand, claims are treated in a mechanistic and formal manner, as a matter of legal evidence and not necessarily as truth. On the other hand, all claims can be judged intuitively, as an attempt to determine "what really happened."

Credibility

Khalili's case, as with the majority of claims, was not rejected on a point of law; rather, it was rejected because he had not been believed. Most cases are dismissed not because they are deemed to fall outside the Refugee Convention or the Human Rights Act but because they are deemed not to be credible by the judge. The way judgments are made about credibility goes to the nub of the uncertainty in asylum decision making.

What will be credible to one person can therefore be not credible to the next, depending on his or her own experiences and beliefs. Indeed this is recognized by the English legal system. Unlike decisions on matters of law, where it is implicitly assumed that there is a right or wrong answer, the courts recognize that credibility is in the eye of the beholder. Although judges are warned not to universalize from their own experience on issues of credibility, there is no expectation that different judges looking at the same pieces of evidence will come to the same conclusion. According to one leading piece of case law, different tribunals "hearing the same witnesses may reach quite different views."[25] As appeals are only allowed from the tribunal on issues of law, rather than interpretations of fact, rejections on the grounds of lack of credibility are very difficult to take further.

Despite or even because of the recognized subjectivity of credibility, there have been attempts to regularize what can and what cannot count as credible. The UNHCR defines a credible account as one that is "coherent and plausible, not contradicting generally known facts, and therefore is, on balance capable of being believed" (1998, 11). The insertion of "capable of being believed" implies that the decision maker does not have to believe the account but rather that it is possible that someone else might. The UK Border Agency has tried to further clarify the issue by providing guidance that divides credibility into "internal" and "external" issues. Internal credibility relates to the coherence of the account and the details provided by the applicant. External credibility relates to the match between the account and "generally known facts." Crucially, credibility is not the same as plausibility (Good 2009). Plausibility refers to the "apparent reasonableness or truthfulness" of the account, without referring to whether the individual is actually telling the truth.[26] As such, "a story may be implausible and yet may properly be taken as credible; it may be plausible and yet properly not believed."[27] In effect what all these attempts at definitions do is substitute one discretion-laden phrase for another.[28]

A further attempt was made to formalize assessments of credibility through Section 8 of the Asylum and Immigration (Treatment of Claimants) Act 2004. The act says that credibility assessments should take into account any behaviors that seem designed to mislead, including a failure to produce a passport, producing a false travel document, destroying a travel document, failing to claim in a safe third country, and failing to claim until after being detained by immigration authorities. However, the application of Section 8 is far from straightforward. Decision makers are also told to give due regard to issues such as the mental health of the claimant. Given that there are many reasons why people might behave in the ways set out in Section 8, not all of them pernicious, judges have often taken this direction under discretion.[29] Sometimes judges refer to Section 8 to support making negative credibility findings; at other times judges may simply refer to Section 8 and then ignore it.

The assessment of credibility in asylum claims involves judgments about spoken words and texts. In asylum and human rights cases there is little of the grand oratory of courtroom drama. As the UK Border Agency did not appear, Khalili's time in court lasted barely an hour and involved a number of cursory and formal questions. Although the judgment of credibility is therefore of central importance, it is rarely simply a matter of judging demeanor in the courtroom.[30] Instead, credibility is often an issue of assessing limited oral evidence against a range of written evidence, looking behind both, to make an assessment of the motivations of those who produced the evidence.

Any attempt to judge credibility raises important and unanswered questions about the nature of coherence, plausibility, and the status of what the tribunal often calls "generally known facts."[31] Credibility is by its very nature ambiguous and uncertain. According to a Canadian immigration decision maker, "It is frequently difficult to articulate in rational terms why one does, or does not, believe another. Decision makers may put a lot of faith in their 'gut feelings' about credibility, but recognize that gut feeling does not amount to a legally defensible basis for a decision" (Maklin 2007, 1103). Everyday language synonyms for the word *credible* include "believable" and "trustworthy." Yet what distinguishes belief from more definitive forms of knowledge is that it is not immediately susceptible to positivistic proof. Equally, trust implies a level of uncertainty. We trust in situations where we are not entirely certain or sure. Trust is built on the lack of knowledge and, therefore, always assumes that subterfuge is a possibility. Attempts to judge credibility therefore work in the space of the partially unknown.

Questions of Evidence

All evidence presented before the tribunal can always be questioned. Official documents, for example, presented to corroborate an account can be seen as persuasive, or they can undermine a claim. Khalili had tried to get hold of an arrest warrant to back his claim. However, judges can equally use documents as evidence that a case is untrustworthy by arguing that false documents are easy to obtain, and the likelihood that a claimant has a false document speaks to the person's general lack of credibility.[32] In one important case involving a Pakistani national, which has been influential in Iranian cases, the judge argued that "we know from experience and country information that there are countries where it is easy and often relatively inexpensive to obtain 'forged' documents. . . . It is necessary to shake off any preconception that official looking documents are genuine, based on experience of documents in the United Kingdom, and to approach them with an open mind."[33]

Medical reports that speak to issues of physical or psychological injury are also often read in two ways. For some judges, they are persuasive; for others, they can be dismissed as based entirely on the story told by the claimant to the clinician.[34] I have also been told by a judge who sat in the same building as the one where Khalili's case was heard that, as far as he was concerned, if a doctor said someone had a particular condition, he thought he was in no position to contradict the statement. Formally at least, the UK Border Agency's own directions also state that a supportive medical report can be taken as a good indicator of a well-founded claim unless there is good reason for supposing otherwise.[35] Medical Foundation reports are usually treated as the gold standard by judges.

Yet judges can also take the opposite tack. In the late 1990s, it became increasingly common for lawyers to submit medical or psychological reports as part of their client's claim. However, serious questions began to be raised about the professionalism and quality of many of these reports, psychiatric reports in particular. As one judge argued, "The quality of reports is so variable and sadly often so poor and unhelpful, that there is no necessary obligation to give them weight merely because they are medical or psychiatric reports."[36] Reports that speak about post-traumatic stress disorder (PTSD) have historically been treated with skepticism by judges. The diagnosis of PTSD in Khalili's medical report was dismissed by the judge as being based on an account that "could easily have been self-serving." I have sat in a training session, led by a judge, for doctors who write medicolegal reports, where the judge expressed extreme skepticism about any claim of PTSD. He told the audience that, as far as he was concerned, anyone could be diagnosed with PTSD, and if he left the building and went into the nearest train station, he would be surprised if 90 percent of the people there did not fit the diagnosis. Therefore, he argued that it was of little use in helping him make his decisions. This particular judge's attitude seems to be fairly widespread. Khalili's lawyer told me that over the last five years, in her experience, judges had been giving less and less weight to reports that claimed PTSD.[37] Reports from the Medical Foundation for the Care of Victims of Torture, whether about PTSD or scars, are on the whole given more weight by judges, but by no means all reports are produced by the Medical Foundation.

Judges can find it hard to assess the expertise of the people in front of them. There are no formal requirements that qualify someone to be an expert in UK courts. Formally the judge simply has to be convinced that the expert in question has sufficient up-to-date knowledge and that the expert is objective. However, it is difficult for a judge, who is not an expert in this area, to gain a sense of relative level of knowledge. Qualifications, professional experience and references in reports are not always entirely transparent. As a result, the judge is largely groping in the dark for standards by which to evaluate the evidence. In assessing the expertise behind medical reports judges usually fall back on formal qualifications. A report by a consultant psychiatrist is often given more weight than one written by a counselor, irrespective of their relative expertise on torture survivors.

The objectivity of reports has been questioned by judges (see, for example, Barnes 2004). Experts are instructed that their duty is to the court rather than to the claimant; in practice, however, they have direct contact only with the claimant's lawyer. Lawyers are highly unlikely to submit reports that are unhelpful for the case. I write expert witness reports for Palestinians claiming asylum in the United Kingdom. In the first few years of writing these reports I once wrote one that said the account given by the lawyer's client was not, in my opinion, plausible. I received an irate phone call from the lawyer, who was obviously completely taken aback by what I had done. Since then, I refuse to write reports where I have serious questions. In this context, reports can be seen as having a partisan edge. As one senior judge put it: "All [experts] suffer from the difficulty that very rarely are they entirely objective in their approach and the sources relied on are frequently (and no doubt sometimes with good reason) unidentified. Many have fixed opinions about the regime in a particular country and will be inclined to accept anything which is detrimental to that regime. This means that more often than not the expert in question, even if he has the credentials which qualify him in that role, will be acting more as an advocate than an expert witness."[38] In one case, a judge suggested that the accuracy of reports produced by an expert, who is widely used for reports on the Middle East, be "treated with caution." The expert later successfully sued the tribunal for defamation after it appeared that the critical remarks were put up in error and should have been deleted from the published decision.

Perhaps the most obvious example of the way in which some forms of evidence can be read as supporting or undermining a case is the use of inconsistencies in judging credibility. Most claims are dismissed for vagueness and contradictions in the claimant's account. Yet at the same time, vagueness and contradictions can be taken as evidence of trauma.[39] At stake here is a particular model of what can and cannot be recollected. In this context, psychological reports, for example, either can be used to explain inconsistencies or vagueness by talking about trauma or can be dismissed because they are based on inconsistent and vague accounts.[40] As one leading judgment argues: "It would be absurd if the ICD-10 criteria were to be read to mean that all persons who suffer from PTSD have a memory loss which prevents them from giving a proper account of themselves in the context of an asylum claim."[41]

Oral evidence can also be read both ways. Too polished a piece of evidence can appear contrived and rehearsed, but if a claimant stumbles and hesitates when asked questions the claimant can seem to be making it up as he or she goes along. As Sandvik has argued more broadly, "Displays of skillful personal testimony may be counterproductive when they collide with ideas about demeanour or authenticity" (2009, 239). Lawyers therefore have a difficult balancing act; they must present cases that are persuasive but not make their cases look too manipulated in a context where everyone is well aware that all evidence is constructed with the precise aim of winning a case. A case that is too neat and coherent can appear too well prepared and duplicitous. Yet a case that is partial and incoherent can equally appear to be disingenuous. Cases have to be presented in a way that makes them convincing but not appearing to be too deliberate and artificial.

Suspicion runs through the processes through which claims for protection by torture survivors are assessed. The issue here is the relative weight given to the different forms of evidence presented by survivors and experts. As individual narratives of survivors are often questioned, there can be a reliance on expert knowledge. Writing in the French context, Fassin and d'Halluin have argued that individual testimony of evidence about mental health is treated with relatively less weight than documented marks on the body (2007, 302). However, in the United Kingdom at least, all evidence, whether documentary, personal, physical, or psychological, is suspect. Although experts may be given more space than survivors, even their evidence is not taken at face value. Indeed, the very idea of legal representation itself implies a gap between what is presented and the fact it claims to represent, opening a space for subterfuge.

Erratic Recognition?

The legal assessment of claims by torture survivors is inherently erratic. Legality may create the hope of greater predictability, stability, and objectivity, but it can also bring with it evidential processes that produce unpredictable and unstable decision making. In this context, the recognition of torture survivors is therefore best thought of as a form of guesswork. This is not to say that most judges are not diligent and professional. Nor is it to say that they do not try to make their decisions in a reasoned and patterned manner (Thomas 2009). In some cases, it is relatively straightforward to come to a decision. These are cases in which the evidence is so strong or so weak that it is hard to come down the other way. However, most cases are not like this; in most cases, evidence is partial or incomplete. Nor is it to say that expert evidence cannot be very persuasive. A medicolegal report, in particular, that can find a high degree of consistency between a client's account and the marks on the person's body can be very persuasive. Yet, in many cases, such reports are not obtainable or when they are they can only provide a restricted amount of information to help corroborate a claim. Nor is it to argue that there are not general patterns of class- and race-based prejudice toward specific types of claimants, creating hierarchies of perceived victimhood. Indeed, it would be surprising if there were not. Rather, it is to argue that the limitations and problems in the evidence mean that in most cases, judges are always reduced to making a series of more or less educated guesses. Legal techniques, or prejudices for that matter, are often of little use in assessing the evidence.

In singling out torture as a universal human rights violation, specific political conflicts are fitted into a universal template. Those seeking recognition and protection must place their claims within the same framework. As with many legal processes, important questions are therefore raised about the ways in which the law translates complex experiences rooted in very specific histories and life trajectories into a universal legal category. In practice, though, the legal specificity of torture often dissolves in asylum claims. The promise of protection for torture survivors is not unique to human rights law and can also be found, in large part, in the Refugee Convention, with its broader category of persecution. Furthermore, Article 3 of the European Convention on Human Rights does not solely protect those who face the risk of torture but covers inhuman or degrading treatment or punishment more broadly. Very rarely, if ever, will the specific nature of torture ever become a point of legal argument. In British immigration tribunals, it is very rare indeed to find a case in which a judge rules that someone has or has not been tortured or is likely to face torture. Instead the issue is treated as a more general one of persecution or ill-treatment.

There are similarities here with claims for civil damages for torture victims. In the United States, the Torture Victim Protection Act allows torture survivors to file claims for civil damages as torture survivors. In England, under the Human Rights Act 1998, a person can seek damages for an alleged act of torture, asserting a breach of Article 3 of the European Convention on Human Rights.[42] However, in practice, it is arguable that the English courts have yet to recognize torture as a standalone basis for civil claims. Claims have been run through the notions of trespass against the person, assault, and battery (Virgo 2001).[43] As one of the lawyers involved in making a claim for torture damages for a British national against officials of the Saudi state, told me, "We did not use 'torture' as a legal term of art, but in a descriptive sense."[44] Perhaps most important, the courts have also refused to recognize civil claims against foreign state officials on the grounds of state immunity.[45]

Deciding whether a torture survivor should receive protection in the United Kingdom is overwhelmingly a debate over facts rather than law. However, the evidence that judges are presented with is inevitably limited and incomplete. As a result, when asked, judges might say they have no idea whether they are making right decisions. One senior judge told me: "Asylum cases are unlike other areas—we do not really even have a sense of what evidence is obtainable. In a stabbing in an inner city, we know what sort of evidence we can reasonably expect, but not in a torture case from Congo. In the end we are really just putting a pin in a piece of paper. . . . A great deal of our work is clutching at straws, evidence is often wafer thin, and cases are often not very well presented . . . but we have to try and make it as fair and accountable as possible."[46] This is not simply a cynicism about particular forms of evidence but a generalized hesitation about how all evidence should be treated and how to give it the appropriate weight. Yet, in the end judges must come to a decision, they must allow or dismiss an appeal. As Lord Justice Sedley has put it: "A possible life-and-death decision extracted from shreds of evidence and subjective impressions still has to be made" (2002, 324). It is not simply that judges can be too skeptical and refuse to give the benefit of the doubt, but rather that they do not even have solid ground on which to base their doubts. The problem of evidence is not unique to claims about torture or even to human rights claims but can be found in asylum claims more generally, where evidence is often scarce. Torture claims, however, create specific problems as they contain notions of both intention and trauma that are difficult to prove. Torture implies an element of the deliberate infliction of suffering, but the perpetrator is always absent in cases before the tribunal. Torture also implies a level of injury, yet clinical evidence and personal testimony can only speak about the causes of injury in an indirect manner. Evidence is hard to come by, and it is even harder to know whether to trust it.

Chapter 3
Clinical Evidence about Torture

When the George W. Bush administration was trying to provide legal cover for its treatment of prisoners in Guantanamo Bay, Abu Ghraib, and Bagram, one of its lawyers infamously defined torture as an act that caused pain equivalent to major organ failure.[1] Some critics pointed out that this set the threshold for pain far too high. Others argued that organ failure is not necessarily accompanied by pain at all. In 1976, the European Court of Human Rights ruled that the use of forced standing, hooding, subjection to noise, deprivation of sleep, and deprivation of food and drink by British security forces on Republican prisoners in Northern Ireland did not amount to torture because they did not "occasion suffering of the peculiar intensity and cruelty implied by the word *torture*."[2] The UK Border Agency Guidance states that in order to count as an Article 3 violation, the incident must "involve actual bodily injury or intense physical or mental suffering" (UKBA no date, 3). Along with the identity of the perpetrator and his or her particular intentions, torture is widely seen as being distinguished from other types of ill-treatment by the amount of pain and suffering it causes.

Clinicians, especially medical doctors but also psychologists and psychoanalysts, have increasingly become central to attempts to understand torture and its implications. In the early 1970s, there were no specialized centers that provided medical or psychotherapeutic care to torture survivors. By 2010, the umbrella organization known as the International Rehabilitation Council for Torture Victims (IRCT) had more than 140 members in over 70 countries. In the early 1970s, there was just a trickle of research papers in medical journals that focused on the implications of torture. By the turn of the century, the number of peer-reviewed articles had become a flood. Doctors and other clinicians had, of course, previously worked with torture survivors, but it was only toward the end of the twentieth century that torture came to be seen as a possible distinct field of clinical knowledge. In this context, clinicians are not only called on to ease the suffering caused by torture but, most important for the purposes of this book, also asked to provide evidence about its nature and scope.

This chapter explores the ways in which clinicians try to make past acts of torture visible through the production of evidence for the courts.[3] In doing so, it examines how medicolegal reports attempt to translate between clinical and legal understandings of pain and suffering, with all the potential for beneficial exchange as well as misunderstanding and confusion that translation can entail. The focus of this chapter is on one particular form of clinical knowledge, the writing of medicolegal reports produced in order to document allegations of torture in relation to claims of asylum or humanitarian protection in the United Kingdom. The ways in which reports are used and assessed in the process of a claim of protection was examined in Chapter 2. This chapter explores the forms of knowledge that go into the actual production of the reports.

The writing of medicolegal reports has to be understood against the background of two processes which appear to be moving in different directions. The first is the long-standing campaign by human rights organizations to have torture recognized as a specific harm, codified in international and domestic law (see Chapter 1). By and large these campaigns have been successful; not only is the absolute prohibition of torture to be found in law, but also torture survivors are, formally at least, singled out for specific entitlements. Yet at the same time, there has also been a growing political skepticism toward asylum seekers. As we saw in Chapter 2, the UK Border Agency and immigration tribunals have, in practice, increased the evidential burden required to substantiate a claim of torture. Medicolegal reports are therefore written in a context where torture is legally recognized as an absolute prohibition, but when it comes to individual cases, there is a great deal of institutional skepticism.

Clinical knowledge seems to provide concrete opinions in a field that is often marked by obfuscation and cynicism. The supposedly universal experience of pain promises to cut through the suspicion associated with asylum claims (see Fassin and d'Halluin 2005). In the absence of other evidence, clinicians work inductively when writing medicolegal reports. The clinician writing the report was not in the room when the torture was alleged to have taken place, so he or she has to infer what happened. Injuries to the mind or body are read as signs of the events that caused them. Unknown events are made knowable, as the symptom is made to speak of hidden and past actions (Crossland 2009, 71; Foucault 1989). In writing medicolegal reports, clinicians must therefore search for traces of the past that can be vague, indirect, or apparently contradictory. Bodies on their own do not speak, but wounds must be interpreted alongside verbal accounts and then filtered through clinical expertise and experience. The central argument of this chapter is that far from being definitive and absolute, clinical evidence about torture is necessarily indirect and often hesitant. Clinicians are faced with a legal system of proof that all too often appears to be demanding a level of certainty that cannot be given.

I begin this chapter with a discussion of the relationship between legal and medical understandings of causation. I then move on to give a description of the writing of one particular medicolegal report, in order to give a sense of the issues at stake. In the second half of the chapter, I examine the general problems and concerns experienced by clinicians involved in writing reports. The description of the particular report is produced following interviews with the doctor, as well as an examination of the case notes, legal documents, and the final medicolegal report. The term *clinician* is used broadly to cover the range of psychiatrists, general practitioners, and psychotherapists who work in torture rehabilitation. I recognize that the term is too broad to capture the nuances of the work; therefore, where useful, I make distinctions between different types of professional expertise. I also use the term *medicolegal report* to refer to reports discussing scarring and psychological issues, regardless of whether they are written by a strictly medical professional.

Uncovering the Causes of Pain and Suffering

The notion of torture found in human rights claims is not just about pain or suffering but about pain or suffering caused in very particular ways. It must involve the complicity or acquiescence of a public official and it must be carried out with specific intentions. It is not the quality or nature of the pain that singles out torture survivors but the specific cause of their pain. In a broader sense, such notions of causation play an important role in many contemporary methods for distinguishing between different types of suffering. It is causal claims that help us separate out those harms that are thought to be necessary from those that can be prevented (Haskell 2000, 280–306). Not all suffering is treated as ethically equivalent, and it is only by making causal claims that notions such as guilt and innocence, for example, can be allocated. There is therefore a reliance on what might be called technologies of causal attribution in order to make causal connections visible. Medicolegal reports can be understood as one such technology. Clinical evidence about torture is above all evidence about the causes of pain and suffering. As Bernard Williams reminds us though, causal claims are never self-evident as there are "many ways of interpreting elements, of deciding what counts as being the cause . . . or enough of a cause" (2008, 56). Claims of causation are always open to question.

In writing medicolegal reports, clinicians must move between clinical and legal models of causation. The law is concerned with stripping away all possible causes, only to leave the legally relevant (Fumerton and Kress 2001, Wright 1987). Although the legal process may allow for uncertainty in the shape of differing standards of proof, as we saw in the previous chapter, once a decision has been made, it is final. Clinical knowledge about causation is much less definitive. The development of laboratory-based tests, for example, has meant that clinicians can increasingly investigate the causes of illnesses and disorders in individual patients. An investigation of causation is also important in order to localize the source of a problem, as well as to plan for future prevention. However, as Sandra Mitchell has argued, notions of causation in medicine can be context specific, and "fraught with exceptions and contingency" (2010, 65). Historically, there has been a tension in medical diagnosis between a focus on symptoms (nosology) and an emphasis on causes (etiology). Furthermore, objects and processes working at levels as distinct as poverty, insects, sexual behavior, and viruses can all be said to cause medical problems. Finally, clinical theories of causation are inherently provisional and always depend on how a patient responds to treatment. It is also possible to treat a patient without coming to a firm conclusion about causation at all (see, for example, Anderson 1992; Luhrmann 2001, 49). Put bluntly, one key difference between legal and clinical perspectives on causation is that clinicians assume that what is known now may be incomplete and subject to revision, whereas lawyers seek more absolute and definitive views in order to come to a final decision. In writing medicolegal reports, clinical uncertainty about causation therefore has to be held against the forms of certainty demanded by lawyers and judges.

The key issue in writing medicolegal reports is how much, and exactly what, a psychological or scarring report can tell you about the likely causes of past events. There are two separate issues here. The first is the extent to which it is possible to come to a firm clinical opinion about the attribution of a specific injury. The second is whether these causes can be said to amount to torture. As Darius Rejali argues, many specific forms of torture do not leave documentable traces (2009). The physically or mentally resilient, and those subjected to perhaps more "careful" forms of interrogation, may carry no or few marks that can be determined on preliminary examination. The leading internationally recognized manual on the documentation of torture stresses that "the absence of such physical evidence should not be construed to suggest that torture did not occur, since such acts of violence against persons frequently leave no marks or permanent scars" (OHCHR 2004, 32). Even if documentable traces are left, there is often no linear or necessary causal relation between a particular incident and subsequent symptoms. Scars can have several possible causes, and individual scars need to be assessed within the context of a broader claim. The psychological impacts of torture can also be indirect, ranging from psychosis to a few sleepless nights.

How can torture itself be said to be a cause of pain and suffering? Causes can be understood at many levels. They can be described, for example, as a blow with a blunt object, being hit with a metal bar, or being interrogated violently in a prison cell. *Torture*, as an abstract noun, operates as a cause at the highest level of abstraction. Torture, in and of itself, is not a stand-alone cause of particular sequelae, or abnormalities following injury. It is electrocution or being hit with a metal bar that creates specific injuries. An opinion about particular sequelae and their modes of infliction does not in and of itself necessarily amount to a claim of torture. Torture is more than simply the infliction of individual wounds; it requires very particular types of intent and perpetrator. In this context, many medicolegal reports will not use the word *torture* to describe specific events, but rather they will set out in detail their opinion on the claim that the client was, for example, cut with a sharp object or even cut with a razor.

Writing a Medicolegal Report

Mehdi Rostami arrived at Heathrow Airport in early 2007 on a forged Bulgarian passport and claimed asylum immediately.[4] He was a forty-five-year-old teacher of English who had left Iran four months previously by boat and arrived in London via India. After being detained briefly, Rostami was released while his asylum claim was processed. The UK Border Agency agreed to delay any decision as his lawyer sought medical evidence to corroborate his claim of torture in Iran. Rostami's lawyer turned to the Medical Foundation for the Care of Victims of Torture. Rostami was already a client of the Medical Foundation, where he was receiving therapy. After an initial delay, Rostami was sent to see Dr. Miriam Douglas. Douglas was a local general practitioner who worked for the Medical Foundation on a voluntary basis for a few days a month. Over the course of a few weeks, the doctor and the client met several times for a series of lengthy interviews, lasting a total of nearly 6 hours, during which time Rostami recounted his story and showed Douglas his injuries.

During these sessions, Rostami told the doctor that he was an activist in the Communist Party, had written several leaflets criticizing the Iranian regime, and had led a number of discussion groups for young people in which they could air their grievances. He explained to Douglas that several years prior to coming to the United Kingdom some plain-clothes police officers had come to his door in the middle of the night and demanded that he accompany them to the police station. He was handcuffed, blindfolded, and taken to a dark cell from which he could hear a recording, played at high volume, of someone reciting the Quran. Within a few hours, the police took him to another cell where they accused him of being responsible for organizing some pro-Kurdish demonstrations the previous week.

Rostami went on to tell Douglas that on being returned to his cell, he was pushed down some stairs and, unable to break his fall, landed awkwardly on his right ankle. He heard a cracking noise, which he assumed were his bones breaking and then he lay in his cell, screaming with excruciating pain. Rostami explained that he was imprisoned for a total of twenty-two days. His captors checked on him several times a day and would punch and kick him each time they visited the cell. Rostami was taken upstairs to the interrogation room seven or eight times during his incarceration. During these interrogations he would be beaten all over his body for thirty to forty-five minutes at a time. He was hit on his chest, face, and head, and the men concentrated especially on his broken ankle. Rostami told Douglas that he thinks he lost consciousness at least twice. He also told the doctor that "the men beat me so much at times that they had no strength left, becoming exhausted themselves."

In his account to the doctor, Rostami described how on one occasion he was sitting on a chair and his torturers hit both of his big toes repeatedly with a hammer until they started to bleed. Several years later, the toenails were still black and continued to fall out. His toes also constantly hurt. Rostami also claimed that on another occasion he was sitting on the bench with his hands cuffed behind his back. His head was then pushed downward and he was forcibly held in this position for four to six minutes. The men hit his back and he felt a searing pain throughout his body. He said that he thought that this was caused by an electric baton, but he could not be sure. Rostami went on to tell the doctor that on three or four occasions he was tortured with water. He would be strapped into a high-backed chair, his arms were held by the wrists, his waist secured by a belt attached to the back of the chair, and his head was restrained so that he could not move it. Water was then slowly dripped onto his head from above for more than an hour. At all times, he could hear the screams and cries of others through the walls. Rostami assumed that there were other people being tortured in neighboring rooms, but he was kept in solitary confinement for the duration of his detention and did not see any other prisoners. He also told the doctor that he was in constant pain all over his body for the duration of his detention. He had bruises and cuts on his body, face, knuckles, and head. Prior to his detention, he had had problems with his stomach once or twice a year, but during his detention this worsened significantly, and he had constant abdominal pain and daily vomiting. On several occasions, he vomited blood, which he was able to see when the lights in the cell were switched on.

Rostami was released after agreeing to a statement saying that he would never demonstrate publicly again. However, the effects of his detention stayed with him. He went to the hospital in Iran and had an x-ray taken, which showed that the bones of the lower leg had been fractured and had healed out of alignment. The surgeon informed him that it was too late to reset the leg and the only option would be an operation to re-break the bones. To this day, Rostami told Douglas, he has a hot, burning pain in his ankle when walking. Rostami also had investigations for abdominal pain and was found to have a stomach ulcer. He described to the Medical Foundation doctor how his neck and shoulders are very tense and stiff "as if there is always someone standing on my back." He also described how, every morning, after rising from bed, he has terrible pain and stiffness in his chest and back. This pain is so unbearable that he has to sit next to his heater to warm his body for thirty minutes to an hour before he can move comfortably. However, Rostami complained to the doctor that the worst thing is the emotional impact of his treatment. His relationship with his family changed for the worse after his detention. He had been a person renowned for his kindness, but he became very irritable and developed a quick temper. He also sleeps very poorly, having frequent nightmares. He told the doctor that he became very nervous in crowded places and started to have vivid memories of his time in detention. All sorts of things would trigger these recollections—his wife shouting at their children, the sight of wooden benches and cement floors, and men in military uniform.

The interviews between Rostami and the doctor took longer than normal, as Rostami became increasingly distressed throughout the meetings. During the physical examination, Douglas also noted several scars across Rostami's body. Some of these looked to her like scars from vaccinations or an appendectomy. Rostami also said that some of his scars were from childhood injuries. However, there were three scars, of various lengths, that Rostami claimed were a result of his treatment in detention. Douglas measured the scars and recorded them carefully in a number of diagrams.

A Short History of the Torture Rehabilitation Movement

Before examining the report that Douglas wrote following her meetings with Rostami, and what she felt able to say about the effects of torture, it will be useful to put the writing of medicolegal reports within the context of the broader history of the torture rehabilitation movement. Above all, the torture rehabilitation movement has to be understood as growing out of a human rights project. Medicine and treatment have followed where human rights concerns have led. James Jaranson, one of the early pioneers of the movement in the United States, has described its goals as being "to influence world opinion in order to stop governments from practicing or from supporting the practice of torture" (1995, 254). Torture is seen fundamentally as a political and an ethical concern, as well as a clinical matter.

In the final quarter of the twentieth century, the torture rehabilitation movement grew as a direct response to the arrival of refugee populations in Europe and North America. Rehabilitation centers developed in Paris, Copenhagen, London, Boston, Toronto, and Minneapolis, reflecting the main dispersal points for refugees. In Europe and North America, the process of documentation and rehabilitation for torture survivors has been intractably caught up in the politics of refugee status and has responded to successive waves of immigration. In the United Kingdom, the Medical Foundation for the Care of Victims of Torture grew out of the local Amnesty International medical group. Initially, a "concerned amateur" streak ran through part of the British movement, with many of the leading members having no clinical qualifications. From the 1990s, however, there was an increased professionalization. The Medical Foundation was increasingly staffed by psychotherapists, psychiatrists, lawyers, psychologists, and trained human rights campaigners, among others. In the early days, there were also staff members who came to the United Kingdom after being held as political prisoners. The emphasis of the Medical Foundation was on the rehabilitation through therapy of individuals rather than on structural change to prevent torture. The emphasis has also always been on what is called the "holistic approach," with clinicians attending to a client's protection needs—writing reports for asylum applications and tackling issues around housing, health, education, or safety, as well as rehabilitation—rather than on what was seen as the narrow medicalization of torture survivors.

There is an ongoing debate among some of those involved in the torture rehabilitation movement as to whether torture survivors should be singled out, both clinically and politically. Whereas the Medical Foundation focused on torture in the early part of the twenty-first century, Helen Bamber, the founder of the Medical Foundation, set up a new organization that switched the focus from torture to survivors of gross human rights violations. From a different perspective, in 2006, in an editorial in the *British Medical Journal*, Metin Basoglu criticized some of the psychiatrists at the Medical Foundation for their "ideological position, which is not supported by any evidence," for implicitly arguing that torture was a unique form of trauma (2006). Basoglu is a psychiatrist with a behaviorist approach to the treatment of mental health problems and has experience with earthquake and torture survivors in Turkey. In his editorial, he argues that "our studies show that natural disasters, for example, lead to just as complex traumatic stress problems . . . as traumas of human design, such as war and torture" (2006, 1230). Doctors from the Medical Foundation responded by arguing, "'We are not convinced that it is valid to generalise from work with other populations, such as earthquake survivors or war veterans, to torture survivors" (Seltzer, Sklan, and Patel 2006).

Many of the clinicians who write medicolegal reports argue for marking out torture as a distinct form of pain and suffering. Yoav Landau-Pope, the former director of clinical services at the Medical Foundation, told me that he thought "deliberately inflicted trauma is always very different from arbitrary trauma, and individual cruelty is different from collective violence, as it goes to the heart of the self."[5] From this perspective, torture survivors should be seen as distinct from other people who have lived through violence or trauma (see also Quiroga and Jaranson 2005, 23). Crucially, this issue needs to be distinguished from whether the aftereffects of torture can be documented to the standards demanded by legal proof.

Research into torture sequelae only really began in the late 1970s, largely on refugees in northern Europe (Eitinger and Weisaeth 1998). Since then, many research articles have been published in medical journals, peaking in the mid-1990s. In the 1970s, led mainly by research in Denmark, there was much talk about the identification of a distinct "torture syndrome" (see, for example, Amnesty International 1977). However, clinical evidence that torture survivors have a discrete and an identifiable set of sequelae has proved elusive (see Allodi 1991; Jaranson 1998; Mollica and Caspi-Yavin 1992; Turner and Gorst-Unsworth 1990).

There has been relative success in identifying the sequelae of specific forms of torture. X-ray studies have been used to investigate head injuries attributable to torture, skin biopsies to differentiate scars caused by electrical shocks from those caused by other types of burns, and myoglobin levels as an indicator of traumatic muscle destruction, among others (see Allodi 1991; Jaranson 1998). However, the tests developed from such research tend to produce a large number of false negatives. They may help identify fifteen people who have been electrocuted or had the soles of their feet beaten, but they will also give negative results on another fifteen people who have had identical experiences. According to anecdotal reports, authorities in Egypt and Turkey have claimed that *falaka*, the name commonly used to refer to beatings applied to the soles of the feet, can be detected through the use of radioisotopes, in order to try to undermine allegations of torture.[6] The police apparently used negative test results to argue that the claims of torture made by human rights activists were false. As such, there is also a real fear that the development of too rigorous tests could raise the standard of proof well above that which is actually required for asylum claims or even legal prosecutions. Perhaps most important, such tests are very expensive and well beyond the budgets of most documentation centers.

In general, research into the consequences of torture faces several major problems. First, it is clearly not possible to carry out the kind of double-blind trials often associated with medical research. A researcher cannot collect one hundred people, electrocute half of them with a cattle prod under identical conditions, use the other half as a control group, and carry out statistical analyses of the results.[7] In an attempt to get around this problem, in the 1970s, a group of Danish doctors carried out experiments on themselves and on anesthetized pigs, using electric batons. However, the doctors were met with demonstrations by animal rights protesters and the trials soon stopped (Genefke 2008). The populations studied are also usually refugees in North America or Europe and therefore not only represent disparate populations but also are far removed in time and space from the initial infliction of torture. Stuart Turner, a psychiatrist who worked with the Medical Foundation in the 1980s and now heads one of the leading general psychological trauma centers in the United Kingdom, has written that "there is no adequate controlled research on the assessment, treatment and clinical outcome of torture survivors" (McIvor and Turner 1995, 709). Research on torture has therefore necessarily often been exploratory.

Reading Pain and Scars

Clinicians report that the most common sequelae they encounter with torture survivors are nonspecific forms of chronic pain (C. de C. Williams and Amris 2007, 7). Rostami's major complaints to Douglas were about pains in his stomach and back, which incapacitated him for long periods. Douglas wrote in her report that the pain experienced by Rostami could well be "somatic pain—that is a manifestation of his extreme psychological distress rather than of any underlying physical pathology caused by his mistreatment." She went on to argue that the pain he reported was frequently found in depressed patients. However, nonspecific, chronic pain famously resists standard medical tests (Charlton

2005; Kumar, Tandon and Mathur 2002). So, although chronic pain might be the most commonly observed aftereffect of torture, it continues to resist attempts at measurement and therefore offers limited space for specific documentation (IRCT 2009, 15).

The largest part of Douglas's report was taken up in documenting the various scars and lesions that Rostami showed her during their interviews. This is common in many medicolegal reports. To help her interpret the scars, Douglas turned to the Istanbul Protocol. The protocol, which has since been adopted by the United Nations, was developed following concerns from the Turkish Human Rights Foundation and Turkish Medical Association that the Turkish courts were accepting the problematic reports produced by state doctors to discredit the claims of torture made by political activists. In the context of highly politicized disputes over the implications of medical findings, the Istanbul Protocol was an attempt to set out a clear methodological route through which torture could be documented and injuries linked to specific causes. The assumption was that the brief and cursory reports produced by the doctors employed by the Turkish police or military would not meet this required level of rigor and therefore would be discredited in the courts.

The Istanbul Protocol sets out five levels, originally developed by the Medical Foundation in the United Kingdom, through which wounds and scars are to be assessed in relation to claims of torture. These are *not consistent, consistent, highly consistent, typical,* and *diagnostic,* going from the weakest probable fit between claimed cause and scar to the strongest (OHCHR 2004, 34–35). The precise definition of each of these words is some way from their everyday usage. *Not consistent* is specified as meaning that "the lesion could not have been caused by the trauma described." *Consistent* is defined as "the lesion could have been caused by the trauma described, but it is non-specific and there are many other possible causes." By describing a lesion as *consistent,* a physician is saying he or she cannot rule out that it was caused in the way claimed, but can say little more. *Highly consistent* is described as meaning that a "lesion could have been caused by the trauma described, and there are few other possible causes." The level of probability here is still quite low, however; saying "there are few other possible causes" does not even necessarily imply that the attributed cause is even the most likely. *Typical* is defined as meaning "an appearance that is usually found with this type of trauma, but there are other possible causes." This category is based on a slightly different logic from the previous two, as it is making a direct causal claim, saying that a particular type of torture usually results in these types of scars, without ruling out other possibilities, or even saying torture is the most likely cause. The last category, *diagnostic,* is defined as implying that a scar "could not have been caused in any way other than that described." This is by far the strongest claim and, in effect, rules out any other possible causes.

As we saw in Chapter 2, British judges now require that doctors use the Istanbul Protocol in writing reports. The irony here is that the criteria set out in the Istanbul Protocol were initially intended as a tool to critique the claims of denial in complicity with torture made by states but are now being used to question the claims made by people requesting protection. An extra gloss was put on the Istanbul Protocol in a 2008 judgment of the Asylum and Immigration Tribunal.[8] In that case, the judge rejected the claim that the submitted medicolegal report was corroborative of the claim of torture and ruled that when claiming a scar was *highly consistent*, report writers had to assess "other possible causes (whether many, few, or unusually few), specifically examining those to gauge how likely they are, bearing in mind what is known about the individual's life history and experiences."[9] This, in effect, means that the doctor has to weigh the claim of torture alongside other possible causes.

Many doctors say that only certain types of scars or lesions really shout out their causes, with cigarette burns and bullet wounds paramount. To give but a few examples, the Istanbul Protocol states, "Burning is the form of torture that most frequently leaves permanent changes in the skin. Sometimes, these changes may be of diagnostic value" (OHCHR 2004, 37). Some types of whipping also leave distinct marks. As the Istanbul Protocol puts it, "These scars are depigmented and often hypertrophic, surrounded by narrow, hyperpigmented stripes" (OHCHR 2004, 37). Such scars can be distinguished from self-flagellation or dermatitis by their length, angle, and location.

However, some forms of torture can result in injuries that leave a nonspecific appearance. Blunt force trauma, such as being kicked by heavy boots, "often leaves no or uncharacteristic scars" (IRCT 2009, 7). The Istanbul Protocol further states, "Anal fissures may persist for many years, but it is normally impossible to differentiate between those caused by torture and those caused by other mechanisms" (OHCHR 2004, 33–24). There can also be no linear causal relationship between a particular mode of torture and its resulting sequelae. For example, *falaka* can sometimes, but not always, leave pains in the shin and swollen feet (IRCT 2009, 7). Furthermore, many forms of torture are expressly designed to leave no marks. Water boarding is famously almost undetectable after the event. Rostami described how he had water dropped on his head and had been electrocuted in a way that left no scars. In addition, even forms of torture that do cause more obvious wounds, do not necessarily result in permanent scars (OHCHR 2004, 34). There is not space here to list all the various forms of torture and the claims that have been made about the scars and lesions with which they are associated. The key point is to illustrate the range of causal certainty in claims about the relationship between specific forms of torture and particular sequelae.

In many medicolegal reports, the clinician can go no higher than *consistent*. As part of this research I examined thirty-five medicolegal reports in detail. Although it is by no means a fully representative survey, it does give some indication of general patterns. In the examined reports, 345 individual or groups of scars or lesions were classified according to the Istanbul Protocol scale. Of these, 129 were classified as *consistent*, 51 as *highly consistent*, 59 as *typical*, and 5 as *diagnostic*. In a further five individual incidents, the clinician said that the scars were *not consistent* with their attribution.

Douglas was able to go as high as *highly consistent* in the classification of Rostami's injuries but no further. In her report, Douglas described the two, 2-cm irregular scars on Rostami's kneecaps as being *highly consistent*: "The scars are most irregular as would be expected when skin is dragged across a stone surface. Another possible cause might be an injury sustained while working outdoors and kneeling on the ground. However, Mr. Rostami's occupation had been sedentary and he has lived in an urban area most of his life so I think this explanation less likely." It is worth noting that Douglas went higher than the Istanbul Protocol definition of *highly consistent* in stating that the attributed causes were the most likely. The other scar on Rostami's shin was described as *consistent* with either falling down the stairs or a beating, meaning that it could have been caused in the way described, but there were also lots of other possible, and equally persuasive, explanations. Hard purple scars such as this, technically known as keloid scars, are nearly always nonspecific in origin, as there is so much swelling. Douglas also gave an opinion on the state of Rostami's toes, noting that there "is tenderness on palpation of the great toe nails, both of which are thickened. This is attributed to damage caused by hammers and is highly consistent with this account. Other possibilities might be a thickened nail due to fungal toenail infection, but this would have a different appearance and would not be tender to palpation." Douglas was keen to stress that the relative absence of obvious physical signs should not be taken as evidence that Rostami's ill-treatment did not happen. She noted in her report: "At first it might seem implausible that he bears so few scars after describing such significant beating. . . . However, a skilled torturer can inflict a great number of blows and leave no scar. Additionally, the scars often fade with time." Of the thirty-five reports I examined, in six cases, the clinician remarked that the absence of scars should not be taken as indicating torture had not taken place.

It is crucial to note here that although it may be hard to give firm causal attributions to particular scars or lesions, individual sequelae do not stand alone. The Istanbul Protocol says that individual scars and injuries have to be assessed in the context of the overall evaluation by the clinician. This means that broader patterns of scars should be taken into consideration. As the Istanbul Protocol states: "Ultimately, it is the overall evaluation of all lesions and not the consistency of each lesion with a particular form of torture that is important in assessing the torture story" (OHCHR 2004, 37). In seven of the thirty-five reports I examined, the clinician wrote that the overall pattern of scars was compatible with the account.

Uncovering the Unseen

How does the writing of medicolegal reports differ from other clinical practices aimed at uncovering the causes of symptoms or sequelae? The word *diagnosis* is often used by clinicians when talking about torture (see, for example, Danielsen, Karlsmark, and Thomsen 1997; Goldfeld et al. 1988; Juhler and Vesti 1989; Mollica and Caspi-Yavin 1992; Van Velsen, Gorst-Unsworth, and Turner 1996). "Diagnosis" is also a key term in the Istanbul Protocol, used to refer to the firm causal attribution of torture and the use of specific techniques (OHCHR 2004, 61). However, the language of diagnosis is at best an awkward fit to the work of interpreting injuries for medicolegal reports. Medicolegal reports are not about diagnosing a discrete disease or illness but about coming to an opinion about the relative consistency of an account of torture with the scars, lesions, and other indicators presented by the claimant.

In practice, most reports are written through a process of classification. Names are given to interrogation techniques that can then be associated with particular injuries. In this way, analogies can be drawn between particular injuries and the accounts that are given of their causes. Although no two scars are ever exactly the same, by making analogies to scars that have been informally classified in similar ways clinicians can draw on their own experiences to make more general conclusions.[10] Placing someone's arms behind his or her back, tying them together, and then hanging the person from his or her hands is known as "Palestinian hanging." It can cause shoulder joint pain; tearing of the shoulder joint; and injury to the nerves that join the spinal cord to the arm, shoulders, and hands. Suspending someone with a horizontal pole placed under the knees and with the wrists bound to the ankles is known as the "parrot's perch" or "chicken kebab" and can cause damage to the cruciate ligaments of the knees.

Many doctors feel that the writing of medicolegal reports shares common features with other types of medical practice, particularly primary care. In both primary care and medicolegal reports, clinicians are confronted by people who may be precise and clear but who can equally be inarticulate in describing their symptoms. The clinician then has to piece together a host of sometimes disparate bits of information, filter statements that could lead in the wrong direction, and finally try to work out what is wrong. It is a process that one doctor described as "peering through the glass darkly" and trying to fit together a series of half-glimpsed symptoms to get a sense of what is going on underneath.[11]

However, the ways in which symptoms and causes are linked are very different in primary care and in medicolegal reports. As Richard Jones has shown in his study of the training of forensic clinicians more broadly, there is a need for a shift in language to make the jump from general medicine to forensics (2003). In general medical practice, clinicians may try to investigate the causes of an illness or injury. However, they might eventually be left without a firm opinion on the cause of a problem. Indeed, a diagnosis may not need a causal attribution, as it is about recognizing a pattern of symptoms that can be treated. The main concern is for the patient to get better. For this reason, an investigation into causation can broadly be thought of as a means to an end, rather than an end in itself. In contrast, in writing medicolegal reports, an opinion about causation is an end in itself, in that a clinician cannot simply write a report about scars without coming to some sort of conclusion about causes. However, in writing medicolegal reports, there is little external space for practical confirmation of an opinion about causation. In general clinical practice, an opinion about causation can be confirmed either by tests or by the patient getting better. In a medicolegal report, the only confirmation of an opinion is how it is treated by the judge, and that explains more about the vagaries of the legal process than the experiences of the client.

In this context, many doctors say they have great difficulty in applying the different levels of probability found in the Istanbul Protocol's categories of *consistent, highly consistent,* and *diagnostic.* The distinction between an indication of *consistent* and *highly consistent* is that there are "many other possible causes" in the former and "few other possible causes" in the latter. Yet, there is no precise guidance on the difference between "few" and "many." Different clinicians can therefore have the same clinical opinion about a scar but classify it differently under the Istanbul Protocol.

The requirement to write about other possible causes can also create concerns.[12] On the one hand, there is no specification as to the level of causal explanation at which the clinician must provide alternatives. Do clinicians have to write about alternatives to blunt objects or military boots? On the other, the requirement to write about alternative explanations means that many clinicians feel they are being asked to push their imaginations to absurd lengths. As one doctor pointed out to me, "How can I, sitting in a surgery in leafy North London, imagine what it might be like to be a fisherman in Sri Lanka and all the other possible causes of a scar?"[13] A common joke is made about whether doctors should speculate about alien abduction as a possible cause. Douglas felt able to suggest that as Rostami was a teacher he was unlikely to have sustained his injuries to his feet and knees through the normal course of events.

Although the Istanbul Protocol was designed to give stability to the often-ambiguous process of linking scars to claims of torture, given how it is being used in the legal processes it can also add another layer of uncertainty and obfuscation.

PTSD and Beyond

In addition to showing the clinician his scars, Rostami told Douglas that he was constantly anxious. He also reported that he had great difficulty sleeping and had frequent panic attacks. On one visit to the Medical Foundation, Rostami saw a police car waiting outside the building and believed it was there to arrest him, so he ran away in distress. He also told the doctor that he had frequent thoughts of suicide and that he had contemplated jumping off a bridge. The dominant popular image of the torture survivor is not solely of physical suffering but also of psychological trauma. The Istanbul Protocol also notes that common psychological responses among torture survivors include avoidance and emotional numbing, hyperarousal, depression, somatic complaints, sexual dysfunction, and psychosis (OHCHR 2004, 46–47). Crucially though, the Istanbul Protocol warns: "The psychological consequences of torture, however, occur in the context of personal attribution of meaning, personality development and social, political and cultural factors. For this reason, it cannot be assumed that all forms of torture have the same outcome. . . . It is important to recognize that not everyone who has been tortured develops a diagnosable mental illness. However, many victims experience profound emotional reactions and psychological symptoms" (OHCHR 2004, 45).

There is not necessarily a causal relationship between any particular method of torture and specific psychological symptoms (OHCHR 2004, 45). Similar symptoms can have different causes, and similar causes can result in different symptoms. Indeed, linear or mechanistic forms of causation are anathema to many forms of psychotherapeutic practice used in the torture rehabilitation movement. A senior clinical psychologist at the Medical Foundation told me: "Overall most people agree that you cannot predict that *x* type of torture will lead to particular types of symptom. In therapy, it is not about diagnosing a particular type of trauma but understanding how it develops. It is not that psychologists are not interested in the cause of the trauma, but rather they want it to emerge. . . . As such, it is not a matter of causation. I cannot set out causal mechanisms but show how trauma develops according to certain psychological principles in an individual case."[14]

Some therapists go so far as to say that the specific cause of trauma is not necessarily the focus of the work. Their clients may be more concerned with housing, family breakdown, or their trip to the United Kingdom than they are with the initial event of torture that led them to flee, and therefore it is these events that they focus on. Even the therapists who do place torture at the center of their understanding of trauma do not necessarily focus on it directly. One therapist told me that in the therapy "you deal with the here and now—torture is still always present—even if not in the form of a history. The way is not to go back and focus on the trauma, as trauma is always emergent—but who knows when it will emerge."[15] Such an approach seeks to understand how people make sense of their past experience, how this impacts their internal processes and their interpersonal relationships, but it does not seek to uncover what "really happened" outside the client's own experience of it.

Within the context of the UK torture rehabilitation movement, the overall dominant approach to mental health issues can broadly be described as psychotherapeutic. Within this area is a great variation in approaches, with no one school dominating. Psychiatrists are also far from being in the majority. Broadly speaking, such psychotherapeutic approaches to mental health have historically paid little attention to particular diagnoses in the course of treatment. The assumption has been that the specific nature of symptoms will vary from person to person and will depend on their own biographical experiences.

Along with the broad psychotherapeutic approach to mental health issues is an alternative approach, increasingly so since the 1970s, which I shall gloss here as medical-diagnostic (see Horowitz 2002). The medical-diagnostic approach has sought to identify discrete disease entities and is an attempt to replace the subjective interpretation of psychodynamic approaches in particular with what is seen as the hard objectivity of scientific method (Timmermans and Berg 2003). Crucially, only physicians are given the professional authority to diagnose, shutting out many of the broader forms of expertise found in the torture rehabilitation movement. The publication of the *Diagnostic and Statistical Manual of Mental Disorders–III* (DSM-III) in 1980 by the American Psychiatric Association marked the mainstream victory of the medical-diagnostic model, in the United States at least. However, in a bid to stop professional disputes, the DSM-III by and large left out issues of causation to focus on symptoms. Mental health problems are therefore organized by observable symptoms, with little attempt to analyze the relations between disorders and their underlying causes. British clinicians, as those elsewhere in Europe, normally use the International Classification of Diseases (ICD), which is produced by the World Health Organization (WHO), rather than the DSM. However, in practice, the ICD broadly mirrors the DSM and has increasingly been brought into line.[16]

One of the few exceptions to the general absence of theories of causation in the DSM-IV is the entry on PTSD, which is defined as an anxiety disorder that can develop following exposure to traumatic events. Sources of trauma can include sexual assault, earthquakes, armed conflict, bereavement, or torture. However, the experience of some form of trauma is central to any diagnosis of PTSD. Furthermore, the causal event is also often embedded in its symptoms, in the shape of flashbacks or nightmares (Young 1993).

In the absence of a Torture Syndrome, PTSD, along with depression, remains the most widely diagnosed mental health disorder in medicolegal reports. The Istanbul Protocol recommends caution in an overly simplistic assumption about the connection between PTSD and torture, saying that there is a "mistaken and simplistic impression that PTSD is the main psychological consequence of torture (OHCHR 2004, 48). In Rostami's case, Douglas had said that his symptoms were diagnostic of PTSD, as he experienced flashbacks, sleeping difficulties, avoidance, and poor concentration. Douglas also added that "Mr. Rostami has severe symptoms of depression and anxiety. In my opinion these are diagnostic of Post Traumatic Stress Disorder . . . in that he meets criteria A (exposed to a stressful event or situation), B (flashbacks, vivid memories, recurring dreams, distress when exposed to a circumstance resembling the stressor such as the sight of benches, cement floors, bearded men, cockroaches etc.), and C (avoidance of circumstances resembling the stressor such as avoiding crowds of youths who are shouting)." In writing her report on Rostami, Douglas pointed out that Rostami had many reasons for being depressed, such as his flight from Iran, his separation from his family, and his relative isolation in Glasgow. However, she concluded, "It is clear that he has been profoundly psychologically disturbed by his torture and detention," drawing a direct line between his treatment in an Iranian police cell and his current psychological issues.

The diagnosis of PTSD has been highly controversial, especially in the context of legal claims (see Marsella, Friedman, and Spain 1992; Summerfield 1999; Young 1995). In particular, it has been claimed that the prevalence of the diagnosis reflects demands for political or economic recognition rather than medical need (Young 1995). Questions have also been raised about the use of PTSD as an evidential tool for uncovering past torture. The Home Office and immigration judges have argued that PTSD is overdiagnosed and easy to fake.[17] As we saw in Chapter 2, Khalili's diagnosis of PTSD was dismissed by the judge as being based on an account that "could easily have been self-serving." As many of the symptoms used to diagnose PTSD—such as flashbacks and nightmares—are self-reported, it is sometimes suspected that the claimant might have simply made them up (Bracha and Hayashi 2008; Hall and Hall 2007). In 2002, the Home Office commissioned a report from Dr. Leigh Neal, a psychiatrist working with the British military.[18] In the report, Neal claimed that "vague comments about stress in general and having a poor recollection of anything are almost invariably associated with malingering." The report was criticized by Dr. Stuart Turner, claiming that Neal had problematically generalized from the distinct case of combat veterans and had failed to take into account the particularities of asylum seekers and refugees, with whom Neal seemed to have very little experience.[19]

A diagnosis of PTSD might initially seem especially useful in medicolegal reports, as a key criteria for a diagnosis includes the fact that the patient has been exposed to a traumatic event. However, crucially, for the writing of medicolegal reports about torture, a diagnosis of PTSD is not confined to survivors of torture but includes people who have experienced trauma more broadly. As such, a diagnosis of PTSD does not, on its own, indicate whether someone has been tortured. According to one of the senior doctors at the Medical Foundation, "Anyone who says that PTSD is diagnostic of torture is talking crap—that is mad psychiatry. It tells you that something has probably happened, but it does not tell you what."[20] Clinical studies have also "found that the development and severity of PTSD symptoms" are not directly related to the proximity or severity of exposure to traumatic events (Kroll 2003, 668). Other factors play a role, whether they are preexisting mental disorders, social support networks, or political motivations, among others. Trauma then is a necessary but not sufficient cause of PTSD.

Many people in the torture rehabilitation movement object to the idea that the complex sequelae of torture can be made to fit into rigid diagnostic boxes. For one, PTSD assumes that the trauma experience is complete and takes the shape of an identifiable event. However, clinicians report that for many clients their issues can be enduring over time, starting well before their abuse in a prison cell and lasting well after, into their flight to the United Kingdom.[21] Helen Bamber, founder of the Medical Foundation, told me that she thought "the symptoms of trauma are so diverse and the DSM is a turgid solution."[22] Similarly, Yoav Landau-Pope, a psychodynamic psychotherapist and former director of clinical services at the Medical Foundation, told me that diagnostic criteria "are not helpful if you are trying to understand someone's experience."[23] Crucially, he felt limitations of the DSM-IV should not be seen as being unique to PTSD or torture but are much more widespread within the mental health field. As Luhrmann has argued, the DSM-IV is based on the assumption that mental health issues can be compartmentalized into discrete disease entities (2001). However, in practice, she claims, mental health issues are not caused by discrete objects like a virus but rather are formed in the human mind, with all the complexity that entails.

Despite all these concerns, it is still relatively common to find a diagnosis of PTSD in medicolegal reports. PTSD is often diagnosed for pragmatic reasons, to further the interest of a patient who the clinician feels meets the diagnostic criteria. Douglas told me, for example, that if the patient showed the right symptoms, she used the diagnosis of PTSD, as in Rostami's case, "because it would benefit the patient and help him get the right treatment.[24] For many clinicians, PTSD is not part of the professional language they use when treating patients, but they use the term in their reports because more psychodynamic approaches, for example, are not given as much weight by the courts. One senior clinician, who had been writing medicolegal reports for nearly ten years told me that he felt diagnostic criteria were largely useful as pegs upon which to hang a more complex analysis of a patient's presentation.[25] A diagnosis of PTSD is a communicative tool, and although it may not be the professional term used within therapy, it can capture some, but not all, of the experience of the person being treated. It is worth pointing out here that such approaches are not necessarily all that different from other forms of clinical practice. Ultimately, clinicians tend to be most concerned with treating the patient, and therefore diagnosis is important to the extent to which it helps find the right course of treatment and to plan prevention. In this process, PTSD can become "PTSD," an instrumental device, perhaps viewed with considerable skepticism but seen as useful to serve specific ends.

In practice, the symptoms of PTSD, rather than the diagnosis itself, can be more important in a medicolegal report, as they allow detailed descriptions of what the client feels happened to him or her and the impact that this has had. As one experienced doctor told me: "If a woman describes washing her genital area obsessively with disinfectant many times a day and is unable to smell a man's sweat without it triggering such powerful recall of her rape experience that she is likely to vomit, then it does give you a pretty strong indication of what happened."[26] Detailing symptoms, rather than concluding that they amount to PTSD, can therefore be more important in trying to corroborate a claim.

Credibility in Medicolegal Reports

On what grounds do clinicians make claims about the causes of injuries? What is the relationship between a cold, detached analysis of injury patterns and a compassionate engagement with the person bearing those injuries? The courts are very firm in arguing that clinicians are supposed to match reported causes with symptoms and assess the extent to which they do or do not match up. Whether the claimant is telling the truth is simply not an issue for the clinician. As we saw in the last chapter, credibility is an issue over which judges reserve the right to make a decision.[27] However, in practice very few doctors say they can write a medicolegal report without assessing whether the person before them is being truthful. A senior doctor at the Medical Foundation told me, "In my opinion you cannot give clinical histories without making a judgment on credibility."[28] The Istanbul Protocol also advises clinicians to make a judgment on whether the person they are examining has made a false allegation (OHCHR 2004, 22). In her report on Rostami, Douglas concluded by writing, "Overall, I have no reason to doubt his claim." This is not quite a positive statement of belief, but it rules out disbelief.

Clinicians broadly share the assumption that writing a medicolegal report is a product of the personal encounter between the clinician and the client, with all the intimacies, detachments, and ambiguities that encounter can produce. The credibility of a verbal account is therefore central to the clinical opinion. One medical doctor, with extensive experience in writing medicolegal reports told me, "Assessment of credibility is actually core to all medical training. No doctor automatically believes what their patient says, but filters it through the prism of their knowledge and experience in order to understand its meaning both in clinical terms and to the patient. Failure to do this leads to misdiagnoses, missed diagnoses, and unhappy patients. The fact that the judges regard credibility assessment as their preserve means that we cannot refer to the C word in our reports, even though they would criticize us if we do not consider alternative causes which may involve implied fabrication."[29] In the context of concerns over credibility, the Medical Foundation puts all requests for medicolegal reports through a process of review, in which a team of lawyers and clinicians decides whether to take a case. One central reason for not taking a case can be that too many consistency issues cannot be explained clinically. These inconsistencies may cause insurmountable problems in later judgments about credibility, and therefore the report is unlikely to be useful in assessing the case. Following her meetings with Rostami, Douglas was initially slightly concerned about one or two inconsistencies in the dates that Rostami had given her, but having sought clarification at the third meeting, she was satisfied that she had clarified them.

Among clinicians, there is a widespread objection to the claim often made by the Home Office and immigration judges that doctors are simply hoodwinked by claimants. Judges often say, for example, that psychiatric reports are based on the account of the claimant and therefore offer little corroborative weight.[30] Some judges even go so far as to argue, to the frustration of many clinicians, that doctors have a professional duty to believe what a patient tells them.[31] Many clinicians argue that although trust between a patient and a clinician is crucial, there is also always a sense that there is more going on than appearances suggest.[32] Clinicians are trained, they say, through analyzing what is said and what is unsaid, what people do and what people do not do, at uncovering the layers of truth and half-truth that often even the patient will not be fully aware of. As Douglas put it, "We are not all dewy-eyed optimists and we know that you have to be careful because it is easy to be carried away by a persuasive witness."[33]

Nearly all clinicians working in the field want to distance themselves from the "culture of disbelief" that is widely seen as facing refugees in Europe and North America, which was examined in Chapter 2 (see also Fassin and d'Halluin 2007). Yet there is still a widespread sense that people requesting asylum can fabricate or embellish some of their claims.[34] In a context where accounts are subjected to minute scrutiny by immigration officials, and the stakes, should a claimant be sent back, are very high, it is perhaps inevitable that some people will misrepresent parts of their account. For those dedicated to the principles of asylum, such half-truths are not thought to undermine the moral basis of the claim, but rather they are treated as an outcome of necessity. The question then is to separate those parts of an account that are true from those parts that are not entirely true and from those parts that are complete fabrications. Perhaps most important, some types of inconsistency, which could be taken as evidence of fabrication, can themselves be seen by clinicians as a sign of the authenticity of the account. Indeed, Juliet Cohen, the head doctor of the medicolegal report team at the Medical Foundation has argued that sleep disorder, depression, weight loss and malnutrition, chronic pain, and brain injury, all of which are associated with torture survivors, can all lead to difficulties in recall (2001). The British Psychological Society has also written that "while some parts of the trauma memory may be recalled consistently and in detail, it is common that other parts will be more vague, have some gaps, in jumbled order and, possibly, contain inaccuracies (2010, 24).

Given the importance of credibility assessments in writing medicolegal reports, scars, taken in isolation, do not tell the clinician a great deal. The assessment of scars is therefore not a simple reading from the body. Page Dubois has argued that in Ancient Greece, torture was seen as leaving marks on the body that revealed a hidden truth untainted by the suspicions evoked by spoken words (1991). Writing in the context of modern French immigration policies, Fassin and d'Halluin have argued that medical reports have meant that the suffering body has become the main legal resource for undocumented migrants (2005). If the rest of their story is not believed, at least the pain written on their bodies cannot be denied. From this perspective, words can always be doubted, but bodies produce undeniable evidence of pain. However, in the context of British medicolegal reports at least, torture does not leave marks on bodies that can be easily read. A scar in and of itself does not tell a clinician much; it must be assessed against the verbal account of the claimant. In this process, neither bodies nor language can be understood on their own, and neither is entirely transparent.

In assessing scars, a clinician compares clinical observations of the body with the attribution made by the client, in the context of what is known about the client's lifestyle and experiences, along with other physical and psychological evidence. Douglas had to match the claimed cause with the appearance of the scar or lesion and assess their relative consistency with what Rostami had told her.[35] In her report, Douglas noted that, although Rostami gave a fluent account of his experiences, at several points he had difficulty breathing, paused, shook his head, and became tearful. She also noted that Rostami had not tried to claim that all his scars were caused by his mistreatment. Words, demeanor, and physical scars were all compared to one another to produce a clinical opinion. These observations were then checked against the various protocols and diagnostic criteria to make sure that their conclusions would be recognized by other clinicians. A psychological assessment is similarly not simply the taking in of a client's own self-reported symptoms; rather, it involves an assessment of the client's appearance, behavior, speech, and subjective mood. The reading of such signs can be difficult for clinicians, aware as they are of cultural differences in physical and emotional presentations. However, in this process neither bodies nor words are taken at face value but are weighed against one another. Language is interwoven with the corporeal and the experiential (compare Buch 2010; Cavell 1987).

Certainty and Objectivity

If clinical notions of causation are provisional and work at multiple levels, they potentially run up against legal demands for the narrowing of claims about the causes of particular injuries and symptoms. The Istanbul Protocol, with its language of consistency and diagnosis, is designed to help translate between these clinical and legal approaches to causation. However, translation is never a clear-cut process, but it necessarily involves some form, however small, of distortion in order to move from one frame to another. In this situation, Sally Merry has argued that as "knowledge brokers, translators channel the flow of information but they are often distrusted, because their ultimate loyalties are ambiguous and they may be double agents. They are powerful in that they have mastered both of the discourses of the interchange, but they are vulnerable to charges of disloyalty or double-dealing" (2006b, 42). Where, then, do the loyalties of those who write medicolegal reports lie? In the British context, it is important to remember that the report is formally written for the court and not for the client. Every Medical Foundation report ends with the signature of the clinician and the following statement: "The contents of this report are true and to the best of my knowledge and belief. I understand that in compiling this report I have an overriding duty to the court and I confirm that I have complied with this duty." Formally, clinicians therefore have a duty of objective scrutiny and should not see themselves as the advocates of the client. Judges are quick to criticize clinicians if they feel that they have too much of an investment in the case and are therefore not being "objective." As we saw in Chapter 2, judges rarely if ever see a report that directly contradicts a claim, and therefore can have a general sense that all expert reports, not just medicolegal reports, have a partisan edge. Such claims, equally unsurprisingly, are routinely dismissed by clinicians, who argue that the reports are based on rigorous clinical expertise. At stake in the debate are differing notions of objectivity and certainty and the relationship between detachment and compassion.

In understanding how and why clinicians assess the accounts of the people they see, it is important to note that although all reports contain a statement that the author understands that his or her duty is to the court, most clinicians admit they would not write the reports unless they had some form of general sympathy for people claiming asylum. Douglas told me, "I would not do this work unless I was generally minded to believe what they tell me. If I thought they were all chancers [opportunist], I would find better things to do with my day off. . . . I have always gunned for downtrodden folk."[36] However, this does not imply that Douglas saw herself as an advocate for individual cases. The Medical Foundation stresses to its clinicians that there is a difference between supporting the general principle of asylum and human rights and seeing themselves as the advocates for an individual client. Reports can do the former but not the latter, and therefore they should never collude in half-truths and fabrications.

In a context in which immigration decision makers constantly seem to be upping their evidential demands, there can appear to be a demand for a level of certainty that cannot easily be given by clinicians. As we saw in the previous chapter, the findings by the doctor who examined Khalili that the scars on Khalili's ankles were consistent with his account, were dismissed as evidentially inconsequential by the judge. In this context, Anthony Good has argued that many expert witnesses can feel pressured to "express greater certainty than they really feel" (2007, 130). Writing about France, Didier Fassin and Estelle d'Halluin similarly argue that the clinical vagueness found in many of the categories used in medicolegal reports "facilitates translating a personal conviction into a psychiatric diagnosis" (2007, 319). The Medical Foundation has therefore put in place a process of legal and medical review, where reports are checked to make sure they stay within the legally defined bounds and communicate their opinions as clearly as possible to judges. Clinicians can find it difficult to translate their clinical opinions into the language of medicolegal reports. This is especially so given that in normal clinical practice, clinicians do not expect their words to be second-guessed and they do not expect to be asked to fully justify how and why they have come to an opinion. As part of this process, reports can go backward and forward several times to try to make sure that the clinician has not overstepped the mark in what he or she can and cannot say and that the clinician communicates his or her opinions as effectively as possible to a legal audience. Although many clinicians find this process reassuring as they enter into a legal realm that they often do not fully understand, others also privately find it infuriating and feel that it undermines their professional expertise.

In negotiating the relationship between clinical and legal certainty, a tension exists between different understandings of objectivity. These can be glossed as *mechanical* and *expert* objectivity (Daston and Galison 2008, 17). Mechanical objectivity, broadly speaking, implies an opposition to the subjective and the impartial. It is the view from nowhere. Mechanical objectivity seemingly offers the possibility of knowledge independent of individual idiosyncrasy. Perhaps most important, it is also a form of objectivity that appears to be transparent and easily communicated. It does not rely on trust in the superior knowledge of the expert. As such, it seems attractive to judges, who are often broadly skeptical of claims of superior expert knowledge and insist that experts set out their reasons for coming to a conclusion.[37] Judges have insisted that clinicians use the Istanbul Protocol or the ICD criteria for the diagnosis of PTSD, for example, as a way of attempting to make their decision-making processes assessable by outsiders. However, such forms of mechanistic objectivity are not necessarily accurate or reliable. Mechanical replicable processes can also consistently be wrong.

An alternative notion of objectivity, based on trained expert judgment, aims to synthesize, highlight, and grasp relationships, drawing out the crucial points (Daston and Galison 2008; Porter 1995). Such expert judgment is not simply the mechanical reproduction of guidelines but the application of accumulated knowledge for specific ends. For the issues here, perhaps the most obvious example of this tension among different forms of objectivity can be found in the use of photographs in medicolegal reports. British doctors, especially those at the Medical Foundation, tend to use the line drawings provided in the Istanbul Protocol to mark the location and nature of scars or lesions (OHCHR 2004, 22). Douglas's report on Rostami was accompanied by a series of line drawings. The drawings showed the nine points where Douglas observed scars on Rostami's body. Many British clinicians feel that photographs can be too intrusive, and in any case photographs risk being misinterpreted.[38]

In the writing of a medicolegal report, the accumulated knowledge produced by past experience often fits uneasily into the broad categories of diagnostic criteria and scales. Even if a clinician feels he or she can come to a relatively firm opinion about the cause of a particular scar, there is still ambiguity in terms of whether to classify this as *consistent*, *highly consistent*, or something else. The part of the Istanbul Protocol that stresses overall assessment of scars, rather than the assessment of any individual scar, is crucial here, as it creates a space in which opinions that go beyond simple accumulated empirical observation can be inserted. One doctor told me, "We say we are making a holistic diagnosis, when we are sure we are right but cannot pin it down."[39] The key term is "clinical impression" and is endorsed by the Istanbul Protocol as the correct basis for writing medicolegal reports (OHCHR 2004, 22). A clinical impression implies a sense of looking at the patient and his or her claims as a whole, based on past experience. It also, crucially, implies a sense of not being absolutely certain.

It is important to point out here that, in the sense of being based on accumulated expertise, the analysis of the injuries resulting from torture is probably little different from much medical practice. The introduction of checklists, categorization, and "evidence-based medicine" across all fields of clinical practice, especially since the 1970s, was an attempt to produce objective forms of diagnosis and treatment that could be repeated over and over again. Yet, in practice, as Timmermans and Berg point out, guidelines and categorization can seldom cover all cases and all decisions (2003, 3; see also Dodier 1997). They argue that all medical knowledge is inherently uncertain, and the introduction of protocols can actually increase rather than decrease some of the messy contradictions of medicine. The gaps produced by applying abstract frameworks to an often inchoate world are always filled by judgment (Daston and Galison 2008). Generalizable protocols are not universal templates that can be replicated and applied in the same manner over and over again but rather must be forced to fit awkwardly into the often incoherent and unpredictable world of clinical practice.

Although the introduction of scales and guidelines, in the shape of the Istanbul Protocol and the DSM, may provide a framework in which causal claims can be made, it does not provide a straightforward mechanistic way of identifying the traces of torture. As one practitioner put it, "Evaluation in this area still depends mainly on clinical judgements and experience" (Wenzel 2002, 612). The Istanbul Protocol scale of *consistent, highly consistent,* and *diagnostic* talks the language of probability, and probability is often seen as being associated with statistics and therefore objective and scientific. Yet along with the laws of statistical chance is another tradition of using probability to talk about the reasonable degree of belief with which someone holds an opinion (Hacking 1975, 14). The claim that something is probable therefore has the connotation of approval. Clinicians cannot apply the Istanbul scale on the basis of statistical probability, as they have no reliable statistical tables on torture to use and must therefore make judgments based on the person in front of them. Ian Hacking points out, "In practical medicine the facts are too few to enter into the calculus of probabilities not because we cannot get more data, but because obtaining more data about different individuals is irrelevant to the case of the patient we wish to treat" (1990, 86). A statement of consistency in relation to scars therefore ultimately comes down not to general rules but to opinions based on clinical experience, of how convinced the doctor is in any individual case.

In this process the technical and the compassionate can become merged. Matei Candea has argued that there has been a tendency in much social science literature to oppose the detached from the engaged, the objective from the ethical, yet this dichotomy ignores the ways in which the two can be bound up with one another (2010). In the context of writing medicolegal reports, it is only possible to follow through on a belief that it is necessary to understand a client in all his or her complexity in terms of the distancing frameworks of protocols and categories. At the same time, the application of technical criteria makes sense only against a background of a compassionate commitment to the client. Skepticism is combined with an ethical conviction about the importance of dealing with the person before the clinician on their own terms.

The Cause of Torture?

Clinicians are rarely, if ever, asked by lawyers to say whether any particular event amounts to torture. Rather, they are requested to express their opinion on the possible causes of specific injuries. The decision of whether a particular injury amounts to torture is one that judges, not clinicians, make at least in the context of medicolegal reports. Indeed, many British clinicians are reluctant to make statements about torture. Douglas did not refer directly to torture in her opinion in the report, but she used the word when referring to Rostami's own account. The Medical Foundation widely advises clinicians against using the word *torture*, taking the position that clinicians should comment on individual injuries and signs of distress, as this is more precise. Furthermore, as torture is a matter of legal definition and not a clinical syndrome, doctors are advised not to stray into areas of legal sensitivity. Medicolegal reports therefore try to link particular physical or psychological wounds to specific events. The level of causation referred to moves between a specific mechanism and a method, between saying, for example, a scar was caused by being hit with a blunt object or by being kicked by a heavy boot. Torture, as an abstract noun, is much less amenable to clinical documentation than are more specific causes of injury.

Yet, clinicians still refer to torture. The word *torture* still peppers medicolegal reports. Clinicians will sometimes conclude their reports with sentences like "I believe that Mr. X was subjected to systematic torture in his home country." What, then, is a clinician saying if he or she writes that someone has been tortured, as opposed to having been beaten by a blunt object or kicked by a heavy boot? What makes torture appear from behind individual scars and psychological symptoms? If a doctor writes at the end of the report, "I believe this person has been tortured," literally, the doctor has to be understood as saying that, based on his or her clinical experience and the evidence that has been presented, he or she has no reason to doubt what he or she has been told. The clinician is saying that the client, who has described the treatment as torture, is capable of being believed, based on the clinical virtues of detachment and compassion. More broadly though, when a clinician makes a statement about torture in a medicolegal report, it has to be understood in the contexts of human rights conventions and the campaigns behind them. The prohibition of torture has been internationally recognized by states. Yet, at the same time, people are still subjected to cruel and inhuman forms of violence, and the infliction of pain is constantly denied. As such, the use of the word *torture* in medicolegal reports draws together claims about individual scars and psychological symptoms to bring into view an objection to a very particular type of cruelty. A claim of torture is therefore at once a clinical judgment and an ethical statement about human suffering.

Chapter 4
Predicting the Future Risk of Torture

How can we know what the future holds? The previous two chapters examined the assessment of evidence about past torture. However, the crucial issue for people claiming protection in the United Kingdom is not the past; rather, it is events that have not yet taken place. What will happen when a particular individual is returned to Algeria, Libya, or the Democratic Republic of the Congo? Might he or she be tortured? If evaluating evidence about the past is hard enough, speculating about the future remains inherently uncertain. Lawyers, in particular, can be somewhat uneasy about predicting forthcoming events. It is dangerously close to what one senior judge, Lord Denning, called a form of "prophesying."[1] Such guesswork appears anathema to the attempts at precision and predictability usually thought to be associated with law.

Human rights practices can look to the future as much as the past. In contrast to, say, the criminal justice system, which concentrates on retrospective punishment, much of the human rights project focuses on the prevention of future harms. The principle of non-refoulement, of not returning people to places where they may face torture or other forms of ill-treatment, is an obvious example. As such, human rights practices can therefore rely on what Fuyuki Kurasawa calls a form of "preventive foresight" (2007, 97). They try to envision possible future abuses and introduce the relevant precautionary measures. Yet, as Kurasawa argues, human rights projects are in a bind, as they are also part of a wider "modernist project" that eschews eschatology in favor of a sense of time without specific meaning, direction, or end point. In this process, the future seems dangerously opaque and inscrutable. The task of prediction is therefore inherently fallible.

This chapter examines how judges try to predict the future occurrence of torture; in particular, how the category of risk is used to try to bring the future within view. For a claim for protection from torture to be successful under Article 3 of the European Convention on Human

Rights, it must show "strong grounds for believing that the person, if returned, faces a real risk of being subjected to torture or to inhuman or degrading treatment or punishment."[2] Risk is a very specific way of trying to grapple with events that have not yet happened. It is not simply about the recognition of danger but is an attempt to calculate its probability. To work on the basis of risk reduction is to try to pin down the future to identifiable problems and work out their respective odds (Beck 2002). In this context, risk can be understood as a technique for taming the future, for making it calculable, visible, and intelligible (Ewald 1991, 207; O'Malley 2003; Zaloom 2009).

Asylum and immigration procedures involve making a distinction between those risks that are acceptable and those that are not, those lives that should be protected and those that can be risked (Fassin 2007, 301). As a technique for divining the future, risk inevitably narrows the vision of the forms of violence and cruelty that can be predicted. Judgments about risk are based on general trends and categories rather than on individuals. Yet, it is individual lives that judges must make decisions about, opening a space of the unknown between the general and the particular. Judicial risk assessments are also very different from those in fields such as insurance and finance, for example, which work on the basis of quantitative variables, with constant real-time feedback and adjustments (compare Ewald 1991; Zaloom 2009). Judicial risk assessments about torture, in contrast, work on the basis of broad political processes, with all the ambiguity and lack of precision that entails and with little prospect for retrospective adjustment.

Risk assessments around non-refoulement apply to people claiming protection under the Refugee Convention, as well as Article 3 cases. However, unlike the Refugee Convention, Article 3 protection is formally absolute. It still applies to those who have committed crimes against peace, war crimes, crimes against humanity, or a serious nonpolitical crime. Those who might face the risk of torture are therefore formally singled out for protection above and beyond those seeking refugee status.

The central argument of this chapter is that through risk assessments, the absolute prohibition on torture is translated into the uncertainties of judicial attempts to predict the future. A right that supposedly has no exceptions or limitations becomes shot through with caveats and ambiguities once it is projected forward in time.

The arguments of this chapter are made through a focus on the cases of two men who the British government attempted to deport to Algeria as security suspects, but whose lawyers argued that they faced the risk of torture on return.

Two Algerians

In early 2002, an Algerian citizen, who would become publicly known by the moniker *U*, was arrested and charged with terrorism offenses.[3] The British government accused U of holding a senior position in a *mujahedin* training camp in Afghanistan and having direct links to Osama bin Laden. U had claimed asylum in the United Kingdom in 1994 but had lived in Afghanistan between 1996 and 1999. He admitted in court that he had returned to the United Kingdom in 1999 to arrange for "volunteers for Chechnya to go to Afghanistan to acquire some basic training."[4] Another Algerian, Ahmed Ressam, who was convicted of plotting to blow up Los Angeles International Airport, had told the American authorities that he had received training in Afghanistan from U.[5] The United States initially sought U's extradition but withdrew the application after Ressam refused to testify. The British prosecution against U was also dropped, but upon his release he was immediately detained on immigration grounds. While U was in detention, a German court ruled that four Algerian men convicted of planning to bomb the Christmas Market in Strasbourg had all received training from those close to U.[6] In August 2005, he was served with notice of the decision to deport him to Algeria on the grounds of national security.

In September 2003, a second Algerian citizen, who would become known as "RB" (and occasionally as BB), was arrested by British police under the Terrorism Act 2000.[7] RB had been detained as the police were looking for a group who were allegedly planning to poison thousands of Londoners by spreading ricin, a toxin 6,000 times more deadly than cyanide, on car door handles across north London. He had arrived in the United Kingdom in 1995, at the height of the Algerian civil war. RB had been studying engineering in France and originally came to the United Kingdom on a six-month visitor's visa, and then seems to have gone off the radar. In 1999, he claimed asylum in the United Kingdom, and subsequently married an Algerian citizen also living in the United Kingdom, fathering three children. While living in the United Kingdom, RB had been a regular visitor to Finsbury Park Mosque. The mosque's imam at the time was Abu-Hamza, who in 2006 was found guilty of "soliciting to murder" and "stirring up racial hatred," in relation to his sermons and sentenced to seven years in prison.[8] When RB was arrested, police found a stamp at his home for the *Dhamat Houmet Daawa Salafia* (Protectors of the Salaafist Call) (DHDS), an armed Islamist group based in Algeria. The group was not illegal in the United Kingdom at the time, but it was on the UN Security Council list of Al Qaeda–linked groups.[9] The initial charges against RB were eventually withdrawn, but he pled guilty in relation to a holding a false French passport and was sentenced to three months in prison. Following his release from prison, RB was detained again and served with notice of the decision to deport him to Algeria on grounds of national security.

U and RB are among dozens of Algerians, Libyans, Iraqis, Jordanians, and others whom the British government has tried to deport on the basis that they are a threat to national security. Even before the September 11 attacks in the United States, the British government attempted to deport foreign "terror suspects," against whom the government lacked the necessary evidence to convict in a criminal court. Many of these people come from places with human rights records that have been widely criticized. Given that the men had now also been labeled as suspected terrorists, they faced considerable dangers if they were returned home. The Special Immigration Appeals Commission (SIAC), a tribunal set up especially to hear immigration cases involving security suspects, ruled that both U and RB should be detained and then deported as they were a threat to national security.[10] The decision was made partly on the basis of evidence presented by the British security services behind closed doors, without the presence of either man's lawyers. The interests of the appellant were represented by a "special advocate," who was given security clearance to see the classified evidence. Once the special advocate had seen or heard the secret evidence, the advocate was barred from contact with the appellant or his lawyers. In open court, both U and RB were represented by the law firm Birnberg Pierce. The firm's senior active partner, Gareth Pierce, is a prominent British civil rights lawyer, who had made her name having the convictions quashed of wrongly convicted members of the Provisional IRA. Her law firm has represented a high proportion of those detained under counterterror legislation. The lawyers argued before SIAC that if both men were returned to Algeria they would face the real risk of torture, and the United Kingdom would therefore be in breach of its obligations under Article 3 of the European Convention on Human Rights.

Challenging Article 3

The concept of risk is not itself mentioned in the European Convention on Human Rights or, for that matter, in the Refugee Convention.[11] Nor can it be found in the UN Convention on Torture, with its explicit prohibition on sending people to a country where they might face torture. Instead the language of threat and danger is used. The notion of risk was only introduced as the principle of non-refoulement was subjected to increased judicial challenge in the late 1980s and early 1990s.[12]

Article 3 has acted, formally at least, as a barrier to the British state sending back terror suspects to Algeria, Jordan, and Libya, as well as to many other countries. However, for many in the British government, this seemed to be an unreasonable impediment. Famously, Tony Blair scrawled the demand to simply "Get them back," across a memo detailing the diplomatic and legal negotiations over the deportation of an Egyptian Islamist.[13] Blair continued, "This is a bit much. Why do we need all these things?"[14] Speaking from the steps of Downing Street, on 5 August 2005, Tony Blair said, "In my view anyone who is a foreign national who is inciting or engaged in extremism in this country should be out." Similarly, in a speech to the European parliament in September 2005, the then Labour home secretary, Charles Clarke, argued that the absolute prohibition on sending people back to countries where they faced the risk of torture was out of balance (2005). Clarke's successor as home secretary, John Reid, made the same arguments when he claimed that when he hears people arguing, "We ought to be prohibited from weighing the security of millions of people in this country, of our own people, if a suspected terrorist remains here when we are trying to deport him. . . . I can't help feeling that they don't get it. They just don't get it" (2006).

Against the background of a political determination to deport terror suspects, government lawyers had to translate the deportation procedures into terms compatible with Article 3 of the European Convention on Human Rights, and the ways in which risk has been assessed by the courts. In 2008, the British government sought to challenge the absolute prohibition on sending people to places where they might face the risk of torture or other forms of ill-treatment. The challenge was reportedly pushed right from the "political center of government."[15] Along with Lithuania, Portugal, and Slovenia, the United Kingdom intervened in a case in which a Tunisian citizen had appealed to the European Court of Human Rights against his deportation from Italy. Nassim Saadi was arrested by Italian police in 2002 on suspicion of involvement in "international terrorism." Although these charges were dropped because of lack of evidence, Saadi was convicted of criminal conspiracy, forgery, and receiving stolen goods, and he was sentenced to four years in prison. Within days of his Italian sentence being passed, a Tunisian military court sentenced Saadi, in absentia, to twenty years in prison for membership in a terrorist organization. On his release in 2006, the Italian minister of the interior ordered Saadi's deportation to Tunisia, on the grounds that he was "disturbing public order and threatening national security."[16] The Italians asked the Tunisian government for assurances that any fears of torture or ill-treatment were unfounded.[17] The Tunisian minister of foreign affairs replied that Tunisian law already protected the rights of prisoners.[18] For the Tunisians there was no need for additional assurances, as their legal system already formally prohibited mistreatment. At this point, Saadi lodged a claim with the European Court of Human Rights against his deportation.[19]

The United Kingdom intervened in the case, arguing that the previous approach of the European Court to deportation and the risk of torture were too rigid.[20] In particular, the United Kingdom argued that the risk of future ill-treatment was inherently subjective. As such, the risk of torture should be balanced against the potential danger presented by the person to be deported.[21] Furthermore, the United Kingdom also claimed that such cases should be subject to a far higher standard: "more likely than not," as the current standard of "substantial grounds for believing" was too loose to apply consistently.[22] However, the European Court of Human Rights responded that the risk of ill-treatment on deportation could not be balanced against the danger presented by a security suspect, as they were separate issues. The judgment said, "The Court considers that the argument based on the balancing of the risk of harm if the person is sent back against the dangerousness he or she represents to the community if not sent back is misconceived. The concepts of 'risk' and 'dangerousness' in this context do not lend themselves to a balancing test because they are notions that can only be assessed independently of each other. Either the evidence adduced before the Court reveals that there is a substantial risk if the person is sent back or it does not."[23] One judge went so far as to call the British argument "intellectually dishonest."[24] In turning to the specific details of the case, the Court ruled that "reliable sources have reported practices resorted to or tolerated by the authorities which are manifestly contrary to the principles of the Convention."[25] Citing reports from Amnesty International and Human Rights Watch, the court ruled that any decision to deport Saadi to Tunisia would be a breach of Article 3.[26]

The relationship between risk and the ability to calculate the future was at stake in the *Saadi* case. Two separate precautionary principles were in conflict. As Jasanoff argues in another context, the move from a focus on harm to a focus on risk (the possibility of harm) opens space for conflicts over how precise risk assessments can be and the amount of risk that is tolerable (1997, 72). The British government had tried to argue that the risk of torture is inherently subjective and should therefore be balanced against other threats and be subject to a far higher standard of proof. For the European Court of Human Rights, however, the two risks were entirely separate. Furthermore, precisely because risks are always unpredictable and the prohibition of torture is absolute, the level of certainty about future events must remain relatively low.

Diplomatic Assurances

Faced with the apparent bind of Article 3, the British government has repeatedly tried to meet its formal obligations through the use of what are known as "diplomatic assurances." Such assurances have been widely used in death penalty cases, in which the United Kingdom has agreed to deport a criminal suspect, but only on the grounds that the suspect is not executed. Crucially, these agreements are diplomatic in nature and not legally binding. Since the mid-1990s, the British government has also sought to use diplomatic assurances in cases of foreign nationals suspected of involvement in terrorism.[27] In particular, in 1999 there was an attempt to send an Egyptian lawyer, Hani Youssef, back to Cairo. This was the same man about whom Blair had scribbled "Get them back." Youssef had arrived in the United Kingdom in 1994 and claimed asylum on the grounds that he had been harassed and tortured by the Egyptian security services because of his involvement with Islamic militants. His claim for asylum under the Refugee Convention was refused in 1998 on the basis that there were "serious grounds" for thinking that he had links to terrorist organizations.[28] Following the refusal of Youssef's claim, the Foreign Office decided to push for assurances from the Egyptian government that if Youssef were sent back to Cairo he would not be ill-treated. However, the initial request was turned down by the Egyptian government on the grounds that it would amount to interference in Egypt's judiciary and national sovereignty.[29] At this point, Tony Blair appears to have become impatient. His private secretary wrote, "The Prime Minister thinks we are in danger of being excessive in our demands of the Egyptians. . . . In general the Prime Minister's priority is to see these . . . Islamic Jihad members returned to Egypt. We should do everything possible to achieve that."[30] Nevertheless, the home secretary felt compelled to release Youssef in July 1999, fearing that there was no way the British government could get the necessary assurances from Egypt.[31] Youssef was later granted "discretionary leave to remain" in the United Kingdom.

Attempts to negotiate formal diplomatic assurances with Algeria also failed, principally over the request for a post-return monitoring system, which was seen as interference in national sovereignty. However, in July 2006, President Abdelaziz Bouteflika agreed to an "exchange of letters" with then Prime Minister Tony Blair. In this exchange, both sides declared the "absolute commitment of our two governments to human rights and fundamental freedoms."[32] It was also agreed that the British Embassy could maintain contact with returned persons who were not detained.[33] The United Kingdom has been more successful in negotiating general assurances with Lebanon, Jordan, and Ethiopia.[34] Throughout these negotiations though there was a tension between the Home Office, which pushed domestic security concerns, and the Foreign Office, which focused on diplomatic relations.[35] The signed agreements are bilateral, in that they are written so that they apply as much to the

United Kingdom as to Libya, Ethiopia, and Jordan. In practice they amount to a restatement of international human rights obligations and a commitment that deportees will be treated in a "humane and proper manner, in accordance with internationally accepted standards." They also stipulate that "independent bodies" will be allowed to monitor the treatment of any deportees after their return.

The precise nature of the monitoring organizations is not set out in the assurances. In Jordan, the National Centre for Human Rights was initially approached by the British Foreign Office to serve as the monitoring body but turned it down, citing "national sensitivities" after protests in the Jordanian parliament.[36] After several false leads and rebuffs, a small Jordanian human rights NGO called *Adaleh* was eventually named as the monitoring organization. Human Rights Watch claimed that *Adaleh* had a weak track record of speaking out against torture and was overdependent on British funding.[37] In Libya, the Qadhafi Development Foundation (QDF) was appointed as the monitoring organization. The QDF was headed by Saif al Islam Qadhafi, Colonel Muammar Qadhafi's second son. The largest NGO in Libya, the QDF was funded by Said Qadhafi's own extensive business interest. In 2006, the US State Department described the QDF as "semi-official" and as following "government policy" (2006).

There are a wide range of views, even among human rights practitioners, on whether diplomatic assurances reduce the future risk of torture. For their harshest critics, assurances do nothing to mitigate risk. Thomas Hammarberg, the Council of Europe commissioner for human rights, has argued that diplomatic assurances "are not credible and have also turned out to be ineffective" (2006). Similarly, Manfred Nowak, the UN Special Rapporteur on Torture, has said, "The plan of the United Kingdom to request diplomatic assurances for the purpose of expelling persons in spite of a risk of torture reflects a tendency in Europe to circumvent international obligations'" (SCFA 2008, 66). The United Kingdom's Parliamentary Joint Committee on Human Rights (JCHR) has also argued that "if relied on in practice, diplomatic assurances . . . present a substantial risk of individuals actually being tortured" (2006, 131). From this perspective, diplomatic assurances can simply not be trusted. They tell us very little about the future risk of torture.

Those who support diplomatic assurances find they are a reasonable approach to a complex problem. From this perspective, critics are simply being unpractical. Former Foreign Office minister Kim Howells argues that those who express skepticism about the value of diplomatic assurances are "condescending" and display "a real leftover from a colonial attitude" (Penketh 2006). Lord Carlile, the government's "independent reviewer of anti-terror legislation," has also supported assurances, dismissing as a "counsel of despair" the idea that no one should be deported because their safety could not be guaranteed (Campbell 2005).

A middle approach has been to argue that the impact of diplomatic assurances must be judged with respect to each individual case. The European Committee for the Prevention of Torture (CPT) has argued, for example, that there may be a place for diplomatic assurances, but "to have any chance of being effective, such a mechanism would certainly need to incorporate some key guarantees, including the right of independent . . . persons to visit the individual concerned at any time, without prior notice, and to interview him/her in private in a place of their choosing" (2006).[38] The UNHCR has similarly argued that diplomatic assurances may be relied on if suitable mechanisms are set in place (2006). From this perspective, the effectiveness of diplomatic assurances is always context specific.

Diplomatic assurance can be understood as an attempt to make the future more predictable by tying assessments of risk down to formal promises and guarantees, and thereby making risk more calculable. The extent to which such assurances bring the future within sight depends, however, on the level of trust placed in formal guarantees. For some, governments should be treated as rational agents who can be taken at their word and are therefore relatively predictable. For others, regimes such as those of Algeria, Libya, and Jordan should always be suspected of subterfuge.

Evidence about the Risk of Torture

I shall now return to the specific cases of U and RB to examine how the courts made calculations about the future risk of torture. The two cases were heard by the security-cleared Special Immigration Appeals Commission. The senior judge on the SIAC, Mr. Justice Mitting, had ruled against the government in several high-profile cases.[39] Large parts of the evidence presented by the Foreign Office were seen behind closed doors, with the lawyers of the Algerian men having no access. In open court, the SIAC heard from the Foreign Office that the Algerian Ministry of Justice had given specific assurances in relation to U and RB. These were mostly restatements of the formal position in Algerian law, and they included the right to appear before a court, the right of habeas corpus, the right to be presumed innocent, and that "human dignity will be respected under all circumstances."[40] U and RB's lawyers objected that torture was not specifically prohibited by the assurances. However, the judge later ruled this had been done through the promise to protect the "human dignity" of the men, albeit in a "universally understood diplomatic language."[41] The lawyers for U and RB admitted that the assurances had been given in good faith by the Algerians.[42] However, they also argued that the government did not have full control over the security services.[43] Furthermore, both men would now be of particular interest to the security forces, as they had been singled out by the British government.[44]

Most of the evidence presented about future risk in both cases concerned events that had already happened. Compared to most asylum and immigration claims, more resources are available in cases before the SIAC for the collection of evidence, and therefore more expert witnesses and reports. The former British ambassador to Morocco and Libya, Anthony Layden, gave evidence for the government. Layden had been appointed as the Foreign Office's key liaison with the Algerian government over those deported with assurances. In his evidence, Layden attempted to paint a picture of Algeria as a country moving away from violence and toward greater transparency and accountability. He acknowledged that torture still existed in Algeria, but he claimed it was decreasing. Layden also acknowledged that the deportees might be detained on arrival in Algeria and that there might be a risk of torture. However, he was adamant that the arrangements that had been put into place had mitigated this risk to a negligible level. The SIAC judgment paraphrased Layden as saying that "his unshakable view was that the assurances given by the Algerian authorities in the case of BB eliminated any real risk that he would be subjected to torture or ill-treatment."[45] Layden also argued that there was no evidence for a lack of support among the Algerian security forces for the political reform process.[46]

In its decisions on U and RB, the SIAC also relied on evidence presented in a previous case that dealt with similar issues.[47] In this, the Foreign Office had presented a US State Department report that argued that Algeria was "emerging from over a decade of terrorism and civil strife."[48] An internal Foreign Office assessment was also presented that claimed that "as Algeria slowly emerges from the shadow of the insurgency, the government's strategy has been to promote national reconciliation."[49] In the Foreign Office's evidence, there was a clear sense of Algeria moving away from a past in which torture had been endemic.

There was an attempt by the Algerians' lawyers to undermine the predictive claims of the former ambassador, by showing that he had previously been wrong. In particular, the SIAC was presented with evidence about what had happened to four other Algerians—known as Q, K, H, and P—who had been deported in recent years with Foreign Office involvement. All had received assurances similar to those provided to U and RB. In particular, the SIAC heard how Q was detained immediately on his return and held on suspicion of terrorist or subversive acts. In U's case, his lawyers presented a witness statement from a trainee lawyer who had visited Algeria. The statement reported a discussion with one of Q's Algerian lawyers, in which the trainee was told that while in detention Q had "heard the screams of people being tortured around him."[50] Layden claimed that Q had not taken up the offer of regular telephone conversations with the British Embassy, but that it had been told by Q's family that he was well.[51] The British Embassy also received a note from the Algerian Ministry of Justice indicating that Q had signed a statement declaring he had not been mistreated in detention.[52]

The Foreign Office's evidence about the general trajectory of Algerian politics was also challenged by a number of academic expert witnesses. Professor David Seddon, an anthropologist by training who has worked on issues of social and political development across the African continent, gave evidence in a written report that it was unsafe to return to Algeria any person alleged to have been involved in "Islamist extremist activities."[53] Later, new evidence was submitted by Dr. Hugh Roberts.[54] For many years, Roberts was one of the few academics working on Algeria in the United Kingdom; he had also worked for the International Crisis Group, specifically on Islamist groups in North Africa. Roberts's written report claimed that since 2007 a number of bombing attacks had occurred that had been instigated by elements within the Algerian government, showing that the regime was far from stable or in control.[55] The SIAC was also shown a report from Amnesty International that claimed that "despite improvements, torture and other ill-treatment remains both systematic and widespread."[56] From the perspective of such evidence, the move away from torture in Algeria was far from inevitable and complete.

Speculating about the Future

On what grounds can judges predict the future? Formally, at least, the judicial assessment of risk is supposed to avoid conjecture. The threshold of demonstrated future risk is said to be more than simple "theory and suspicion."[57] A "mere possibility" does not suffice.[58] The European Court of Human Rights has argued that although judgments about the future may be speculative, they must be "cautious" and "careful."[59] English judges talk about an "informed guess."[60] What can this mean in practice?

One place to start when making an "informed guess" about the future is in the past. Judges argue that past events can be treated as a good guide to the future.[61] As the academic James Hathaway, who is often approvingly cited by judges, has argued, "Where evidence of past maltreatment exists . . . it is unquestionably an excellent indicator of the fate that may await an applicant upon return to her home" (1991, 88).[62] However, the past is, at best, only a partial guide to the future. Even if a claim of past ill-treatment is not accepted, it is open to the courts to decide that a risk might exist in the future. The same is true the other way around. Even if past events are accepted as having taken place, the court may rule that there is no future risk. The fact that something happened in the past is no guarantee that it will happen again. Judges can argue that events such as regime change, a reform process, or simply the passing of time have driven a wedge between past abuses and their possible future reoccurrence.[63] However, one leading judgment has also argued that judges should not treat the assessment of past events and future risks as two separate processes.[64] Rather, all evidence should be treated in the round. In this process, the distinction between the past and the future is blurred, if not erased, as events that have not happened are brought together with those that have.

The Decisions

In a series of judgments, the SIAC ruled that U and RB would not face a "real risk" of torture if returned to Algeria. The visions of the future found in the reports written by the academics on the general situation in Algeria were roundly dismissed. Although it was accepted that Roberts was an expert on Algerian society and he had expressed his views independently, his report was described as "speculative" and was criticized for its lack of sources.[65] The judgment also described his evidence as having "little weight," as he was not an expert on law or human rights.[66] The judgment also claimed that the judges were "unpersuaded" by Seddon's report, as its conclusions were, they claimed, "belied by what has in fact occurred."[67] In contrast, the judges were impressed by the evidence presented by Layden, the former British ambassador, who they described as "forthright," "impressive," and a "realist."[68]

It is possible to see the preference for the evidence of the former ambassador over that of the academics as part of a battle over relative expertise, with diplomatic knowledge taking precedence. In this case, information gathered from confidential meetings and political negotiations was prioritized over archival and interview research.[69] However, I want to focus not so much on the relative authority given to forms of expertise but rather on the temporal models through which judgments about the future were made.

In reading the past and present for indicators of the future, evidence about previous handling of individual returnees was treated, in the judgments, as not particularly useful. Although the judges felt they could not rule out that the Algerians who had previously been deported had been mistreated on return, the possibility was rejected as improbable.[70] The SIAC judgment claimed, "That evidence does not satisfy us on balance of probabilities that 'Q' and 'H' were exposed to the sounds of actual or pretended ill-treatment of others with the intention or effect of breaking their moral resistance. We cannot exclude the possibility that they heard such sounds, but that is all."[71] In particular, Mitting ruled that the reports of past torture were of doubtful credibility, as they either were not sourced or came from campaigning Algerian lawyers.[72] More important was a general sense that Algeria was moving away from torture. The SIAC ruled that "Algeria is making a sincere, broadly supported and generally successful attempt to transform itself from a war-torn authoritarian state to a normally functioning civil society; solemn diplomatic assurances given by the Algerian State to the British Government about individual deportees are reliable and can safely be accepted."[73] For Mitting, Algeria was firmly on the path to reform and democracy, and would not be easily thrown off this path.[74]

In the decision-making process, the future was brought into sight through a reliance on formal assurances and legal reform. Assurances were seen by the SIAC as being central to any judgment about future safety. They argued, "In a country where the rule of law is firmly embedded, it can safely be assumed that an assurance given to another state will be fulfilled."[75] The SIAC also argued that it was in the long-term interests of the Algerian state to comply with the assurances as Algeria "wished to be accepted by the international community as, a normally-functioning civil society."[76] The judges went on to add that it was "barely conceivable, let alone likely, that the Algerian Government would put . . . at risk" its growing economic ties with the United Kingdom.[77] Mitting ruled that a formal monitoring agreement was not necessary, as given all the attention that had been paid to the cases it was not "realistic to suppose" that ill-treatment "could occur without the fact of breaches becoming known."[78] Finally, the judges cited evidence shown to them in a closed session that "powerfully supports the proposition that it is in the Algerian state's interest" to abide by the assurances.[79]

The future had not been made completely clear, however. The judges ruled that "we cannot wholly exclude the possibility that the assurances will be breached in future in the cases of U or others or that they will be subjected to treatment which would infringe Article 3; but that is no more than a 'mere possibility.' "[80] Equally, in another ruling, Mitting was careful not to rule out the possibility that people suspected of terrorist activity might be tortured in the future. He wrote, "Nevertheless, it would be naïve to conclude that no person suspected of terrorist activity, in particular foreign terrorist activity, is at risk of torture or ill-treatment at the hands of Algerian security forces."[81] However, this risk was not deemed to reach, as a matter of principle, the required level or warrant a stay on deportation. As was argued in a third case, any "attempt to predict if and when such adverse developments might occur is futile. SIAC cannot be concerned with long-term political speculation. All that it can do is to evaluate current conditions and to see if they are likely to be stable in the medium term."[82] Long-term predictions were dismissed as entirely speculative. The SIAC members limited themselves to the short-to-medium term.

The SIAC decisions that U and RB could be safely deported to Algeria were appealed on the basis that the use of secret evidence was unfair and the decisions unsound.[83] The Court of Appeal ruled that the question of whether RB or U faced a real risk of torture on return to Algeria was a matter of fact, not law.[84] The Court of Appeal's jurisdiction is generally limited to questions of law, and the court ruled that the evidence was assessed in an adequate manner and the appeal on this issue was not allowed.[85] The decision was upheld in the House of Lords.[86] However, appeals were allowed on other grounds, and the cases were sent back to the SIAC. Although originally granted bail, both men were eventually detained until their cases were decided.

Torture, Risk, and the Future

What type of future can be imagined through the category of torture? And how does the focus on risk limit the possible futures that can be brought into view? The risk of torture is not self-evident, as risks do not exist independently in the world. Instead, any understanding of risk is a product of the devices we have for measuring it (Ewald 1991, 207; Power 2007). At first glance this may seem an absurd thing to say about torture, as what could be more real than pain and suffering? However, torture is not simply pain and suffering but a very specific way of understanding the infliction of violence. Thinking about torture in terms of risk therefore implies setting down markers that can be measured, of freezing the ebb and flow of violence, so that its likely occurrence can be calculated.

Risk does not arise from a precise and known danger. Indeed, if the exact nature and occurrence of the threat were known, it would not be a risk. Rather, risk is a generalization, based on a distribution of factors across a wider population. There are two important consequences of this. First, risk is not a quality that can belong to individuals alone but to general categories (Castel 1991). The specifics of individual life trajectories get subsumed. Judges may speak of individual risk factors and personal circumstances, such as being a senior political activist, as crucial for any decision. However, this is still to view any individual as a representative of a general class or category. There is simply no individual evidence of what might happen in the future, and judges therefore have to infer from similar cases. At the same time, the specificity of torture as a distinct form of violence is lost. Instead, there is an examination of the general procedures of a state and its relationships with its citizens, rather than of the complex dynamics that can lead to acts of torture and create individualized vulnerabilities. Cases therefore turn less on the individual circumstances than on general political processes.

At this stage it is perhaps useful to draw on historian Reinhart Kosel-leck's distinction between prophecy, progress, and prognosis as approaches to predicting the future (2004). For Koselleck, prophecy (of which judges are so mistrustful; remember Lord Denning), draws no sharp distinction among the past, present, and future (compare Empson 2006). All events are tied together by a greater purpose, determined by fate or divine intervention. Prophecy anticipates an end that is already given. This gives events an "already, but not yet quality" (Cava-nagh 1998, 223). Nothing entirely new can occur, and prediction is therefore relatively unproblematic as long as one can read the signs correctly. In contrast, Koselleck argues that the notion of progress draws sharp distinctions among the past, present, and future.[87] Prophecy has a limited horizon of expectation, but progressive time remains open to an unknown future, which has no goal. In such a context, prediction is inherently difficult, if not impossible, as the future is fundamentally different from the past and the present. For Koselleck, prognosis represents a middle ground between the determinism of prophecy and the contingency and openness of progressive time. Through prognosis, the future is not already made, but neither is it totally unpredictable. The past and present remain guides, and the future is a domain of finite possibilities. As such, predictions continue within the domain of known experience. A fourth way of apprehending time can be added to Kosel-leck's distinctions, namely that of the cyclical time of calendars (Gell 1992, 69–92). Cyclical-calendar time is divided into set units that run subsequently, yet repeat after a given period. Cyclical-calendar time is one of the favored temporal frames of bureaucracies, as it allows the planning of regular events and processes. Although all four ways of looking at the future imply a different metaphysics of time, in practice they can all coexist in the same place, as they are deployed for different ends (Bloch 1977; Howe 1981). However, whichever form of temporal foresight is used, it can play a crucial role in legitimating decisions that are made in the present.

Judicial risk assessment works on the basis of prognosis rather than on prophecy, progress, or calendars. The messianic qualities of prophecy would seem anathema to the self-images of law, progress opens up an unknowable future, and cyclical-calendar time assumes that all the variables are known, which is obviously not the situation in immigration and asylum cases. In contrast, prognosis allows the future to be predicted in situations of relative uncertainty. Through prognosis, although change is imagined, the basic lines of prediction are limited and the future therefore remains a known quantity.

The prognostic forms used by judges have more parallels with diviners than prophets. In E. E. Evans-Pritchard's classic account, divination is used to help make decisions about the future under conditions of uncertainty (1976; see also Turner 1975). To uncover the traces of unknown future events in the present, diviners use deductive or inductive reasoning to read patterns in the past or present. The similarities with judicial methods for viewing the future are pertinent. Judges and diviners both use formal techniques based on internally closed principles as an aid to making decisions about the future. In doing so, diviners and judges may use very different models of causation to link the here and now with the yet to come. Yet, they both work under conditions of inherent uncertainty and try to blur the boundaries between the contemporary and the forthcoming. In contrast, however, although diviners are always grappling with the relationship between their predictions and events as they actually occur, judges' predictions exist in a moment of frozen time and cannot be judged, by other judges at least, against subsequent events. Any decision about the future that is made by judges only ever takes place in the present. Legally speaking at least, such decisions cannot be assessed against what actually happens. The decision is right or wrong, according to the evidence presented before court, at the time the evidence is taken, irrespective of what later happens. There is no power of legal hindsight. Even if someone is later tortured, as long as the judge came to a decision using the correct legal procedures, the decision cannot be appealed on those grounds. The only avenue open is a fresh claim. The limited space that is available for an appeal is based on the inherent irrationality of the initial decision or whether the judges did not follow the law correctly. Only if an appeal is made to the European Court of Human Rights can new evidence and therefore a new decision about the future be made.

The legal assessment of risk works on the basis that future dangers can be measured and that these measurements can be taken from events that have already happened or that can be seen in the present. In deciding the cases of U and RB, the judges relied on formal procedures and guarantees, in the shape of Algerian law, Peace Accords, and above all diplomatic arrangements. Priority was given to the legal and diplomatic evidence presented by the Foreign Office over the political analysis provided by the academics. When considering the nature of these formal commitments, it is worth bearing in mind that Algeria had already signed the International Covenant on Civil and Political Rights in the late 1960s and was one of the first states to sign the UN Convention Against Torture in 1986. Algeria had already made the formal promise not to torture. Yet, although the Foreign Office acknowledged that torture had taken place in Algeria, they argued that the new bilateral commitments they had received minimized the risk of it taking place in these individual cases.

The form of prognosis used by the SIAC assumed that Algerian history is moving forward in one direction. In the cases of U and RB, words such as "emerging" and "transformed" were used to understand Algerian politics. There is a sense of general progress toward a better future, even if the precise goal is undefined. A clear trajectory is created, leading from the past through the present and into the future.[88] A similar approach was taken toward Libya. The British government wanted to deport two Libyan citizens, alleging they were linked to "Islamist terrorist groups."[89] Although the SIAC eventually rejected the use of diplomatic assurances to send people back to Libya, it still used the language of evolution to describe the change in attitudes that had taken place in the Libyan regime. The judgment said, "The evolution in its [the Libyan regime's] outlook towards the West is genuine and a change set for the long term, even if only because the inner circle has seen that as the route to the survival of the regime."[90] In these assumptions about movement through time, the potential for breaks, disjuncture, and countercurrents within Libya or Algeria were put to one side. There was a set direction for change, and the possibility of unpredictability was dismissed as mere conjecture. Subsequent events in North Africa have, of course, shown the unpredictability of political developments. The protests and armed uprising which began in December 2011 were not considered even slightly possible by most observers just a few months beforehand.

The Algerian state was also treated as a unified and rational actor. The SIAC ruled that as Algeria wanted to be accepted as part of the international community, the costs of mistreatment and international censure would outweigh any short-term benefits. The direction of travel for the Libyan state was similarly argued as being set by "pragmatic self-interest."[91] Indeed prognosis can only work if the actors are assumed to be rational; otherwise, their actions are unpredictable. It was for this reason that the SIAC ultimately rejected the diplomatic assurances provided by Libya as a ground for reducing future risk. The Libyan state was personalized in the figure of Colonel Muammar Qadhafi, and he was described as "mercurial."[92] More important, it was argued that "the way in which Colonel

Qadhafi sees his pragmatic interest in his survival may itself be unpredictable and need not to western eyes, be rational or in his self-interest."[93] The Libyan state was treated as too personalized to be trusted.

Finally, there was also an assumption that the state can be made transparent. The Algerian state is treated as "solemn" and "sincere" and the monitoring mechanisms set up by the Foreign Office in Algeria were therefore seen as capable of producing clear and reliable information. In a parallel case involving the Jordanian citizen Abu-Qatada, the SIAC acknowledged that the Jordanian security services practiced torture but ruled that the intense scrutiny of Abu-Qatada's treatment by human rights activists and the media meant that he was unlikely to be mistreated. The judgment said, "If he were to be tortured or ill-treated, there probably would be a considerable outcry in Jordan, regardless of any MOU [Memorandum of Understanding]. The likely inflaming of Palestinian and extremist or anti-Western feelings would be destabilising for the government. The Jordanian Government would be well aware of that potential risk and, in its own interests, would take steps to ensure that that did not happen."[94] Such assumptions about transparency potentially ignore the fact that torture is inherently difficult to monitor (Rejali 2009). It leaves few marks on the body and usually takes place out of sight. The irony is that much of the information used to assess the reliability and transparency of the monitoring mechanism was itself far from transparent, as it was the product of confidential diplomatic and security assessments and had been presented in closed session.

The assessment of the future risk of torture produces a picture of politics as formal, pragmatic, and transparent, which puts to one side the possibility of temporal conflicts, breaks, and countercurrents. Indeed, the calculation of risk is only possible if this is the case. It is hard to see how judicial risk assessments could take place otherwise. Without these assumptions a realm of uncertainty and unknowability is opened up. Foresight requires predictability. The crucial point here is the way in which this skews the assessments in favor of particular visions of violence. Crucially, it is for the person claiming protection, or at least for the lawyers, to present a likely narrative of future risk. They cannot simply try to disrupt the trajectory presented by the Home Office, as judges try to avoid assessing the future in a void. Instead, claimants must try to construct their own historical trajectory that places the risk of torture center stage, using the same emphasis on formal structures and temporal continuity. As one of the lawyers representing the potential deportees told me, "Lawyers like patterns and predictability; they are the basis on which we work."[95]

The forms of reasoning adopted by the judges in torture cases are in practice little different from those found in most refugee cases. The same focus on formal structures, generalized risk calculations, and the use of prognostic predictions can be found in both. In many ways the specifics of torture or persecution are lost under a general concern with the rule of law and democratic structures. However, the prohibition of torture is treated as absolute, with no get-out clauses. It is the absoluteness of the prohibition of torture that produces arrangements such as diplomatic assurances, where the future is tamed through formal promises. Regardless of whether the assurances work as effective guides to the future, they single out individuals for protection. A relatively privileged category of people, whose lives cannot be opened up to a very specific and limited set of envisioned risks, is distinguished from those groups fearing other forms of violence. For these individuals, the future is seen in entirely negative terms, through a concern to prevent the complicity of the British state in possible future harm, rather than a wider commitment to a more just political order. The aspiration is to the prevention of a narrow set of wrongs, rather than the creation of the good (Beck 1992, 42). The aim is inherently limited in that its ambition is to stop people from being tortured, rather than promoting positive values more broadly. Perhaps most important, though, is that although the principle of non-refoulement in cases of torture is said to be absolute, the ways in which the future is brought into view necessarily produce uncertainty. Risk assessments create broad spaces of unknowability between the general and the specific, the principle and the practice. When applied to concrete situations, an absolute principle is turned into an informed guess.

Chapter 5
Prosecuting Torture

In July 2005, Faryadi Sarwar Zardad, an Afghan citizen, was found guilty by an English court of conspiracy to torture. Although he was tried in London, he was prosecuted for crimes committed in Afghanistan in the mid-1990s. Zardad was the first and, at the time of writing, the only person to have been charged, prosecuted, and convicted of torture in the United Kingdom. Zardad's prosecution was launched on the basis that torture was so heinous a crime, such an affront to "civilised values," that perpetrators should be prosecuted no matter who they are, where they commit the act, and who they violate.[1] Unlike what happens with respect to nearly all other crimes, the British state claims universal criminal jurisdiction over torture. The jurisdictional reach of English criminal law is extended beyond its normal limits, as torture is seen as such an outrage to humanity that it "shocks the conscience." Such an attitude is widespread and many states have taken a similar approach. The US Court of Appeals, for example, ruled in 1980 that the "torturer has become like the pirate and slave trader before him *hostis humani generis*, an enemy of all mankind."[2] The crime of torture seems to transcend the usual boundaries of states.

This chapter asks, what does it mean to prosecute the crime of torture as an affront to humanity? Previous chapters have explored attempts to protect survivors of torture; this chapter examines the prosecution of those responsible for the perpetration of torture. Perpetrators have been singled out for specific condemnation, as the crime of torture is said to hold a special "stigma."[3] It seems to take a particularly cruel individual to deliberately inflict pain on another human. Under what conditions then, is it possible to legally determine that someone intentionally commits such an act?

Assigning guilt for torture is an act of cultural and political interpretation. Torture involves acts that can be covered by seemingly more mundane crimes, such as assault or grievous bodily harm. Given the particular stigma attached to torture, there is a possibility that the often banal processes through which violence is inflicted can fail to match the levels of revulsion applied to torture as an abstract crime. Ascribing culpability for torture therefore requires a leap of imagination, that someone can be placed in the special box of reprobation reserved for those responsible for such a heinous act. By placing torture in the category of being among the very worst crimes that anyone can commit, it raises the stakes in any prosecution.

The central argument of this chapter is that the history of the ways in which torture has been criminalized under English law means that the potential spaces for attributing culpability are unevenly distributed. If torture is an international crime that speaks beyond the borders of states, criminal prosecutions for torture also take place in the context of disparities in state sovereignty. For events in Afghanistan or elsewhere in the world, a restricted range of charges can be applied under the principle of universal jurisdiction, with torture paramount. However, the full scope of the criminal law, and charges such as assault, is open for the prosecution of British citizens or for events that took place within the United Kingdom. There is therefore a structural prejudice toward imagining that an Afghan, rather than a British citizen, has committed torture. Prosecuting a crime in the name of humanity can therefore gloss over inequalities in the spaces available for assigning guilt. The law is weighted in favor of seeing other people, in other places, as guilty of torture, and British citizens as responsible for other, apparently less serious crimes.

Very few prosecutions are attempted for the crime of torture. However, torture is not so rare as to be almost nonexistent, as the number of prosecutions would suggest. The near total absence of torture prosecutions therefore raises questions about why the abstract crime of torture seems so hard to apply to specific cases. This chapter focuses on a comparison of the successful prosecution of Zardad with the unsuccessful court-martial of the British soldiers charged with the ill-treatment of Iraqi detainees, with which I started Chapter 1 of this book. The cases against the British soldiers, with one exception, collapsed, despite the fact that the British army admitted that its soldiers had beaten and abused the Iraqi detainees during interrogation, resulting in the death of one of the detainees.

It is admittedly very difficult to compare the two trials. The events in both cases were very different and took place in very different legal and political contexts. It may be pointed out, for example, that only the Zardad case involved a charge of torture, whereas the British soldiers were charged with assault, inhuman treatment, and negligence. Yet, no criminal charge is self-evident. Investigations only take place, people are arrested, charges are made, and sentences are given as part of a series of often contingent decisions made by police officers, prosecuting authorities, and judges (Lacey 2009). Evidence needs to be gathered, charges need to be determined from a range of possibilities, and cases need to be made persuasive to judge and jury (Innes 2003; McBarnett 1983). Specific crimes are forged from the raw materials of social harms, rather than found.

In addition, the two cases involve very different jurisdictions, in the shape of criminal law and military law, and are therefore not directly comparable. However, like crimes, jurisdictions are also not self-evident. Rather, jurisdictional boundaries are historically contingent devices that separate categories of person (Ford 1999). The changing boundaries among military law, human rights law, criminal law, and humanitarian law, for example, help to legitimate some forms of violence over others (Berman 2004). To point out that the two cases involved different criminal charges and different jurisdictions is therefore to start the conversation rather than to end it. We need to examine how and why this is the case, rather than take it for granted. Both cases were widely thought, by many people, if not all, to involve incidents of torture. The cases can therefore be compared in order to explore why only one resulted in a legal conviction for torture.[4]

This chapter starts by briefly outlining the criminalization of torture in the UK. It then sets out the two separate cases, those of Zardad and the British soldiers, following those cases through investigation, charging, arguments in court, and their respective verdicts. The chapter then moves on to compare the notions of responsibility applied in both cases. It concludes by examining the political arguments over the applicability of the charge of torture.

The Criminalization of Torture

Despite the ubiquitous condemnation of torture, its widespread criminalization only took place in the late twentieth century. The eighteenth-century campaigns for the abolition of torture rarely, if ever, resulted in a specific crime of torture; instead, it resulted in the prohibition of evidence obtained under duress. It was only after the end of the Cold War that it became widely possible to charge people with the crime of torture, especially in domestic courts. It is true that the Geneva Conventions of 1949, along with their additional Protocols, prohibit the use of torture.[5] The Geneva Conventions set out a number of "grave breaches"—including torture—for which states are required to prosecute perpetrators, although what this amounts to is not defined.[6] Crucially, though, the Geneva Conventions only apply to international armed conflict. The additional Protocols of 1967 have a broader remit but still apply only to what amounts to full-scale civil war, rather than to broader armed disturbances and tensions. The Geneva Conventions are therefore not universal in their scope, and they cover distinct categories of person in particular contexts. Furthermore, they provide no definition of torture. A wider reference to torture was included in the 1993 statutes of the International Criminal Tribunal for the former Yugoslavia.[7] The Rome Statute of the International Criminal Court of 1998 also included torture in its list of crimes.[8] These statutes were incorporated into English law through the International Criminal Court Act 2001. However, under the Rome Statute, torture was still only a crime if it occurred in the context of an armed conflict on the one hand, or as part of a widespread or systematic attack directed against any civilian population on the other. Torture was therefore only criminalized in specific situations.

The wider extension of the criminalization of torture has to be understood in the context of parallel and related developments that took place in the human rights field (see Chapter 1). The UN Convention Against Torture of 1984 says that all state parties shall criminalize torture, as well as prosecute or extradite perpetrators, no matter where the crime took place.[9] The drafters of the convention were originally of the opinion that this did not require that states make the offense of torture a unique and specific crime (Burgers and Danelius 1988). Perpetrators could instead be charged with related crimes, such as assault. Through the years, however, the Committee Against Torture has come around to arguing that states must make torture a specific criminal offense. Many states still argue that torture is already covered in their wider criminal law and that there is therefore no need to specifically criminalize torture. However, the committee has since roundly criticized this approach on the grounds that torture, as a crime committed by public officials, has a special stigma.[10] In part this is a symbolic stance about signaling the specific abhorrence of torture. It is also a practical argument, in that it is aimed at ensuring that all possible acts of torture are prohibited under domestic criminal law.

Torture only became a specific and universal crime in the United Kingdom in 1988, following the ratification of the UN Convention Against Torture.[11] Prior to 1988, people accused of such acts could be charged with other crimes. Following the Mau Mau uprising in Kenya during the 1950s, for example, a British officer was convicted of disgraceful conduct of a cruel kind (Anderson 2005). Similarly, in Northern Ireland in the 1970s, following the allegations of mistreatment of Republican detainees, two army privates pled guilty to assault and causing bodily harm. The Criminal Justice Act 1988 states, "A public official or person acting in an official capacity, whatever his nationality, commits the offence of torture if in the United Kingdom or elsewhere he intentionally inflicts severe pain or suffering on another in the performance or purported performance of his official duties."[12] Similar laws were put into place in Scotland and Northern Ireland. This definition differs from that in the UN Convention Against Torture in that it does not require any specific purpose for an act to be considered torture, other than the intentional infliction of severe pain or suffering.[13] Nor does it make an exception for suffering inflicted as part of "lawful sanctions."[14] At the same time, however, English law provides for the defense of "lawful authority."[15] The Committee Against Torture has argued that this is a potential loophole in the law, but the British government claims that it is necessary in order to prevent people such as surgeons, who inflict pain as part of the proper conduct of their duties, from being prosecuted.[16] The English law reflects its roots in human rights principles, in that unlike international criminal law, it says that only people acting in an official capacity can be held accountable for acts of torture.

In terms of English law, perhaps the most original part of the criminalization of torture was its universal nature. Historically, English law has worked under the principle that a jury in a criminal trial should be summoned from the locality where the incident occurred. English criminal law has also generally been seen as applying to a definite territory. As an exception to this rule, the Offences Against the Person Act 1861, established the jurisdiction of English courts over murder, manslaughter, and bigamy committed anywhere in the world, but only if the perpetrator were a British subject. More broadly, piracy and slave trading were also widely recognized, not just by the United Kingdom, as crimes that could be prosecuted irrespective of where they took place and by whom they were committed. The motivation behind the extraterritorial extension of jurisdiction in these cases was largely practical, as both activities took place at sea, outside normal state reach. The extraterritorial principle was further extended through the incorporation of the four Geneva Conventions of 1949 into English law in 1957. Under the Geneva Conventions Act, English courts were given jurisdiction over grave breaches of the conventions, including torture, no matter where they occur, as long as it is within the context of an international armed conflict.[17] The British government has historically been broadly opposed to any general extension of the extraterritorial principle. In the international arena, throughout the drafting of the UN conventions on genocide, apartheid, and torture in the 1970s and 1980s, the British argued against universal jurisdiction, claiming that it was impractical and unworkable (Burgers and Danelius 1988, 58). In this context, universal jurisdiction has been incorporated into English law in an ad hoc manner, resulting in great variation in its scope from crime to crime.[18] English courts have universal jurisdiction over the crimes of torture, hostage taking, and war crimes in international armed conflicts ("grave breaches" of the 1949 Geneva Conventions). They do not have universal jurisdiction over genocide, crimes against humanity, and war crimes in internal armed conflicts. Under the International Criminal Court Act 2001, perpetrators of such crimes who are not legally "resident" in the United Kingdom cannot be prosecuted. Failed asylum seekers, for example, cannot be charged.

Despite the English courts having universal jurisdiction over torture from 1988, the law remained, in effect, dormant for ten years. Then in 1998, the Spanish magistrate Baltizar Garzon requested the extradition of former Chilean president Augusto Pinochet from the United Kingdom, where he was visiting for medical treatment. Pinochet was wanted in Spain for various crimes against Spanish citizens, including torture. As a former head of state, Pinochet claimed immunity from prosecution and hence extradition. In March 1998, the House of Lords ruled that certain crimes, such as torture, were not covered by state immunity from criminal prosecution.[19] However, Home Secretary Jack Straw decided that Pinochet was not well enough to stand trial and he was allowed to return to Chile. Until the case against Zardad, this was the only time that the specific crime of torture had been put to the test in a English court, and even then it was indirectly, as the case involved Pinochet's extradition to face charges, not his actual prosecution.

Investigating Zardad

In 1999 the veteran BBC journalist John Simpson interviewed the Taliban foreign minister, Wakil Ahmed Muttawakil, about why the Taliban were willing to provide shelter to Osama bin Laden. The foreign minister retorted that the British were sheltering a man named Zardad, who was responsible for abuses in Afghanistan before the Taliban came to power. A year later, Simpson made a short documentary for BBC News. The film claimed that Zardad was a former warlord who was responsible for looting, raping, and murdering at a place called Sarobi, on the main road between Kabul and Pakistan. Simpson explained that he had tracked Zardad down to a small suburban house in south London. The report ends with Simpson concluding that the British government will probably not be bothered to try a man accused of war crimes in Afghanistan, and he will be allowed to slip away.

After the report was broadcast, the story received further interest in the British press, and Simpson sent the file to the UK Parliamentary Joint Committee on Human Rights, as well as to the Metropolitan Police.

The Revolutionary Association of the Women of Afghanistan (RAWA) also started a campaign to have Zardad arrested (RAWA, no date). RAWA had been founded in the late 1970s as a secular organization, campaigning for woman's rights under the Soviet-supported government. Working from exile throughout the 1980s and 1990s, it would only return to Afghanistan after the fall of the Taliban. Following the announcement of the investigation, the Afghan Embassy in London said it had known that Zardad was in London, but it had not made any attempts to have him extradited. The embassy added that the way the British authorities dealt with Zardad was "not our business" (Morris 2000).

The Zardad case file was sent to the antiterrorist branch of the Metropolitan Police for further investigation, but it appeared to stall for a while. Eventually, fearing that Zardad was about to leave the country, the police arrested Zardad and released him on bail. It was almost a year later, when Zardad's bail was to be reviewed and the case had passed on to another police officer, that the collection of evidence sped up.[20] The new police officer assigned to the case, a detective sergeant, started searching the Internet for people who could help him. Unlike many criminal investigations, the case had to work backward. Rather than starting with the victim and having to find the perpetrator, here the police had the perpetrator and were looking for victims. In this task, the police were helped by RAWA and an organization called the Afghanistan Justice Project (AJP). The AJP had been founded after the fall of the Taliban by Patricia Gossman, a US citizen and former Human Rights Watch researcher, in order to pressure the Afghan government, donors, and the international community to hold perpetrators of human rights abuses to account. During the investigation, British police officers made several trips to Afghanistan. While there, they were under orders to stay in the British Embassy or on the British army base, unless given armed support by the British or American military. When they did go to Sarobi to take photographs, they did so under US military escort. The prosecuting and defense lawyer also made several trips to Afghanistan. Everywhere they went, they too were accompanied by US or British soldiers. In July 2003, Zardad was re-arrested and eventually charged.

The Two Trials of Faryadi Zardad

The trial of Zardad was opened by Lord Goldsmith, the attorney general. It was extremely rare, if not unique, for such a senior figure to lead a prosecution in an English court.[21] The case was heard by Mr. Justice Treacy, who was among the most senior judges at the Central Criminal

Court, otherwise known as the Old Bailey. The remainder of the prosecution was led by James Lewis QC, one of the most highly paid criminal lawyers in the United Kingdom, who had represented the Spanish government in the extradition of Pinochet. The defense was led by Anthony Jennings QC, who died in 2008 and was described in his obituary in the *Times* as "one of the finest courtroom performers of his day" (2008). The trial was to last twenty-five days and, as well as being the first prosecution for torture in the United Kingdom, it would also make legal history in other ways. Many of the witnesses gave evidence by video link from the British Embassy in Afghanistan. The Home Office was concerned that if all the witnesses had come to the United Kingdom, every one would claim asylum. Special legislation was therefore passed in parliament to allow the witnesses to give evidence through a video link to Kabul. After twenty-five hours of deliberation, the jury could not reach a decision, and a retrial was called.

The retrial started in June 2005, with the same judge and the same legal teams, except that Goldsmith was not present. Zardad was charged with one count of conspiracy to torture and one count of conspiracy to take hostages. The formal charge in relation to torture read: "Between 31 December 1991 and 30 September 1996 in Afghanistan you agreed with others that a course of conduct would be pursued which, if the agreement was carried out in accordance with those intentions would necessarily amount to or involve the commission of the offence of torture." In its opening remarks, the prosecution argued that Zardad acted as the sole authority over a swath of territory in which he wanted to "create an atmosphere of fear and terror, using indiscriminate and unwarranted violence."[22] The prosecution alleged that he was a commander in Hezb-e-Islami, which had been formed to fight the Communists, and later became one of the key players in the internal Afghan fighting of the 1990s. For the prosecution, torture was a key part of Zardad's attempt at control. In particular, the prosecution argued that Zardad and his men ran a number of checkpoints at which they murdered, looted, and raped those who tried to pass through.

The Evidence of Torture

Eleven eyewitnesses gave evidence about twelve separate incidents of torture. The eyewitnesses included Afghans, as well as some European aid workers. Nine of these witnesses were victims of torture themselves, and two saw it perpetrated on other people. Nearly all the Afghan witnesses gave their evidence via satellite link from the British Embassy in Kabul. The first eyewitness called, though, was an Afghan refugee living at the time in the north of England. He described being stopped several times at a checkpoint outside Sarobi by Zardad's men, and then being heavily beaten, as well as having a spike driven through his knee.[23] Testimony from other witnesses included descriptions of being whipped with bicycle chains and electric cables, as well as being beaten with fists and guns.

Most of the incidents described did not involve Zardad in the direct infliction of violence. More often than not he was not present at all, but the acts were carried out by men the witnesses said were under his command. In one incident, however, the witness claimed that Zardad himself had tortured him. The exchange under examination from the prosecution went as follows:

Question: What happened when you got to Commander Zardad's base?

Answer: I was beaten there by Commander Zardad.

Question: How were you beaten?

Answer: I was beaten with a Kalashnikov. My hand and head were broken. . . .

Question: Were you bleeding?

Answer: Yes.

. . .

Question: How long were you whipped with this cycle cable?

Answer: For four months.

Question: Was Commander Zardad ever there when you were being beaten with this cycle cable?

Answer: Yes, he used to stand there or stay there.[24]

Despite the frequent mention of scars and other injuries resulting from torture, medical evidence was presented in only one case, and no mention was made of the Istanbul Protocol.[25] The contrast with immigration and asylum cases (see Chapters 2 and 3) is stark.

Zardad was the last man to take the stand. Under examination and cross-examination, he claimed that he had been a general commanding about one thousand men.[26] He denied, however, that he had controlled the checkpoints, as he said he was always on the front line fighting. Hezb-e-Islami and its intelligence branch did have some checkpoints in the area, he claimed, but they were not under his command. He did admit though that he had responsibility for his soldiers, saying, "Every military commander has a responsibility to address his troops and give them orders. They have responsibility to order them for good acts and prevent them from bad acts."[27] Zardad accused the European witnesses of working for the intelligence services and the Afghans of working for his enemies. They were all simply lying, he said.

The Nature of Torture

The case against Zardad had to be made to fit the charge of torture. One of the prosecuting lawyers told me when I interviewed him that "the real charge was mass murder, but we could not charge him with that, as we do not have universal jurisdiction for that."[28] The first element of the charge of torture under the Criminal Justice Act 1988 is that it must be intended to cause severe pain and suffering. As such, the existence of pain and suffering was a key theme running through the witness testimony. One exchange with a survivor went as follows:

Question: When they beat you with the cable, for how long [did it] go on?

Answer: [Two or three] . . . minutes, but there were days when it continued for 10 to 15 minutes.

Question: What effect did that have upon you?

Answer: What do you mean, from what aspect?

Question: How much pain was there?

Answer: Only I knew that and my God, how painful it was.

Question: Was it painful enough to make you cry or scream?

Answer: Yes, but even if it was not that painful, we pretended and we started crying so that they do not beat us any more.[29]

Despite this emphasis on pain, there was not a particularly intricate debate, as there often is in human rights forums, over the precise intensity of pain and suffering required to count as torture. The judge told the jury, "You must not water down the question of pain or suffering."[30] The judge also reminded the jury that suffering did not have to be physical but could be mental as well. However, the jury was not given precise directions over the exact levels of pain needed to qualify as torture. Some of the events recounted seemed to involve straightforward murder, for which Zardad could not and had not been charged. However, the prosecution argued that the events could count as torture as long as the jury was convinced that the victims had suffered before they had died.[31]

The second requirement of the charge of torture is that it be carried out by a "public official" as part of his or her "official duties." Given the situation of civil war and general chaos in Afghanistan in the 1990s, the question of whether Zardad was a public official was open to question. What did a public official look like in 1990s Afghanistan and what were his or her official duties? In a pretrial hearing, the defense had argued that as there was an "official government" in Kabul at the time, to which Zardad was opposed, he was therefore part of a rebel faction.

Treacy ruled that there was no evidence that Zardad was a de jure public official, but he left it open to the jury to decide, as a matter of fact, whether Zardad acted as a de facto public official.[32] In the course of the trial, the issue of whether Zardad was an effective public official did not come up. A key part of Zardad's defense was that he was a soldier who respected high moral values; he could not argue that he did not control men and territory.

The third part of the crime of torture under the Criminal Justice Act 1988 is intent, in the sense of intending to cause pain and suffering. As such, the crime of torture reflects a wider sense in common law, that people can only be held criminally responsible if they commit the act knowingly. This is the mens rea element of a crime, the requirement of a guilty mind. In the narrow sense of specifically intending to cause severe pain and suffering, the issue of intent was not particularly significant in the Zardad trial, as no one was arguing that the incidents had taken place accidentally. Rather, the defense's claim was that torture did not happen at all, or at least that Zardad was not responsible when it did. However, under the Criminal Justice Act, intent to torture does not simply refer to the intention directly to cause pain and suffering but also to assist or encourage such acts. Direct involvement is therefore not required. The issue then becomes one of proving that a person who was not directly involved was instrumental in ordering that the acts should take place. Zardad was not charged with taking part in every act of torture about which the witnesses spoke. Rather, he was charged with conspiracy, of agreeing with others that torture should be carried out.[33] The defense argued that this meant the jury had to be sure there was a "meeting of minds."[34] For there to be a conspiracy, Zardad and his men had to intend the same consequences.

At the trial, whether Zardad was involved in a conspiracy to torture came down to whether there was a checkpoint and the extent to which Zardad controlled what went on there. Was Zardad a military commander who headed a disciplined fighting force who followed his orders, or a leader of a ragtag band of bandits? The prosecution argued that the road past Sarobi had strategic importance as the only direct route between Kabul and Pakistan. Zardad controlled the area around the road, including the checkpoint, and therefore was responsible for what went on there. A former senior commander in Hezb-e-Islami recounted that Zardad had been ordered to remove the checkpoint by his party's leader, Gulbuddin Hekmatyar, but he had refused. Such evidence was said by the prosecution to speak to Zardad's power and influence. The defense, in contrast, argued that not all the incidents of alleged torture were carried out by Zardad's men, and even if they were, they were not carried out under his orders. The defense pointed to one witness, for example, who gave evidence that he had been detained at the checkpoint and that he was told by the armed men that "we are going to take you to the commander, but if he asks you if we have taken anything from you, say no."[35]

The retrial differed from the first trial in several ways. The defense thought the turning point in the second trial came when the jury saw what looked like a checkpoint in the background of a video showing Zardad, despite the fact he had previously denied that the checkpoint existed.[36] The prosecution also, in the words of one of the lawyers, was able to go higher up the "food chain" in terms of evidence about Zardad's position in Hezb-e-Islami.[37] In addition, more witnesses were brought to give evidence in London, rather than by video link from Kabul. Finally, the prosecution was also able to avoid many of the confusions of the first trial. The first time around, for example, the prosecution had tried to bring up what they called "Zardad's human dog," a man who was allegedly kept in a pit and set onto victims by Zardad. However, the attempt to translate the allegation broke down into farce, with lawyers resorting to making barking noises. No mention was made of the issue in the second trial.

The Verdict

After deliberating for less than a day, the jury came back with a guilty verdict on all counts. In passing his sentence, Treacy stressed the severity of the crimes of which Zardad had been convicted, which he called an affront to the "civilised international community." He went on to say that Zardad had shown a "total disregard for humanity."[38] Treacy sentenced Zardad to twenty years in prison and recommended deportation afterward.

Investigating the British Army in Basra

In September 2003, a British army medical doctor responded to shouts of help from a soldier of the Queen's Lancashire Regiment, to find an Iraqi detainee collapsed on the ground. The doctor's attempts at resuscitation failed and the prisoner, Baha Mousa, died on the floor. The medic put the death down to cardiorespiratory arrest. The commanding officer of the QLR was informed of the incident and was told that Mousa had attempted to escape and could have banged his head while being restrained.[39]

Two days later, officers from the Special Investigations Branch (SIB) of the Royal Military Police arrived to investigate the incident.[40] A pathologist was also brought in from the United Kingdom to conduct an autopsy on Mousa. The doctor concluded that the cause of death was postural asphyxia and ligature strangulation.[41] The postmortem also revealed ninety-three separate injuries to Mousa's body. By this time, the Military Police investigation had widened to include other incidents of violence by British troops against Iraqi detainees. As the investigation progressed, three soldiers were detained by the police. Interviewing the Iraqi detainees though was delayed because of a lack of interpreters. Many of the soldiers involved in the incident returned to the United Kingdom in the next month, further hampering the process. In the meantime, the Brigade commander had personally apologized to Mousa's father and an official statement of regret was published in a local newspaper.

By the end of 2004, the story of Mousa's death had made it into the British press (see, for example, Fisk 2004). This came several months after the first newspaper stories and pictures from Abu Ghraib. In the following months and years, a number of high-profile cases involving the mistreatment of Iraqi detainees by British troops also made headlines. After a court-martial in Germany, pictures were released of young British soldiers forcing Iraqi prisoners to simulate oral and anal sex. The secretary of state for defence announced that he was "profoundly disturbed" by what he had seen but was of the view that the "incidents depicted do not reflect typical behaviour and standards of the British Army," and announced an inquiry into the lessons to be learned (Ministry of Defence 2004). Colonel Jorge Mendonca, the commanding officer of the soldiers who had been holding Mousa and the other detainees, had since returned to the United Kingdom and been awarded the Distinguished Service Order.

The case file on the death of Mousa was not sent to the military prosecutors until June 2004. When this happened, a further pathology report was ordered, and additional interviews were conducted to link suspects with individual victims. In early March 2005, the attorney general expressed concerns about many of the investigations arising from incidents in Iraq (Townsend 2005). He went on to say that he had become particularly worried that the Mousa case was only referred to the military prosecutor more than nine months after the incident had occurred, and then at a level involving junior ranks only. Soon after, charges were formally announced, including against the commanding officer of the regiment.

The Trial of Payne and Mendonca

The court-martial started in early September 2005, in the southern garrison town of Bulford. Presiding over the case was a civilian judge, for the first time in a British court-martial. The evidence was to be heard by a panel of senior army officers, all above the rank of colonel. The prosecution was led by Julian Bevan QC, a high-profile criminal lawyer who had been involved in the prosecution of the police officers who fabricated evidence in the case of the "Guildford Four."[42] The defense lawyers included Geoffrey Cox, who was also a Conservative MP, and Lord Thomas of Gresford, the former Liberal Democrat shadow attorney general.

The prosecution's case was that in September 2003 a number of Iraqi civilians were arrested following a raid on a hotel by soldiers of the QLR. The men were taken to the battle group headquarters and detained in a temporary detention facility, before they could be transferred elsewhere. While the Iraqis were waiting, they were subjected to "tactical questioning." Over a day and a half, the detainees were kicked and punched, hooded with hessian sacks, made to maintain stress positions for long periods of time, and deprived of sleep, in temperatures rising to 60 degrees Celsius (140 Fahrenheit).[43] The prosecution alleged that the general abuse included the denial of food, threats to life, being punched, being covered with urine, and being repeatedly beaten when the detainees failed to stay in the stress positions demanded by the soldiers. The prosecution also argued that the abuse was not carried out on the spur of the moment but was systematic and deliberate, and although it was carried out by relatively low-ranking soldiers, it was only made possible by the negligence of the commanding officers.

Corporal Donald Payne was charged with the common law offense of manslaughter for the death of Baha Mousa. It was alleged that Payne had restrained Mousa and smashed his head against the floor, having previously beaten and abused him. Payne was also charged with trying to pervert the course of justice for his attempts to cover up what had happened. Payne pleaded guilty to a charge of inhuman treatment.[44] In doing so, he became the first British soldier to be found guilty of a war crime. Two other soldiers were also charged with the war crime of inhuman treatment, but they pled not guilty. Colonel Jorge Mendonca was charged with negligently performing his duty by failing to take reasonable steps to ensure that Iraqi detainees were not ill-treated. Another soldier was charged with assault and actual bodily harm, and a warrant officer and a major were also charged with negligence.

The Elements of the Offenses

The charge of "inhuman treatment" is a product of the International Criminal Court Act 2001, which gives the Rome Statute of the International Criminal Court effect in English law. It defines inhuman treatment as the infliction of "severe physical or mental pain or suffering upon one or more persons."[45] In practice, it is a lesser offense than torture. Inhuman treatment implies no deliberate intention to cause suffering for specific ends, such as obtaining information. The prosecution argued that the use of stress positions was not in and of itself a form of inhuman treatment, but that the length of time for which the positions were used and the violence necessary to maintain them was.[46] Payne was also charged with manslaughter for his part in the death of Mousa. The prosecution argued that although Payne had not intended to cause the death, the banging of Mousa's head on the floor and the subsequent kicking of Mousa had passed over the lawful threshold.[47] Finally, Mendonca was also charged with negligence under the Army Act 1955. In order for negligence to be found, the prosecution had to show that Mendonca had a duty to ensure the detainees were not ill-treated and that he failed to carry this out.

Who Killed Baha Mousa?

The key issue in the court-martial was identifying the people directly responsible for inflicting the violence against Mousa and the other detainees. Witnesses were called from Iraq, as were other British soldiers, who all testified in person to the ill-treatment of the detainees. There was evidence throughout the trial that Mousa had been abused at multiple points.[48] For this reason, it was hard to say which of the scores of beatings Mousa received had been responsible for his death. The second pathologist's report said that it was not possible to say that any particular injury caused the death.[49] Payne was at a disadvantage though in that he had been directly identified by some of the Iraqi detainees.[50] The identification of the other perpetrators was made more complicated by the fact that for most of the time the detainees were wearing hessian sacks over their heads.[51] Many soldiers who gave evidence simply also said that they could not remember who was where and when, leading the judge to claim there had been "a more or less obvious closing of ranks."[52]

The prosecution argued that although Mendonca was one step removed from the treatment of the detainees, he was still the commanding officer and as such he was responsible for the conduct of his soldiers.[53] In particular, he was responsible for insufficient guidance in the handling of prisoners, as there seemed to be no adequate orders or training in place for the guards to ensure that they treated the prisoners according to the law. Furthermore, prisoner handling practices, such as the use of hooding and stress positions, amounted to "at the very least bad practice." Finally, the prosecution argued that there was no adequate monitoring in place.[54] The prosecution admitted that a commanding officer may be very busy during operations and therefore might delegate the day-to-day handling of detainees to junior officers. However, the prosecution also claimed that once Mendonca became aware of the use of the "conditioning techniques," he should have stepped in and stopped the procedure until he had satisfied himself that the techniques did not contravene international law.[55] For the prosecution, Mendonca knew that his major, to whom he delegated the treatment of detainees, had little experience in the handling of prisoners.[56] Mendonca also knew that his soldiers were angry at the recent murder of a captain from the same regiment by Iraqi insurgents.[57] Mendonca had apparently been previously warned by a brigadier that members of his regiment had been behaving too "robustly" toward Iraqi civilians. Yet, knowing all this, Mendonca failed to make sure that proper procedures were in place to protect Iraqi detainees.

Much of the evidence at the court-martial focused on the chains of command, forms of training, the exact nature of army doctrine, codes of practice, and different interpretations of international law in order to understand who had the responsibility to do what and when, as well as who knew what and when. A large part of the case hinged on the evidence of Major Anthony Royce, who had been responsible for the handling of detainees in the period immediately before the death of Mousa but not during the events themselves. Royce said that he had been told by the Brigade intelligence officer to "condition" prisoners. Worried that this was counter to the training he had received prior to coming to Iraq, he claimed to have double-checked with the Brigade's legal adviser and was again told that "conditioning" was acceptable, despite the fact that this seemed to be similar to the techniques prohibited in Northern Ireland in the 1970s. Royce gave evidence that in the early summer of 2003 he discussed with Mendonca the approach to "conditioning" and "maintaining the shock of capture." Royce also told the court that he had informed Mendonca that he had discussed and cleared the use of stress positions with Brigade headquarters.[58]

The Decision and Its Aftermath

Before the defense could begin its submissions, the judge ruled that there was no case to answer.[59] For the judge, Mr. Justice McKinnon, there was no clear evidence about which of the many injuries inflicted on Mousa, by several different people, had caused his death. Payne could therefore not be singled out for manslaughter.[60] McKinnon also ruled that the evidence from Royce that he had had a discussion with Mendonca about the conditioning process meant that Mendonca had fulfilled his duty toward the detainees and therefore could not be found guilty of negligence.[61]

After the trial collapsed, the British army and the Ministry of Defence expressed regret over the death of Mousa (Ministry of Defence 2007). Payne was jailed for one year after pleading guilty to inhuman treatment and dismissed from the army. Mendonca resigned from the army in May 2007. According to the press, he feared that he would face internal disciplinary measures (Condron 2007). Mousa's family launched a civil case against the Ministry of Defence, alleging a breach of the right to life and the prohibition of torture and inhuman or degrading treatment or punishment, under the Human Rights Act.[62] The following year, the secretary of state for defence conceded the case and agreed to pay £2.83 million (US$4.62 million) in response to ten separate claims of abuse by British troops.[63] Two months later he announced a public inquiry, headed by a judge, to look into the circumstances surrounding Mousa's death. The inquiry, which started in July 2009, was given no power to allocate individual criminal or civil liability. Any person giving evidence was immune from disciplinary action and his or her own testimony could not be used to decide whether to prosecute him or her. The focus of the inquiry was therefore the provision of training, policies, and the chain of command, and it would conclude by making formal recommendations for the future.

Guilt in Faraway Places

Throughout both the Zardad trial and Payne and Mendonca court-martial, the claim that criminal trials cannot even begin to come to grips with complex situations like Afghanistan or Iraq was an important issue for the defense and prosecution. Mendonca had tried to argue that it was impossible for most people to understand the events in Basra, which were "beyond the ken of the vast majority of people who now criticise our soldiers and operations and call into question our leadership. . . . Take a British soldier, put him into a helmet and body armor in 58 or 59 degrees [136 Fahrenheit] and have hundreds of Iraqis throw bricks, petrol bombs and grenades at him and then marvel at his restraint in not opening fire."[64]

The claim that English law is at best a clumsy device with which to understand such events was even more significant in the *Zardad* case. The defense team members told the jury in their opening speech that they were "dealing with events, many, many miles away, a number of years ago."[65] As they put it, "You are in the unenviable position of having to put yourself into a culture, into a historical conflict and try to imagine what was going on, a time of tribal, religious factions, disputes; a time when perhaps many of the normal things in our society were suspended."[66] For the judge and the prosecution in the *Zardad* case, however, such differences were something that could be overcome. Treacy warned the jury that they would be hearing about a strange country, but that they would become familiar very quickly with the background.[67] The prosecution also saw the space between an English court and an Afghan roadside as inherently bridgeable. After the trial, one of the prosecuting lawyers told me that he thought the jury could look at the evidence objectively: "Twelve people in London are as good as anyone—as it is as simple as right and wrong."[68] He argued that the prosecution had been able to create a link between events in Afghanistan and London through visual images and eyewitness testimony so that the "jury could see these were real people, powerless Afghans."[69]

When Is Torture Not Torture?

Perhaps the biggest contrast between the two cases is in the charges brought against the defendants. Zardad stood accused of beating, stabbing, shooting, whipping, and killing people as they came through his checkpoint in order to retain control over the region. The soldiers of the QLR were accused of beating, kicking, hooding, using stress positions, and, in the case of Payne, killing Iraqi detainees as they sought to maintain the "shock of capture" as part of a "tactical questioning process." Zardad was charged with torture and hostage taking, whereas the British soldiers were charged with inhuman treatment, assault, manslaughter, and negligence, but not torture.

To understand the different charges used in both trials, it is important to examine the applicable laws and jurisdictions in both cases. British troops in Iraq were accountable under the Army Act 1955, which covers specific military offenses and discipline.[70] Under the Army Act, British troops are also liable for any criminal offenses they commit under English law, including the International Criminal Court (ICC) Act 2001 and the Criminal Justice Act 1988. A charge of torture is available under both the ICC Act and the Criminal Justice Act, but, as we shall see later in this chapter, with different definitions. The prosecuting army lawyers decided that the ICC Act was the most appropriate law with which to charge several of the soldiers for abuse of the Iraqi detainees. One of the prosecuting military lawyers explained the choice of charges to me in the following way: "The charges were selected that were felt to present the best chances of conviction before a military court. In the case of

Payne and others, the setting was occupied Iraq. . . . The protagonists were military. Consequently, it was considered appropriate to see the charges within that context."[71] The ICC Act, with its general framing in terms of the laws of war, was felt to be the suitable law. The choice of laws, with their different definitions of torture, had important implications for the ways in which the charges were drawn up.

Under the ICC Act, the distinction between inhuman treatment and torture is made in terms of intent. Charges of torture and inhuman treatment require the same levels of pain and suffering, but torture also requires, in addition, that the pain be inflicted for specific purposes, such as "obtaining information or a confession, punishment, intimidation or coercion or for any reason based on discrimination of any kind."[72] The army lawyers concluded that Payne was inflicting pain for his own enjoyment and therefore his acts did not qualify as one of the specific forms of intention required for torture under the ICC Act.[73] However, even under the admission of the prosecuted soldiers, the use of conditioning techniques, such as forced standing and sleep deprivation, was intended as part of a wider interrogation strategy and was therefore designed to obtain information, rather than simply to bring enjoyment. Yet, the position of the prosecution was that these methods in and of themselves were not liable to cause severe pain and suffering. Rather, it was the extra beatings administered by Payne and others that brought it above the necessary threshold. These extra beatings, it was argued, were not committed with the necessary intent.

Had the soldiers been charged under the Criminal Justice Act, there would have been no requirement of a specific purpose for the infliction of pain and suffering other than it be deliberate. Pain inflicted simply for enjoyment could still be torture. Furthermore, about the same time as the British soldiers were acquitted, the House of Lords said that the conditioning techniques used in Northern Ireland in the 1970s, which had strong resonances with the techniques used in Basra, could be understood as torture using contemporary standards.[74] Within the framework of English criminal and human rights law, the use of stress positions and other related techniques could therefore, on their own, pass over the necessary threshold to count as torture. It was only under the ICC Act that they did not. Through the prosecution of Payne, Mendonca, and the others, events that might be understood by many human rights or criminal lawyers as torture were being framed in terms of international criminal law, resulting in the seemingly less grave charge of inhuman treatment (Simpson 2007a).

In contrast, there was a much more restricted range of crimes under which Zardad could be charged. Because of the limited number of charges available under the principle of universal jurisdiction, the full scope of English criminal law was not open to the prosecutors. It was torture, hostage taking, both, or nothing.

Who Is Responsible?

Criminal law can be seen as an instrument for the attribution of responsibility, in that people are not legally culpable for events for which they are not responsible. However, in complex political events, how do we allocate responsibility? How does a sense of individual culpability relate to an attempt to understand the responsibility of wider organizations and doctrines in making events possible? In this context, as David Kennedy argues, to sort and separate the tangle of administrative, political, and individual responsibility for the abuse of detainees is not a "matter of 'getting to the bottom of it' or 'finding out what happened.' It is a cultural and political project of interpretation" (2006, 143). He continues, "It may be possible to identify the bad act precisely—torture of this person here, in this prison—and to assign responsibility to one administrative unit, perhaps to this guy. . . . But it may also be possible to set in motion a broad ethical and legal discourse about the legitimacy of everyone until nothing can be pinned on anyone. And it is not clear that justice will be done, or seen to be done, either way" (2006, 156). The events at the heart of the Payne court-martial and the Zardad trial clearly did not involve lone individuals but took place within a much larger context in which political violence was used by broader organizations and groups of people. In both cases, however, the prosecutions took very different approaches to the attribution of responsibility, and command responsibility in particular.

Mendonca's responsibility was understood through the framework of negligence. As one of the military prosecutors told me, they decided on the disciplinary charge of negligence, as "the prospect of any conviction of a decorated senior officer for a war crime would have been unlikely before a court-martial."[75] Negligence here was conceptualized as a failure to fulfill a professional and formal responsibility. This was not understood in ethical terms but as a purely factual matter. The wider issue of the moral duties of commanding officers was put to one side (see, in contrast, Bonafe 2007). The questions being asked by the judge were whether the officers had specific duties in the chain of command, if they knew what those duties were, and whether they carried them out (Rasiah 2009). This had the effect of reducing the court-martial, in large measure, to a debate about the policies and procedures followed, irrespective of the outcome in terms of the ill-treatment of Mousa and the other detainees. Mendonca, the prosecution argued, was negligent in this regard because he failed to clearly instruct the soldiers and to monitor their behavior. The effect of arguing that the "conditioning" was not in itself illegal, but that it was the extra violence inflicted by Payne and others that toppled it over the edge, was that the prosecution limited the reach of the investigation and the severity of the charges faced by senior officers. They did not have to go up the chain of command to see who had ordered the "conditioning."

Rather than negligence, the specific form of responsibility applied to Zardad was conspiracy. Conspiracy charges allow the assignment of individual guilt in situations where violence has several sources. The criticism of such charges is that they are broad and all encompassing, allowing courts to assign guilt on the basis of thin evidence (Meierhenrich 2006). The charges against Zardad were not simply framed in terms of command responsibility. Such a charge, as in the case of negligence, requires evidence of orders, structures, and policies, and is therefore most often successful if "committed in the typical hierarchical military context of the conduct of hostilities" (Bonafe 2007, 617). During the trial, the prosecution had tried to set out the command structures in Zardad's faction. However, one overriding theme throughout the case was the general violence and chaos running through Afghanistan at the time. There was a constant stressing of the weakness of institutional, political, and legal structures. For this reason, formal command responsibilities, as manifested in policies and procedures, were much harder to demonstrate.

Zardad's deliberate involvement in conspiracy to torture was inferred from his purported behavior and character.[76] The judge told the jury that they were entitled to look at all the actions and all the words surrounding an incident or incidents in order to read off intention.[77] By arguing that torture reflected a wider pattern of behavior, the prosecution attempted to argue that the jury could deduce a general agreement to carry out torture. In this way, events that did not constitute torture, such as shooting, could still be considered by the jury.[78] The defense, in contrast, argued that Zardad should be seen as an honorable and dignified commander of men, and that torture was simply out of character. Although they recognized that terrible things had been happening in Afghanistan, they urged the jury to make a distinction between the atrocities that took place in Afghanistan and Zardad's personal responsibility.[79] In the closing speech, the prosecution stressed that for much of the 1990s, men such as Zardad had been "regarded throughout the civilized world as peasant freedom fighters."[80] To support this claim, the jury watched a video that showed Zardad addressing his men. In the video Zardad was translated as saying: "We are not fighting for money, nor do we work for money. So my request to you is that no one should steal or loot and that you should treat people with respect. If anyone is going to disrupt the security or loot any house or steal, you all listen, those people will face punishment. Consider these peoples. Honour yourselves. . . . These people should be treated with respect and their honour and dignity should be protected.''[81] For the defense, the video showed that far from conspiring to torture, Zardad actively sought to prevent it among his troops.

Character also came up in Mendonca's trial. A key part of Mendonca's defense was that he was a diligent and hard-working commanding officer. Although he could not be in every place at once, he was serious and disciplined about abuse.[82] One officer who had served with Mendonca said he was among "the best . . . I have ever worked with. . . . There was—there was no—no tolerance whatsoever . . . to the abuse of detainees. It was entirely against—it was entirely against the mission, and it was entirely against the very clear direction that the commanding officer had given in terms of what we are trying to achieve and how we were going to achieve it.''[83] In contrast, turning the argument about Mendonca's character on its head, the prosecution argued that given Mendonca's previous behavior, it was fair to suggest that he could have inferred the risk to the detainees.[84]

Although Mendonca and Zardad were both seen as military commanders, the nature of their responsibility was portrayed in very different ways in the two trials. Zardad was seen as responsible for torture because he was an inherently violent individual in a lawless land. A discussion of his character became central to showing that he was not only capable of, but also culpable for, such an abhorrent crime. In contrast, Mendonca's responsibility was largely framed in terms of the ways he did or did not deviate from formal and agreed-on procedures. His culpability was reduced to a debate about bureaucratic and administrative processes within the chain of command. Rather than being seen as a man capable of a heinous crime, he was charged with simply being someone who had not done his job properly. Interestingly, Barack Obama has indicated that a similar approach will be taken toward any American who might be charged with torture, or other crimes, in Guantanamo, Bagram, or elsewhere. The key issue will be the extent to which the accused followed the various pieces of legal advice produced by the Department of Justice and other branches of government. Responsibility is reduced to the ability to follow formal rules rather than an issue of ethical judgment.

The Politics of the Trials

What can we make of the fact that the first person ever to be convicted of torture in the United Kingdom was an Afghan, whereas the British soldiers responsible for the ill-treatment of Iraqi prisoners, and the death of at least one, had their cases dismissed? For critics of trials for acts carried out in faraway places, such prosecutions are inherently partial and political. On one level, criminal law fails to adequately come to grips with the "complicity of multiple agents in the making of war" (Clarke 2009, 19). Throughout the prosecutions of Zardad, Mendonca, and Payne, the complex nature of the injustices experienced by the people of Afghanistan and Iraq, with all their superpower involvement, was reduced to a very limited set of activities carried out by a few men. On another level, criminal prosecutions, for the critics at least, are inherently selective in the crimes and people they seek to prosecute (Cryer 2005, 191). In the prosecutions, not only were debates over the illegality of British and American actions since the September 11 attacks on US soil being left to one side, but many figures, guilty of far worse acts, were being lauded as international statesmen. The fact that only Zardad, and no British citizen, has been charged with torture only emphasizes the partiality of the charge. Finally, criminal prosecutions of this type can be seen as an attempt to prove the moral standing of the prosecutor, rather than the guilt of the perpetrator (Simpson 2007b, 83; see also Koskenniemi 2002; Makua 2001). In the aftermath of British involvement in the 2001 invasion of Afghanistan, it was very handy that the English courts were claiming to be bringing justice to innocent Afghan victims, by prosecuting a cruel warlord. Furthermore, given the widespread opposition to the invasion of Iraq, the prosecution of a few soldiers allowed politicians to try to take the moral high ground once more. For their critics, the prosecution of such cases is partial at best and conspiratorial at worst.

For their defenders, however, such criminal trials are necessary in order to end impunity and bring justice to the victims. From this perspective, such prosecutions are insulated from the charge of selective justice and political interference, as judges are able to work autonomously (Hirsh 2003). These trials are therefore part of what is best about liberal criminal law (Bass 2000). The fact that Mendonca and most of the other soldiers were not convicted does not undermine the value of the *Zardad* conviction, as each case has to be viewed on its own merits.

For nearly everyone involved in both trials, the cases were seen as being inherently political. *Politics* here seems to refer to a sense of partial self-interest. The defense in the *Zardad* case told the jury that the Afghan government has a political interest in seeing Zardad on trial, as it restricted culpability for the events in 1990s Afghanistan to one person.[85] Equally, a senior investigating police officer on the case told me that he felt that such trials should be carried out by an international court, as that would lead to greater levels of fairness and stop cases from being affected by "shifts in the political winds."[86] For many people around the Mousa case, the prosecution and its collapse were inherently "political'" too. Ben Wallace, the Conservative MP for Lancaster, home of the QLR, said the attorney general should be censured for launching the prosecution in order to appease his own guilt about Labour Party involvement in the invasion of Iraq (*Daily Mail* 2007). The British press made wide reference to the apparent £23 million (US$37 million) cost of the case, calling it a politically motivated "witch-hunt" (*Times* 2007).

For many of the people involved in the trials, their purported selectivity was also a crucial issue. At the start of the trial, Payne's lawyer had said that it was "deeply unfair" that Payne's senior officers were facing lesser charges. The defense team for Zardad pointed out that many of the more senior figures, who were responsible for far graver crimes, now had roles in the Afghan government. Amnesty International also said that it had concerns over "the independence and impartiality of the investigations" in the *Payne* and *Mendonca* cases (2007). A military lawyer involved in the *Payne* and *Mendonca* prosecutions told me that they decided on the charges given the nature of the court-martial, and thought they were unlikely to secure convictions with more serious charges.

For the prosecution in the *Zardad* case, however, the selectivity of the case was not an issue. As the prosecution team told the jury, "Of course we cannot set the world to right. We cannot cure every injustice. But what we can do is give justice to the poor unfortunate victims in this case who have nowhere else to turn. . . . Mr. Zardad has the benefit of being tried by what we believe is the best and the fairest system of criminal justice in world."[87] One of the senior lawyers behind the decision to prosecute Zardad went further than this when he told me, "Of course the trial was selective. But all prosecutions are selective. If you are a black man on the streets of London, you are far more likely to be charged than a white man."[88] For him this was not a good thing, but it was part of life, and it did not mean no one should be prosecuted. As one of his colleagues also told me, "You are never going to be able to prosecute everyone, but you have to prosecute who you have."[89]

The crucial issue is not whether the trials were "political" or "selective." There is no sense that the prosecution was somehow manipulated by the lawyers and police officers involved. Yet, there is also a politics inherent to all such trials as they deal with political issues, such as relationships between states, the monopoly on violence, and the legitimacy of political regimes (Simpson 2007b). Furthermore, all criminal prosecutions, not just those for high-profile crimes such as torture and inhuman treatment, are inherently selective, as not all possible crimes are prosecuted. Prosecutors need to make decisions about which crimes to prosecute and under which law, and prosecutor discretion is built into most common law systems. As such, neither the *Zardad* nor the *Payne* and *Mendonca* trials were simply the expression of the political interests of the British government or a neutral procedure of impartial and universal justice but a combination of the two. The very structure and possibilities of the trials assumed a wider political context in terms of who was on trial and how they got there (Clarke 2009; Koskenniemi 2002; Simpson 2007b). Indeed, both prosecutions were only possible (and in one case necessary) because of the presence of British troops on foreign soil.

The contrast between the successful prosecution of Zardad and the collapsed court-martial was not the result of a deliberate series of decisions but rather was shaped by the jurisdictional architecture within which torture is prosecuted. The relative spaces available for discretion in both cases were weighted in favor of seeing other people in other places as guilty of torture. This is not to claim that there is bias or malignant intent among any of the police officers, lawyers, army officers, or jurists involved in either case. Rather, it is to argue that the full array of criminal and military law was available for the charging of Payne and Mendonca. The prosecutors narrowed the charges to inhuman treatment and negligence, but other charges were potentially available. Others involved in the case were charged with assault. None of these charges was available in the *Zardad* case. Torture and hostage taking were the only available options. As such, the jurisdictional arrangements through which torture was prosecuted produce an unequal geographic distribution of potential culpability. There was simply more space available to imagine that an Afghan, rather than a British soldier, was responsible for torture.

Attributing culpability for torture though is not simply an issue of the choice of laws but also one of imagination. It is a question of how much and what types of evidence are needed to create a persuasive case that someone is capable and guilty of torture. As we have seen in previous chapters, torture can present large evidentiary barriers, not least because it is often—although not always—deliberately inflicted in a way that leaves few traces (Rejali 2009). It is therefore worth comparing the evidence needed to make that leap of imagination in the two cases. When I showed him a draft of this chapter, one of the military lawyers involved in the prosecution of Mendonca and Payne told me that he was "surprised that the court convicted [Zardad] where the charges were conspiracy and found the link to events by individuals at a checkpoint could be held to fall within a common design. I am absolutely certain that a court-martial would never have convicted in such circumstances."[90] Zardad was found guilty despite the huge problems involved in investigating crimes conducted years earlier in a faraway place. In the

Zardad case, little or no forensic evidence was available, and the prosecution had to rely on eyewitness testimony, much of it via a satellite link from Kabul. In contrast, in the *Payne and Mendonca* case, the Military Police were on the scene in a matter of days, several forensic and other medical reports were available, and numerous eyewitnesses and victims were willing to come forward. Yet only one of these cases reached a guilty verdict and the court-martial of the British soldiers collapsed because of lack of evidence. The contrast between the evidence that was successful in achieving a conviction in the *Zardad* case and the evidence that is often needed to corroborate claims of torture in asylum cases, despite the formally lower standard of proof in the latter, is also stark. There seem to be disparities in the evidentiary thresholds that must be passed, in practice, but not in theory, in order to make torture legally imaginable. There is a further contrast between the ways in which Afghans can be found by English courts guilty of committing torture and the difficulties Afghans face in being recognized as victims in immigration and asylum cases.

Prosecuting Torture

Very few people are ever charged with, let alone found guilty of, torture. We therefore need to ask why convictions are so rare. The answer, unfortunately, is not simply that cruelty and brutality are uncommon. At the time of writing, no British citizen has ever been charged with torture in an English court. It is not just the United Kingdom that seems reticent to bring charges of torture against its own citizens. The US soldiers involved in the Abu Ghraib photographs were not charged with torture; rather, they were charged with dereliction of duty, conspiracy to maltreat prisoners, assault, and indecent acts, among others. The first person charged and convicted of torture in a US court was Charles "Chuckie" Taylor, Jr., the son of former Liberian president Charles Taylor. The younger Taylor, a US citizen, was convicted of torture and conspiracy to commit torture in Liberia between 1997 and 2003 while he headed the Anti-Terrorist Unit during his father's presidency (Human Rights Watch 2008). The Taylor conviction, in 2008, was the first brought under the US federal Extraterritorial Torture Statute of 1994.[91] Torture in the United States is criminalized only for crimes committed outside the United States; for crimes committed within its borders, other charges have to be used.

For many of the people who advocate the use of torture as a specific criminal charge, it carries a particular moral weight, as torture is seen as being carried out by people acting in the name of the state.[92] As such, it is qualitatively different from common assault. However, this creates an inherent tension, in that under domestic jurisdictions, it is the state that must charge its own officials. The "special stigma" attached to the charge of torture and the fact that the acts that it describes are covered by other laws means that the specific charge of torture is often avoided. The particular status given to torture as a "heinous" crime means that it is only reluctantly used as a specific charge by states against their own citizens. Charges such as assault or dereliction of duty are preferred. Torture is reserved for acts carried out in other places by other people. Even when charging their own citizens through other laws, states select carefully who is charged. There is a temptation to focus on those who actually inflict the pain, rather than on those higher up the chain of command. Even though they were not charged with torture following the events at Abu Ghraib, the junior soldiers faced the most serious charges. When senior officers were charged, it was for disobeying orders rather than for abuse. It was the same in the case of Mendonca and Payne.

There may be more space to use the charge of torture in international courts, which seek to operate above and beyond the limitations of domestic politics. It is probably the International Criminal Tribunal for the former Yugoslavia (ICTY) that has tried and convicted the greatest number of people for the crime of torture. Those charged with acts of torture include Slobodan Milošević, the former Yugoslav president; Vojislav Šešelj, the former leader of the Serbian Radical Party; and Radoslav Brðanin, vice president of the government of the Republic of Srpska, as well as several generals and prison camp commanders.[93] However, prosecutions are limited at the ICTY to contexts where broader crimes against humanity or war crimes can be shown and will also focus on those with "greatest responsibility" (OPICC 2010). Many acts of torture and many torturers are simply not within the jurisdiction of international criminal law or high up its list of priorities.

To prove a charge of torture under English law requires proof of severe pain and suffering. However, in both the *Zardad* and *Mendonca* cases, there was no fine-grained calibration of the level of suffering required to reach the crucial threshold. Instead, it was left to the jurors to decide as a matter of fact. What is more, in contrast to asylum cases, the testimony of torture survivors was largely allowed to stand on its own. In both trials, there was little or no medical evidence, and forms of pain were dealt with by direct witness testimony. It is interesting to note that the ICTY has suggested that some acts—rape in this particular case— may not require specific proof of suffering, as the acts in and of themselves are enough to provide this evidence.[94] The implication is that, for criminal trials at least, a focus on levels of pain seems not to be a major evidential stumbling block, at least in cases in which the defendant is not a British citizen.

The crime of torture also requires evidence of intention. It needs proof of the deliberate infliction of pain and suffering and the belief that the person being charged is capable of deliberately perpetrating a crime that is often described as a barbaric affront to humanity. A focus on intention therefore raises the game, as it requires persuasive evidence that the person in the dock can be counted among the cruellest villains. In the *Zardad* case, the jury was persuaded that Zardad was capable of acts of torture. In doing so, the wider structural and political causes of violence in Afghanistan in the 1990s were put to one side. Responsibility was focused on the actions of one man, his character and motives. A similar strategy was adopted in the aftermath of Abu Ghraib, where although the charge of torture was not used, it was argued by the American military that the abuse was isolated and the result of a few "bad apples" rather than a systemic and deliberate policy. In contrast, during the *Payne and Mendonca* court-martial, there was an attempt to spread responsibility further. However, in spreading the case further, rather than focusing on wider political causes, the issue of responsibility was turned into one of orders and policies, in which individual culpability disappeared behind a maze of procedures, and the charge was reduced to negligence. Where ill-treatment is part of a broader policy, prosecuting torture requires evidence criminalizing entire governmental structures, something that, at least in the case of democracies, the courts seem loathe to do.[95] Torture appears most attractive to prosecutors when responsibility can be kept narrow.

The prosecution of torture is carried out in the name of a wider humanity. Yet the legal charge always takes place within a particular geopolitical architecture. Torture may be seen as a crime that transcends boundaries, but it is always prosecuted in a world of nation-states, with all the inequalities and hierarchies that this entails. The prosecution of Zardad was only possible because British troops were in Afghanistan and could provide protection to the investigating team. The Afghan state was not going to protest the investigation. British soldiers were only in Iraq, and immune from Iraqi law, because of the American and British invasion in 2003. Equally important, the criminal charge of torture also exists in a jurisdictional structure where there is a structural prejudice toward charging other people, from other places with torture, leaving a far greater scope of potential charges from British citizens. Torture is a universal crime, but it is prosecuted in a world of hierarchy, meaning that legal culpability is unevenly distributed.

Chapter 6
The Shame of Torture

This chapter is about the shame of torture. With some notable exceptions, torture appears to be one of the few things people will nearly universally say is wrong. The dishonor of exposure would therefore seem to be powerful. Who would willingly admit to being a torturer? Although shame can lead to denial, it also carries a sense of the vulnerability of reputation to the gaze of others (Piers and Singer 1972). As Thomas Keenan has argued, "The concept gathers together a set of powerful metaphors—the eyes of the world, the light of public scrutiny, the exposure of hypocrisy" (2004, 436). If guilt is the product of a transgression, shame is a response to failure. It is a reaction to falling short of a professed goal. Institutions can, of course, not feel shame in an emotional sense, although people who act in their name might well do. However, shame can be understood as a political process as much as a psychological one. The impact of shame lies in the social implication of being caught, and it is enforced through external censure rather than through remorse.

Human rights organizations, of many different hues, seek to expose violations and bring about change through the use of shame. Human rights shaming is thought to work because it forces states to bring their actions in line with the normative values that they claim to uphold. Many human rights practitioners will say that their aim is not to embarrass states. However, even if they do not intend to produce shame, in the sense of the full glare of naked exposure, human rights monitoring still works with the implicit assumption that transparency will be a significant motivating factor in bringing about change. Often without means of direct enforcement, human rights organizations rely on the persuasive power of ignominy.

Human rights shaming has an international dimension. The threat to expose wrongdoing from outside narrow national boundaries is thought to be particularly powerful against states sensitive to their reputations on the world stage. Amnesty International's Campaign Against Torture in the 1970s worked in large measure on the basis that the power of shame was the most persuasive tool they had in the fight against torture (see Chapter 1). At the same time though, there was also a recognition that exposure by individual human rights organizations alone was not going to bring about all the necessary changes. Amnesty International, together with several other human rights NGOs, was therefore instrumental in the eventual adoption of the UN Convention Against Torture. If shame requires standards that can be judged against, and exposure when these standards are not met, the idea was that international conventions and their monitoring mechanisms could provide both. Although the relationship can sometimes be tense, international NGOs and the international human rights monitoring mechanisms often depend on each other for information and political support.[1] International mechanisms though have a relative advantage over NGOs in that they are forums within which states have agreed to bear themselves to exposure.

Torture seems to be the perfect human rights violation for shaming strategies. Indeed, Kenneth Roth, the executive director of Human Rights Watch, argues that shaming works best for civil and political rights, such as freedom from torture, as they provide the greatest clarity over perpetrator, responsibility, and remedy (2004). Torture is ideally suited for such practices because, he argues, "it is fairly easy to determine the violator (the torturer as well as the governments or institutions that permit the torturer to operate with impunity) and the remedy (clear directions to stop torture, prosecutions to back these up . . .)" (2004, 68; see also Rejali 2009). According to Roth, the shame of being exposed as torturers is a powerful weapon in the hands of human rights organizations.

The United Kingdom also seems to be the ideal candidate for shaming strategies, given its self-image as a bastion of human rights and the rule of law on the international stage. As the previous chapters have shown, since the start of the war on terror numerous allegations of British involvement in torture have been made. This involvement has included the use of evidence obtained through duress, the transportation of security suspects to places where they might face torture, and the complicity of British security officials in torture inflicted outside the United Kingdom by other states, not to mention allegations about British troops in Iraq. Nongovernmental organizations have turned to international monitoring mechanisms to try to make these allegations stick and to mobilize the persuasive power of shame.

The central argument of this chapter is that the shame of torture easily dissipates within bureaucratic regimes. Human rights monitoring is not simply a transparent form of information gathering, revealing information to the wider world; it can hide as much as it reveals. The particular methods through which monitoring produces information about torture lead to a focus on formal standards and further monitoring mechanisms. As a result of the technical ways in which human rights obligations are interpreted, the shame of torture is dispersed into arguments about procedure. If shame relies on an audience as well as on a sense of failure, the focus on broad policies means that it is never clear when failure takes place or if anyone is watching.

This chapter focuses on the two most prominent international human rights monitoring organizations that investigate torture: the European Committee for the Prevention of Torture (CPT) and the UN Committee Against Torture (CAT). The chapter starts with a description of a visit by the CPT to a group of detainees, it then moves on to compare the CPT and the CAT, before describing the ways in which the CAT has interacted with British officials. It concludes by examining the "impact" of the CPT and the CAT, and the nature of human rights shaming strategies around torture in general.

The Visits to Belmarsh Prison

In February 2002, a Maltese lawyer and Lithuanian medical doctor stood outside Her Majesty's Prison Belmarsh and demanded to be let in. Belmarsh is a high-security prison in south London, built in the functional red-brick style of modern penitentiaries. Inside were four men who had been arrested three months earlier under UK anti-terrorism legislation and were being detained indefinitely without charge. They included Mahmoud Abu-Rideh, a wheelchair-bound Palestinian refugee. Abu-Rideh was born in Jordan to Palestinian parents and spent five years as a teenager in an Israeli jail, where he claims he was tortured. He had then traveled to Pakistan and Afghanistan, before being granted asylum in the United Kingdom in 1998. Three years later, he was detained by the UK government and accused of being "involved in fund raising and distribution of those funds for terrorist groups with links to Al Qa'eda."[2] The Lithuanian doctor and the Maltese lawyer asking to be allowed into Belmarsh Prison were representatives from the Council of Europe's Committee for the Prevention of Torture. Concerned about what they had heard about the treatment of the men in Belmarsh, they were making an emergency visit to the United Kingdom.

Abu-Rideh and the other security detainees at Belmarsh were being held under a system that had been developed by the British government in response to the tensions between the international prohibition of torture and the security policies of the UK government. This is the same system that was discussed in detail in Chapter 4. In the atmosphere after the attacks of September 11, the British security services suspected the four men of being involved in terrorism, but it lacked the evidence to convict them in a criminal court. This was either because the secret service wanted to protect its sources or because there was a very real possibility that the evidence against them had been collected through torture. The next step would have been to deport them. However, Abu-Rideh was a stateless Palestinian and therefore had no state to be deported to; all the detainees also faced the risk of torture if returned to their home countries. The British government had therefore developed a system under the Anti-terrorism, Crime and Security Act (ATCSA) 2001, whereby the home secretary could "certify" someone he believed was a "risk to national security."[3] Such people could be detained if their removal from the United Kingdom was practically impossible or prevented by law.[4] Many of the people the British government tried to deport to Algeria, Libya, and Jordan examined in Chapter 4 were held at some point under this system. It was also under this system that Abu-Rideh and the other detainees were, in effect, being held indefinitely without trial.[5]

During their visits to the United Kingdom, the CPT delegation met with the detainees, prison officers, civil servants, and senior police officers, as well as on several occasions with Amnesty International and the leading British civil liberties organizations, Liberty and Justice. Liberty is one of the most high-profile civil liberties organizations in the United Kingdom, with its origins between the two world wars. Justice is a smaller organization, with an emphasis on legal issues, and the UK affiliate of the International Commission of Jurists. The CPT also held a meeting with the government-appointed independent reviewer of antiterror legislation, Lord Carlile of Berriew. Lord Carlile is a former Liberal Democrat member of parliament and a practicing lawyer. Although he sits on the board of several civil liberties organizations, he has also come under criticism from Liberty for what they see as his support of government antiterror policy (Liberty 2006). Finally, the delegation met with Gareth Pierce, the lawyer for many of the detained men. The CPT does not seem to have met with any high-level ministers during these visits.[6]

After the first visit, the CPT delegation sent its recommendations to the British government. At the time, the report was confidential and was not released until a later date. In a polite, diplomatic, and formal tone, the CPT noted one allegation of physical ill-treatment, where a detainee, who was not named, claimed that he had been painfully restrained and punched. The CPT recommended that police and prison officers should "bear in mind that all forms of ill-treatment, including verbal abuse, are not acceptable."[7] The report also expressed concerns that detainees were being given only delayed access to lawyers and that some of the evidence being used in the review of their detention was secret.[8]

Several months later, as requested, the United Kingdom sent its response, phrased with the same formal politeness as the CPT's report.[9] The document had been put together by civil servants at the then Lord Chancellor's Department (later the Ministry of Justice), after pulling in information from other parts of the government and being checked over by legal advisers. The reply agreed that ill-treatment was to be avoided and set out the formal policies and procedures for the use of force. It went on to say that without specific allegations, it was difficult to comment on the claims of ill-treatment.[10] There was also an admission that there had been some problems in ensuring detainees had access to lawyers, but these were largely procedural and had since been sorted out.[11] The tone, however, was slightly more combative when it got into the issue of secret evidence, expressing "surprise" about the CPT's concerns.[12]

Believing that the treatment of the Belmarsh detainees was still a live issue, the CPT delegation decided to return to the United Kingdom in March 2004. This time, the delegation was led by the same Maltese lawyer, but an Icelandic psychiatrist had replaced the Lithuanian doctor. Since the previous visit, several other people from Libya, Algeria, and Egypt had been detained under the ATCSA, most of whom had previously claimed asylum. These included detainee "P," an Algerian who had been refused asylum in the United Kingdom in the late 1990s. P wore prosthetic limbs, as he had lost one arm entirely and had the other amputated above the elbow, following a bomb explosion. While in the United Kingdom, he had been arrested in 2001 and charged with "possession of articles for suspected terrorist purposes" and conspiracy to defraud, but the charges were eventually dropped. P was detained again in January 2003 and certified under the ATCSA, accused of being an "associate of Algerian extremists engaged in active support for various international terrorist groups, including nationals associated with Usama Bin Laden."[13] In particular, he was accused of being linked to the same plan to bomb the Christmas market in Frankfurt as detainee U (examined in Chapter 4) and of plotting to launch a number of biological and chemical weapons attacks in the United Kingdom. Abu-Rideh's mental health had deteriorated considerably since the last visit of the CPT delegation and he had been moved to Broadmoor Hospital, a high-security psychiatric hospital outside London. The psychiatric staff at Broadmoor had argued that a high-security hospital was not the most appropriate place for someone with Abu-Rideh's mental health needs, but this had been overruled by the home secretary. Gareth Pierce, the lawyer for detainee P and Abu-Rideh, had tried on several occasions to challenge the conditions under which the men were being held, arguing that the conditions were causing a deterioration of their physical and mental health.[14] However, in the case of P, the mental health team at Belmarsh argued that if he cooperated with his treatment his condition would improve.

The second CPT delegation was particularly worried that the conditions of detention at Belmarsh and Broadmoor did not suit the detainees' status as people who had not been accused or convicted of any criminal offense.[15] Noting that Abu-Rideh had suffered severe weight loss and that his "mental state also appeared to have deteriorated considerably," the delegation said that it was "clinically inappropriate" to keep him in an establishment "commonly tasked with the care of dangerous and violent patients."[16] The report concluded with the relatively harsh words, that for some of the detainees "their situation . . . could be considered as amounting to inhuman and degrading treatment."[17] Following the visit, P's mental health also declined and he too was moved to Broadmoor.

There was a longer-than-normal delay in the release of the British government's response to the CPT's recommendations. A significant court case at the end of 2004 had effectively made many of the CPT's recommendations out of date by outlawing the system of detention.[18] Nevertheless, the British government eventually responded in detail. The strongest language was reserved for "categorically" rejecting the claim that some of the treatment of the detainees could be considered "inhuman and degrading treatment."[19] The argument that conditions of detention were not appropriate for people who had been neither accused nor convicted of a crime was met with a claim that a "more relaxed regime" had been put into place.[20] The replies confirmed that the Home Office would not rely on any evidence that it knew or believed to have been obtained through torture by a third country.[21] The claim that "secret evidence" is a significant procedural disadvantage was once again dismissed.[22]

The Monitoring Committees

International human rights monitoring mechanisms are an attempt to shine a light into the darkest recesses of places of detention. They try to hold states to account for their treatment of detainees through a careful combination of transparency and persuasion. In the mid-1970s, two Geneva-based NGOs, the International Commission of Jurists (ICJ) and the Swiss Committee Against Torture (SCAT) began lobbying for a UN-based system for monitoring places of detention in order to prohibit torture. The assumption was that only an international body would have the necessary moral and political authority to fulfill the task. The ICJ is an international group of lawyers, with its roots in Cold War criticisms of the human rights record of the Communist bloc. The SCAT, later renamed the Association for the Prevention of Torture (APT), had been founded by Jean-Jacques Gautier, a retired banker and committed Christian, with the specific aim of establishing an anti-torture monitoring mechanism. Taking its model from the International Committee of the Red Cross, SCAT had submitted several draft proposals to the UN Commission on Human Rights for an international torture monitoring body. However, as in the rest of the UN human rights system, many states, and the United States and the former Soviet Union in particular, were keen to avoid any restrictions on sovereignty (Normand and Zaidi 2008). Any monitoring mechanisms they agreed to had limited powers to investigate allegations or to issue binding decisions. It soon became clear that it was going to be difficult, if not impossible, to get widespread agreement from UN members for a universal system of visits to places of detention.

The UN body that was eventually created had a very restricted mandate. Formally, the UN Committee Against Torture monitors compliance with the UN Convention Against Torture and Other Cruel, Inhuman or Degrading Treatment or Punishment 1984 (see Chapter 1). Crucially, the routine business of the Committee Against Torture does not include the power to visit signatory states directly, and the committee instead relies on written reports and oral presentations given in Geneva.[23] The committee then issues its own recommendations to the reporting state.[24] The recommendations issued by the CAT are advisory rather than binding. The committee is made up of ten part-time members and is supported on a part-time basis by members of the Office of the High Commissioner for Human Rights (OHCHR).[25]

The Convention Against Torture contains perhaps the most detailed definition of torture in any international instrument. However, there are few explicit statements by the committee clarifying what this definition might mean in practice. In part this is because of a deliberate case of constructive ambiguity. Members argue, for example, that they do not want to create a clear distinction between torture and cruel, inhuman, or degrading treatment or punishment, as this will create a line to which states will automatically move. By leaving the division between the two categories unclear, the committee has more room to operate when censuring states.

After the failed attempt to get a body with the power to inspect places of detention directly through the United Nations, NGO and diplomatic attention shifted in the early 1980s to the Council of Europe.[26] It was hoped that it would be easier to reach consensus at the Council, which would then provide a model for the rest of the world to follow. In 1987, the Council of Europe adopted the European Convention for the Prevention of Torture and Inhuman or Degrading Treatment or Punishment, setting up the CPT.[27] The convention entered into force in February 1989 and by 2010 had been ratified by forty-seven states, stretching from Ireland to Russia, and Iceland to Malta.

Like the CAT, the CPT cannot issue legally binding decisions or recommendations. Instead, the mandate of the CPT is "by means of visits, (to) examine the treatment of persons deprived of their liberty with a view to strengthening, if necessary, the protection of such persons from torture and from inhuman or degrading treatment or punishment."[28] The CPT carries out periodic visits to signatory states, as well as ad hoc visits, should it have particular concerns. The CPT has the power to enter a member state at any time and to visit people deprived of their liberty.[29] The recommendations produced by the CPT are in principle confidential, as are all their discussions. However, in practice, virtually all states visited by the CPT have taken the decision to release the recommendations addressed to them, after they have written their own responses.[30] The committee has more than forty members, elected from all the members of the Council of Europe. They are part-time members, but they are supported by a full-time secretariat based in Strasbourg.

The CPT does not attempt to define what torture is. From the outset, there was a desire by the Council of Europe to prevent the CPT from stepping on the toes of the European Court of Human Rights. For this reason, the CPT is resolutely not the guardian of Article 3 of the European Convention of Human Rights. Broadly speaking, the CPT takes the line that all forms of ill-treatment are prohibited (Bennett 2005, 2). The CPT has developed its own principles, but it has not sought to relate these systematically to international human rights obligations.[31] It does not seek to define torture; rather, it focuses on broad principles of prevention, such as conditions of detention, size of prison cells, and access to lawyers.

Although the CAT and the CPT are both set up to monitor the prohibition of torture, they are very different mechanisms. For one, the normative references of the CPT are much wider than those of the CAT. Whereas the CAT is limited to the UN Convention Against Torture, the CPT can draw on whichever standards it chooses. At another level, the mandate of the CPT is much more limited than that of the CAT, as it focuses on places where people are deprived of their liberty, rather than, as in the case of the CAT, anywhere torture or other forms of ill-treatment might occur. The resources of the CPT are also much greater than those for the CAT. Although the CAT relies on a handful of civil servants at the OHCHR, the CPT secretariat is made up of more than twenty people. Most important, whereas the CPT makes direct visits to places of detention, the CAT is always one step removed in Geneva.

The general consensus among commentators, activists, and practitioners is that the CPT is a much stronger body than the CAT, both in terms of resources and expertise. Common complaints about the CAT include that its members do not have the necessary levels of knowledge to grasp complicated legal issues and that they do not understand the implications of their formal independence (Bank 2000; Crawford 2000). In contrast, the CPT is widely seen as a model for other human rights monitoring organizations. Indeed, in 2006 a new subcommittee of the CAT was established and was modeled on the CPT. The Optional Protocol to the Convention Against Torture (OPCAT) created a new body to ensure a "system of regular visits undertaken by independent international and national bodies to places where people are deprived of their liberty."[32] As of the time of writing, the Subcommittee on Prevention of Torture (SPT) had not visited the United Kingdom.

Despite these important differences, the two committees have a great deal in common. Both are concerned with prevention rather than holding states to account. The CPT and the CAT are fundamentally future-oriented institutions. They do not seek to allocate individual responsibility as might happen in a criminal trial, but rather they seek to oversee and prevent. As Silvia Casale, the former president of the CPT, told me in an interview, "We are not trying to make a legal case . . . but trying to find the gaps and propose reforms. . . . We use individual cases to understand wider processes, and ask what is it about the system that could allow this to happen."[33]

Perhaps most important, both the CPT and the CAT are the products of political compromises and have to operate through persuasion rather than by direct enforcement. They therefore make their claims very carefully, and their language is diplomatic and formal. The combination of the need for politeness, an emphasis on formal procedures, and the focus on the future rather than the past all means that most of the CPT and CAT recommendations are phrased in terms of policy. At the same time, given the political spaces within which the CAT and the CPT operate, the roles and processes of both committees are constantly changing, as they are produced through the interaction of international diplomats, civil servants, and NGOs.

The UN Committee Against Torture

On an autumn day in late 2004, Jonathan Spencer, a senior British civil servant from the Department of Constitutional Affairs, sat in a conference room overlooking the shores of Lake Geneva. With the hum of simultaneous translation in the background, he began presenting the United Kingdom's report to the UN Committee Against Torture. A written report had been submitted a year previously. Normally there is at least a two-year delay before the CAT is able to scrutinize the reports. However, against the background of the United Kingdom's role in the invasion of Iraq, its support for the United States in the war on terror, and the pictures from Abu Ghraib, which had been revealed in the previous year, the United Nations had decided to bring the United Kingdom report forward. Spencer began his presentation by stressing that "the United Kingdom regards torture as an affront to and a denial of the inherent dignity and right to respect which is an inalienable birthright of every human being." The United Kingdom delegation, of almost thirty people, was one of the largest the CAT had ever seen. Representatives of about a dozen British NGOs, as well as an American diplomat who was shadowing the United Kingdom delegation in preparation for the US report that was due to be submitted in the forthcoming year, were also in the audience.

This was the fourth time since the early 1990s that the United Kingdom had appeared before the CAT as part of the routine reporting cycle. According to one estimate, more than 70 percent of states, historically, have overdue reports (Bayefsky 2001). The United Kingdom always submits its reports, even if occasionally they are several months or years late. This time, the report ran to more than one hundred pages. It covered the criminal offense of torture, the training of personnel, procedures of arrest, conditions in prison, and domestic monitoring mechanisms, among other things. Despite being the focus of much activity and protest in the United Kingdom, the ATCSA was given just half a page.[34] In the oral presentation, however, Spencer argued that there was "an emergency that threatens the life of the nation" and that the provisions of the ATCSA "were a necessary and proportionate response to the emergency." He also argued that the "the UK government does not believe that any material used against the detainees has been obtained by torture."[35] In relation to Iraq, Martin Howard, from the Ministry of Defence, claimed that military personnel were "instructed that prisoners, detainees and civilians should be treated with dignity and respect and should not be subjected to torture, abuse or inhuman or degrading treatment."[36] Howard went on to say that allegations of ill-treatment of civilians in Iraq by military personnel were fully investigated and that they had not been involved in "systematic human rights abuses." He also denied, contrary to claims by several human rights organizations, that hooding was still in use.[37]

The afternoon before the UK presentation, the CAT had met with a delegation of British human rights NGOs, including Amnesty International, Human Rights Watch, Liberty, Justice, and Redress. The British NGO delegation was one of the biggest to appear before the CAT. They had also submitted several "shadow reports," outlining the key issues they felt the CAT should focus on. Human Rights Watch, for example, was pushing "diplomatic assurances." Liberty and Justice had come together to focus on the procedures of ATCSA, while Redress emphasized the formal frameworks for the legal protection of torture survivors.

To a great extent, the CAT relies on information supplied by NGOs, as it has limited investigatory powers to supplement the information it receives from states. Members are unpaid and only work in Geneva for five weeks a year. The rest of the time they have other jobs. Although the CAT is supported by UN civil servants, none of these work for the CAT full time. As such, NGOs can play a central role in setting the committee's agenda, determining the questions the committee members ask, and eventually affecting the recommendations that the committee makes. During sessions examining state reports, members sometimes refer directly to information from human rights organizations. More often than not, however, members simply quote from the NGO reports, without indicating the source. There is also a great deal of informal lobbying that can go on in the corridors outside the meeting room, as NGOs try to slip in last-minute questions.

Following the UK presentation, the ten CAT members took their turn to ask the delegation questions. Taking the lead was Felice Gaer, the American member of the CAT. Gaer was the director of the American Jewish Committee's Jacob Blaustein Institute for the Advancement of Human Rights and a veteran of US human rights delegations. Among other things, she asked whether the UK government thought diplomatic assurances were a "safeguard against return to torture or a loophole to permit it" and asked for clarification on whether evidence potentially obtained under torture was used in domestic British courts. When she had finished, other committee members asked whether it was right to "leave someone in legal limbo" under the ATCSA and requested further information about investigation of deaths of detainees in custody in Iraq. Depending on how they are counted, more than seventy questions were asked by the CAT. Following the questions, the United Kingdom delegation was then given just over a day to prepare its answers. In its reply, the United Kingdom delegation denied that ATCSA created a legal limbo, reiterated that evidence obtained through torture was not used, and argued that diplomatic assurances were in compliance with the United Kingdom's international obligations.

As the CAT has limited investigatory powers, it cannot and does not make factual determinations, or even firm allegations. Its members therefore pose highly qualified questions. They ask states to comment on existing allegations, using phrasing such as "I have a feeling that . . .," "There are strong allegations that . . ." or "Could you comment on . . .?" When disagreements over basic facts arise, the committee members are in no position to determine whom or what is correct. In general, the questions concern broad policies, institutional arrangements, or statistical clarifications. The polite tone and broad nature of the questions make them relatively easy for states to avoid answering. When the UK delegation gave its replies, the general questions invited general answers, whereas specific questions were met with a mass of information. In this context, specific substantive issues almost always give way to issues of principle and procedure.

Two weeks after the CAT had heard the presentations, it issued its conclusions and recommendations. In these, the CAT noted that it remained concerned about whether there was an absolute prohibition of torture under the criminal law in force in the United Kingdom and recommended that the government review its domestic legislation accordingly.[38] As was examined in Chapter 5, the Criminal Justice Act 1988 criminalized torture, but it also provides for the defense of "lawful authority."[39] The committee members also expressed concern about the use of diplomatic assurances but said that the arrangements being used were "not wholly clear" and therefore could not be assessed.[40] The "resort to potentially indefinite detention" under the ATCSA was also singled out, and it was recommended that the United Kingdom should "review, as a matter of urgency, the alternatives."[41] The recommendations of the CAT also included a request for further "reflection" on the government's intention not to rely on evidence obtained by torture and the making public of all investigations into alleged misconduct by its forces in Iraq, including those surrounding the death of Baha Mousa (see Chapter 5). Finally, the United Kingdom was asked to consider developing a statistical database on issues relating to the Convention Against Torture.[42]

The language of the recommendations makes it clear that they are not obligatory. Like the CPT, the Committee Against Torture must walk a diplomatic tightrope. As Andreas Mavromatis, the veteran former chair of the CAT explained to me, "We need to go softly. We cannot throw everything at them. The purpose is not to point fingers but to save lives. . . . We cannot demand too much as otherwise they will close the door on us."[43] It is also very rare for the CAT to tell states that they are in direct contravention of the Convention Against Torture. Although in 2007, for example, the CAT recommended that the United States "should rescind any interrogation technique, including methods involving sexual humiliation, 'water boarding' and 'short shackling,'" the language is ambiguous as to whether the United States has used these techniques and whether they were in direct breach of the convention.[44] At no point was the British government told its actions were in breach of the Convention Against Torture.

The United Kingdom responded more than one year later to the recommendations. By this time, the ATCSA had already been superseded and replaced by a new law. The UK response began by saying that it did not consider it necessary to review domestic law prohibiting torture.[45] The response also claimed that when releasing information about investigations into abuses in Iraq the United Kingdom had to balance the interests of transparency with those of privacy and fair trials. The response ended by setting out more details about the diplomatic assurances that had been obtained from Libya, Jordan, and Lebanon for the extradition of terror suspects.[46]

Human Rights Monitoring and the Construction of Risk

For human rights monitoring to take place, torture has to be made "monitorable" and amenable to particular forms of assessment. Having limited investigatory powers, monitoring mechanisms are forced to take their information from the sources that are available. Files are produced, statistics taken, and policies written from which information can then be read. As a future-oriented institution concerned with prevention rather than punishment, the CAT understands torture through the lens of risk. The parallels with judicial decisions about the risk of return to torture are substantial (see Chapter 4). In both cases, to work on the basis of risk reduction is to try to make the future measurable, or at least monitorable, to pin it down to identifiable problems (Knight 2009). The CAT and CPT therefore work on the basis of broad categories. In order to produce monitoring information, the CAT and the CPT cut through the complex processes that result in detention and ill-treatment, highlighting some and ignoring others. As Sally Merry has argued about human rights indicators, but in terms also applicable to human rights monitoring in general, the result is a "world knowable without the detailed particulars of context and history," converting "complicated contextually variable phenomena into unambiguous, clear and impersonal measures" (2011). Monitoring is not a transparent process of information gathering but one of abstraction and generalization, and its procedures can obscure as much as they reveal. Such processes are not unique to human rights monitoring, and they can be seen as part of a broader process of "technical governance." As Tania Li has argued, only those issues through which a technical solution can be proposed are highlighted (2007, 126). Broader goals of political and social transformation are rendered as technical questions of procedure, documentation, and the adoption of the correct policies.

It is important to note here that the blind spots of the CAT and the CPT are not simply a problem of expertise or knowledge. Many members of the committees are well aware of these problems. Rather, the problems are an issue of the political space within which both committees operate and of their institutional limits. Given limited resources, sources have to be created from which information can be read at speed. Neither organization is designed as a fact-finding body. The CAT therefore focuses on policies and procedures, which the United Kingdom was more than happy to provide. It also uses statistics as a stable surface from which the possibility of torture can be read. The CPT, in contrast, sees situations head on, but it too has a very limited knowledge. Its visits last a number of days, weeks at most, and it therefore has to rely on a great deal of background information. It has only a snapshot. These snapshots can be very illuminating, but they are snapshots nevertheless.

What types of knowledge then does the monitoring process produce? Government officials and NGO activists from the United Kingdom broadly agree that neither the CPT nor the CAT tell them anything they did not know already. There are few, if any, new facts or bits of information produced by engagement with the monitoring committees. Light is not shone into new corners. As an official at the Ministry of Justice who liaises with both the CPT and the CAT told me, "Very rarely do any of the questions raise a new issue. In nearly all cases though we already have well-established lines."[47] Another British civil servant with extensive experience with both committees described them to me as "huge information-gathering exercises. . . . The policy questions are normally fairly predictable, as we will have heard them before so will have the policy responses ready. I can't say it doesn't raise new issues, but would be surprised if it did."[48] Indeed one former senior government minister complained to me that the monitoring organizations often got things wrong.[49] Activists and lawyers broadly agree that the reports and replies seldom tell them anything new. At most, the way things are phrased can sometimes be enlightening. The process can produce ways of characterizing policy by the British government that can be very revealing. If the government's responses appear to be particularly careful, they can cause activists to ask what is being planned.

After collecting information, the next step of the monitoring process is judging risks of torture and ill-treatment. As was argued in Chapter 4, the risks of torture are not self-evident, as conceptualizations of risk do not exist independently in the world and are in large measure a product of the systems that monitor them (Ewald 1991). The theory of risk that both committees work with is implicit rather than explicit. As Silvia Casale told me, "We do not have a worked-out theory . . . as it is not really our job . . . other people have done this."[50] There is little analysis of the causes of torture and ill-treatment: the focus instead is on its visible, or at least the monitorable, manifestations. As it is procedures, policies, and legislation that the committees have easiest access to, it is precisely around policies, procedures, and legislation that the understanding of torture is built up. There is therefore a concern with issues such as access to lawyers, rules of evidence, the criminal law on torture, and the formal distinction between convicted prisoners and the Belmarsh detainees.

The risk of torture is also linked to the cultural attitudes of officials. Both committees particularly emphasize the training of police officers, prison guards, soldiers, lawyers, judges, and the general public. Training is seen as necessary for, in the words of one CAT member, a "shift in mentalities" and as such the eradication of torture is seen as an issue of "cultural change." Similarly, as Silvia Casale has argued, "We are concerned about anything that is disrespectful because our experience is that torture and other forms of ill-treatment, more or less serious, occur when you have an environment in which respect for the person breaks down" (Bennett 2005, 4). In this context, the CPT often recommends that staff be reminded that ill-treatment is unacceptable. A concern with individuals and wider political causes can seep into the work of both the CPT and the CAT. However, because of their political and resource limitations, the default position is always a concern for technocratic and managerial processes. As with judicial assessments about non-refoulement, monitoring through risk therefore abstracts torture away from individual cases and the specifics of violence toward a focus on general categories and processes.

The Impact of Shame

Given the focus on policies in human rights monitoring, what role does shame have? Can a state be ashamed of its procedures? In truth, it is difficult to get a sense of the impact of CPT and CAT recommendations, as they become part of the general stream of politics. The influence of human rights monitoring can be diffuse and indirect because their conclusions, recommendations, and communications can take on a life of their own (Merry 2006a). Nongovernmental organizations, courts, and even governments use the committees' recommendations in their own political struggles. In this process, it is impossible to say whether something changed because of the CAT or the CPT, or whether it is the result of other pressures. There is no obvious causal link. Political change does not happen simply for one reason but rather because of an accumulation of factors. However, it is possible to look at the rhetorical approach to the recommendations, the ways in which they are formally integrated into the policy-making process, and the locations where references are made to them. By doing so, we can begin to understand the spaces that the recommendations open for political debate and those they close down.

As we saw in Chapter 4, under the government of Tony Blair the political rhetoric of the United Kingdom was that human rights had to be rebalanced in favor of protecting the general population and that those who argued for the rights of terror suspects were naïve at best and dangerous at worst. Human rights obligations were therefore not absolute and given once and for all. The British government seemed to be saying that it had nothing to be ashamed of. Although they did not make direct attacks on the CAT and the CPT, maybe because they were too low profile to warrant the effort, successive ministers criticized the international human rights regime. In one famous incident, Professor Manfred Nowak, the UN Special Rapporteur on Torture was reportedly harangued in a meeting with Charles Clarke, then British home secretary and the man who introduced the ATCSA. Clarke accused Nowak of wasting his time and told him he should concentrate on places with a real human rights problem.

It is of course important to attach a certain level of skepticism to political rhetoric, as there is a strong sense of playing to the crowd in many of the attacks on international human rights mechanisms. These public criticisms also seem to have died down after 2007 and the resignation of Tony Blair. However, at a practical level, the general sense is that the British government and its civil servants treat its liaisons with the CAT and the CPT as a bureaucratic task to be dealt with efficiently, rather than as a source of guidance, accountability, and moral authority. As an administrative task, it is also fairly low down the list of priorities and one that looks outward to diplomatic relationships rather than inward to political change. As the civil servant who had been responsible for liaising with both the CPT and the CAT told me, "Other departments have other priorities. . . . It is not that there is malice, just people are busy, the reports are low down the list of things to do."[51] Similarly, as a Home Office legal adviser told me, "The CAT process is merely about providing legal comment and explaining the position. . . . We do not really have an international law problem in this area. This is not the same as saying we have done everything the UN has asked."[52] Lord Carlile, the government's independent reviewer of anti-terror legislation, told me that he had never once discussed the CAT or the CPT with the government.[53]

All this does not mean that the recommendations are not taken seriously. After all, the British government will devote thousands of hours to them and write some of the longest reports. However, it is to say that the recommendations do not have bite in and of themselves. The former chief executive of the National Offender Management Service, responsible for all the United Kingdom's prisons, including those holding the ATCSA detainees, told me that although human rights monitoring recommendations do not drive policy, the prison service will try to cooperate "if it is reasonable."[54]

The feeling among many activists is that the United Kingdom works with the CAT and the CPT primarily to show that it is engaging at a formal level, rather than just listening to what it is being told. Although the formal role of both committees is to produce a dialogue, there is very little evidence that this ever actually takes place. Benjamin Ward, deputy director of Human Rights Watch's Europe and Central Asia Division, a lawyer, and former UN employee, told me, "The UK generally tries to engage on soft issues, but when push comes to shove they will not give in . . . when it comes to the hard edge, they will not listen. . . . The purpose of engaging is to assert that it is compliant, rather than to take part in a dialogue. . . . The UK thinks it really has nothing new to learn."[55] It can seem that way to members of the monitoring organizations as well. Silvia Casale told me, "Sophisticated countries like the UK allow themselves the latitude to disagree, as they know that human rights soft law is not binding. . . . The UK government's attitude tends to be that they are not going to reconcile their positions, and they will sometimes delay the publication of a report in the hope that the issue will have gone away."[56] Even some senior officials seem to hold similar views. As Phil Wheatley, the most senior person in the British prison system, put it to me, "We engage because we have signed a treaty and it is important in broader foreign policy terms that we engage with them, as we expect other states to do the same."[57]

Given the widespread feelings about the government's relatively relaxed responses to monitoring recommendations, many NGOs try to hold up the recommendations to "public opinion," hoping that wider exposure will bring about the desired changes in policy and practice. As Sally Merry argues, NGOs mobilize the monitoring committee recommendations "to generate public support or governmental discomfort" (2006a, 71). In this way, NGOs attempt to use the recommendations to get press coverage, which in turn might lead to increased political scrutiny, which might lead to some type of policy or legal reform, which might then lead to practical change (see also, Keck and Sikkink 1998).

However, although anything with the word *torture* in it can get a certain amount of attention, it is often very difficult to get the TV and newspapers to pay attention to the CAT and the CPT recommendations. In large part, this is because of the equivocal way they are worded, which reduces their impact as a headline. A top line that says "UN body recommends more training for prison officers" is not going to grab much attention. At most, it is usually the legal correspondents who are interested, but their stories can be buried deep in the newspaper. The delay in the release of the CPT reports also means that their impact is already somewhat diminished and the British government has had time to prepare its responses. By the time of the 2004 CPT report, which condemned the treatment of the detainees in Belmarsh as inhuman and degrading, the regime in question had already been abolished by a domestic legal decision. Although civil servants and politicians were very nervous about public responses to the criticism, it was largely missed by the press and not picked up by Liberty in public until two weeks after its release.

Some activists and lawyers feel that using the CPT's recommendations as a lobbying tool can actually be counterproductive. Eric Metcalf, the human rights policy director at Justice and previously a government lawyer advising on immigration issues, told me that "there is a sense that the UK can sometimes feel maligned by the Council of Europe."[58] There is a similar feeling within the CPT itself. As Silvia Casale stated, "Sometimes I advise people not to quote the CPT as the UK can be very sensitive about criticism from Europe."[59] The particular history of British relations with the rest of Europe, and the streak of Euro-skepticism that runs through much of British politics and the popular press can reduce the impact of using CPT recommendations in wider campaigns.

Perhaps the key way in which the recommendations of the Committee Against Torture are kept alive is through the inquiries and reports of the British parliament's Joint Committee on Human Rights (JCHR). The JCHR is an all-party committee from both houses of parliament. Since 2002, the JCHR has conducted follow-up inquiries looking at the ways in which the British government has responded to the recommendations of UN human rights committees. In the words of the JCHR's legal adviser: "We decided we were going to take the concluding observations of UN human rights committees and give them life . . . we try to bridge the gap between diplomatic rhetoric and practice."[60] Following the release of the CAT's recommendations, the JCHR held a five-day inquiry and received written evidence from human rights organizations such as Justice, Human Rights Watch, and Amnesty International, as well as from government departments. Senior ministers, civil servants, and police officers gave oral evidence, as did NGO activists. The JCHR report looked at many of the same things as the CAT, such as the use of diplomatic assurances and the investigation of allegations of torture. In many ways, the inquiry was more thorough and systematic than the original CAT report. The report's conclusions were also relatively hard hitting (JCHR 2006). The experience of many NGOs is that the JCHR attracts more press coverage than do international human rights monitoring mechanisms and is therefore taken more seriously by government. However, in many ways the JCHR is similar to the CAT. Like the CAT, the JCHR does not look at individual cases but rather at broader processes. It also hears only oral evidence and reads written reports, and it does not have direct investigatory powers of its own. Perhaps most important, its recommendations are nonbinding, and although they are responded to in detail, there is space for disagreement and, if need be, they can be ignored. It appears, for example, to be the only parliamentary committee that ministers have refused to attend.

The final area where the CAT and the CPT recommendations are invoked is in court cases. Although the CPT reports were not initially designed to be fact-finding, they are sometimes used in courts with other forms of evidence. With one or two notable exceptions, these are largely immigration and asylum cases, and they refer to detention conditions in places such as Russia and the Ukraine, rather than the United Kingdom.[61] It is very hard to find mention of the CAT recommendations in English case law.[62] One decision of the House of Lords even goes so far as to describe a recommendation from the CAT as "having no value."[63] In large part, this relative lack of reference to the CPT and the CAT recommendations is due to their very nature. They are not authoritative on facts, and they make generally vague jurisprudential claims. More important, the language of the CPT and the CAT, phrased in terms of diplomatic politeness, is often not very hard-edged and therefore not very persuasive in a legal context.

Court cases, however, did make a big difference in the areas in which the CAT, the CPT, and the JCHR had expressed concern, even if the committees were not directly mentioned. Litigation rather than shame was most persuasive. In December 2005, the Law Lords ruled that the courts could not hear evidence that might have been obtained through torture by officials of a foreign state.[64] Much of the evidence used to certify people such as Abu-Rideh was obtained by security forces in places such as Pakistan, Afghanistan, Algeria, and Syria. The Home Office argued that it would be nearly impossible to prove that all evidence was untainted. However, the Law Lords ruled that if the courts are unable to conclude that there is not a real risk that the evidence has been obtained by torture, the courts should refuse to admit the evidence. Passing mention was made in the judgment to the concerns expressed by both the

CPT and the CAT over the possibility that evidence obtained by torture was being used in British courts. However, the stress was not on human rights issues but rather on the ban on torture as having its roots in over 400 years of English common law.

Prior to the ruling about evidence, the regime under which the ATCSA detainees were held was also declared unlawful by the House of Lords.[65] The ruling argued that the detention of Abu-Rideh and others was a disproportionate deprivation of the right to liberty and was discriminatory on the grounds that it applied only to noncitizens in an arbitrary manner. This ruling came just a matter of weeks after the CAT recommendations were released, but they were not mentioned at all. Although the CPT had sent its report to the United Kingdom in mid 2004, the report was not published until after the Lords had come to their decision, and therefore no reference could be made to their criticisms of the Belmarsh regime.

In response to the Lords' decision, a new regime was introduced by the home secretary that applied to noncitizens and citizens alike. The detainees remained "certified" as suspected terrorists, but they were released on bail and kept under house arrest in a system known as "control orders." Abu-Rideh was released in March 2005 but had to wear an electronic tag, live at a designated address, and observe a curfew from 7 A.M. to 7 P.M. If he wanted to meet with people outside his immediate family, he had to get permission from the Home Office. He was banned from having a mobile phone or computer. P was also released around the same time and placed under similar bail conditions. However, after his initial release, he was re-arrested in the summer of 2005 and then placed once more under house arrest. Fed up with his living conditions, P agreed to leave voluntarily to Algeria in early 2007. On arrival he was detained, but he was released after three days. Abu-Rideh tried to commit suicide several times during his house arrest. In the days after the House of Lords' ruling on the use of secret evidence, Abu-Rideh was given a travel document by the British government, something he had been asking for for years, and agreed to leave the United Kingdom voluntarily. The travel document had a "right of return" clause written into it, but that was cancelled as soon as he left the country. Abu-Rideh is now believed to be in Syria or Jordan.

The Shame of Torture?

Is there any evidence of anything resembling shame in the ways the British government and its civil servants approach human rights monitoring mechanisms? Critics might dismiss human rights shaming as an unenforceable irrelevance. From this perspective, strong states such as the

United Kingdom will inevitably follow their own interests. Shame is far too soft an emotion for the hardball of international politics (Hafner-Burton 2008; Hathaway 2002; Wachman 2001). This critique would claim that at best states will respond to human rights recommendations in a cosmetic and an instrumental way in order to gain access to international financial support, military assistance, or diplomatic kudos, but they will manifest little real commitment (Risse, Ropp, and Sikkink 1999).

A perhaps less cynical view of international human rights monitoring would point to the vast resources that the United Kingdom puts into the reporting process, and the often high-level discussions that go on about how to respond to criticisms. From this perspective, the British government is worried about being shamed by international human rights organizations and responds in order to limit the negative impact. Serious efforts are therefore put in to engaging with monitoring mechanisms because they have a persuasive normative force and cannot simply be ignored (compare Franck 1998). A related line of argument is that the United Kingdom is rarely shamed by international human rights monitoring because a consciousness of human rights obligations is built deep into the domestic political fabric. States such as the United Kingdom are forced to take their obligation to prohibit torture seriously because of their own internal pressures to do so, from parliament and in the courts to NGOs, activists, and lawyers (Çali and Wyss 2009; Helfer and Slaughter 1997). Even if the recommendations of international human rights monitoring mechanisms are not directly fed back into the system, the British government is already working in the same general direction.

There is a danger, in asking whether and why the British government experiences shame in the face of its international obligations, of treating the state as a unified entity. The British government's interaction with the CPT and the CAT is far from being a seamless web. The liaison with both committees is coordinated by the Ministry of Justice, which needs to seek detailed information from other parts of government—a necessarily time-consuming task. Even if the Ministry of Justice moves quickly to meet the deadlines set by the committees, other parts of government have their own commitments and priorities to manage. This has important implications. Individual people may be ashamed if they are exposed as torturers, but the impact is diffused when the accusations are about rules of evidence, the monitoring of diplomatic agreements, and procedures on arrest. Although individuals within government may be worried about many of the government's practices and policies, these are dispersed into bureaucratic chains. Many of the officials with whom I spoke would privately admit to being worried about "some of the things going on," largely the apparent complicity of the secret services in the ill-treatment of detainees elsewhere in the world, but this ill-treatment always took place elsewhere and was carried out by other people.

Shame implies a vulnerability to being exposed for failing to reach professed ideals and goals. However, it is not clear what human rights monitoring exposes and precisely what ideals are not being reached. Little, if no, new information is provided by the monitoring organizations. Not only are officials rarely surprised by the information produced (if not the normative stances taken by the committees), but NGOs, parliamentary bodies, and journalists nearly always already know the information the monitoring committees present to the world. What is more, it is not clear who the information is being exposed to. If shame requires an audience, it is not obvious that anyone is watching. Government officials largely know what is going on, and the press is rarely interested.

Perhaps most important, if shame requires a sense of failing to meet standards or goals, what these standards or goals are is far from self-evident. When international human rights monitoring mechanisms talk about torture and other forms of ill-treatment, they tend to talk about broad institutions and policies. A concern with torture is often dispersed into procedural issues. To say that this chapter has not really been about torture is to miss the point, as it has focused on the two leading international torture monitoring organizations, and what they talk about is largely procedures and policy. In this context, the ambiguity in the ways in which torture is defined, and the technical ways in which its obligations are interpreted, give the United Kingdom plenty of wiggle room. There are always more policies and procedures to which civil servants can refer.

Shaming strategies can produce spaces for the deflection of responsibility. This is not simply because denial can be an immediate response to shame; rather, it is because it is not always clear what there is to be ashamed about. Through the monitoring process, human rights indicators can become confused with human rights. There can be a slippage between the process of collecting information and the practices designed to prevent human rights violations. Indeed, the very question of compliance with the international prohibition of torture immediately shifts attention from the question as to whether states are complicit in torture. The shame of human rights monitoring is supposed to produce a transparent and precautionary response. Yet a focus on transparency creates space for the endless deferral onto ever more policies and protocols.

Conclusion

The legal prohibition of torture seems absolute and definitive in principle. All too often though, it breaks down when it comes to specific cases. Torture is so hard to acknowledge, not because survivors find it hard to express what has happened to them but because we find it so difficult to say, hear, and name what is in front of us. The law seems to provide the opportunity to protect survivors and prosecute perpetrators with definitional coherence and the possibility of enforcement. Yet, in practice, legal processes create a set of requirements for recognition that very few people can meet.

Suffering, Compassion, and Doubt

Compassion in the face of another person's needless suffering underlies much of the ethical objection to torture and the legal mechanisms that have been put into place to protect survivors. Compassion, inasmuch as it draws on notions of sympathy, implies a sense of suffering another's pain along with that person (Moyn 2006). It is to say "I know your pain."[1] This does not suggest that another person can know the pain in its entirety, but rather that the person can imagine what the pain might be like, even if he or she falls short when doing so.

Compassion as the basis for recognition has its critics. Hannah Arendt, for example, argues that the prioritization of compassion marks a retreat from reason and institutionalized politics (1973). Arendt sees compassion as inherently limiting. As she argues, compassion "cannot reach out further than what is suffered by one person. . . . As a rule it is not compassion which sets out to change worldly conditions in order to ease human suffering, but if it does, it will shun the drawn out wearisome processes of persuasion, negotiation, and compromise, which are the process of law and politics" (1973, 86–87). Recent critiques of compassion have gone further than Arendt. Miriam Ticktin, for example, argues that an emphasis on compassion can mean that people are reduced to being seen as passive suffering bodies (2006a; see also Berlant 2003; Brown 1995). Survivors are treated as victims in need of protection rather than as active agents in their own right. In this context, the granting of rights and entitlements can depend on an emotional response rather than on the recognition of complex wants and needs (Ticktin 2006b). As such, torture survivors can be diminished to docile figures, stripped away from their wider social relations.

Much of the modern critique of compassion implicitly opposes emotion to languages of justice based on rights (Fassin 2010; Povinelli 2002). There is, though, a danger of drawing the line between emotions and rights too firmly. The prohibition of torture is, after all, a right based on an opposition to suffering, combining legal and emotional responses. It is this merging of the compassionate and the technical that marks attempts to recognize torture. Compassion never stands alone, unmediated. The focus on suffering is not simply a response to experiences that exist in the world. It is only through classifying, sorting, and prioritizing that traces of past cruelty are given meaning. It is not the suffering of the survivor in its full complexity that legal processes try to recognize. Such an attempt would only serve to reproduce the horrors described and would be of little help in coming to a decision. Rather, legal processes are concerned with the forms of suffering and pain that meet specific requirements of evidence, procedure, and categorization.

Despite the technical requirements of proof, the evidential demands made by law are unstable. For an act to be considered torture, for example, the intensity of the pain and suffering is of central importance. Yet the law provides no precise point at which pain tips over into severe pain and an act becomes torture.[2] In 1999, the European Court of Human Rights ruled that the level of severity was "relative; it depends on all the circumstances of the case."[3] The English courts have taken a similar position.[4] There has been a partial move from the idea of an absolute threshold of pain and suffering to one based on context, and a greater, although not absolute, focus on the intention of the perpetrator. Either way, legal processes offer no firm guidance on where the threshold of suffering sits. Although words such as *severe* and *aggravated* are widely used, these too also fail to produce a stable and an absolute line. Torture is therefore a category that claims universal application, but its threshold of pain and suffering is constantly shifting when applied in concrete circumstances.[5]

The level of pain and suffering necessary for an act, legally, to count as torture has to be judged from case to case. Elaine Scarry has famously claimed that through torture, pain is objectified on the body (1988). The sheer brute presence of pain and suffering seems, at first glance, to offer concrete and persuasive proof of torture. As Amnesty International said in the 1970s, "Pain is a common human dominator, and while few people know what it is to be shot, to be burned by napalm, or to starve, all know pain. Within every human being is the knowledge and fear of pain, the fear of helplessness before unrestrained cruelty" (1973, 17). Yet, rather than providing a solid basis on which to judge claims of torture, the specific nature and causes of pain and suffering are difficult to read off often inscrutable bodies and minds. When courts or tribunals make judgments about torture, the survivor is rarely, if ever, allowed to speak. The survivor's testimony is seldom accepted at face value. Concern for suffering is instead filtered through technical forms of expertise. Clinicians try to uncover the causes of pain through the use of medical protocols and categories demanded by judges and lawyers to fit suffering and cruelty into a legal framework of innocence and guilt. But stable, legally admissible knowledge about torture is still hard to pin down. Torture survivors can have many observable symptoms, or they may have none. Other forms of evidence can also be partial or nonexistent. General documentation that a regime inflicts torture may be available, but evidence that it happened at a particular time to a particular person is hard to confirm.

In the context of these evidential problems, torture survivors are often faced with what seems to be an institutionalized disbelief about their claims, where the default position of immigration officials, judges, and the general public is that they are not telling the whole truth. However, this disbelief stems not just from a failure to engage with the claims of asylum seekers but rather is, at least in part, caught up within attempts at compassion itself. In the sense that it is an attempt to say "I know your pain," compassion can also bring with it a claim to knowledge about the survivor that can undermine the claim. The recognition of a shared humanity can produce an acknowledgment of the all-too-human potential for duplicity. The combination of the possibility that the other is not being entirely truthful and the sense that we do not know enough about the person to make this judgment at all adds to a feeling of uncertainty about whether compassion is well placed in any individual case. If another person suffers just like me, that person can therefore respond in equally unpredictable and confusing ways. Such suspicions are not about a fundamental chasm between the witness and the survivor, but rather they are a recognition of similarity. Compassion does not therefore turn people into passive victims but treats them as active agents, and it is this that opens spaces of doubt.

Although a focus on suffering may set the general framework within which torture survivors seek recognition, more often than not inclusion within its terms is beyond the reach of any given individual. For the political theorist Wendy Brown, victimhood is the default state for much contemporary politics (1995). Yet, if this is true, it is also important to note that it is really hard to be recognized as a victim. A generalized concern with suffering is no guarantee that recognition of the suffering of a particular person will follow (Fassin and d'Halluin 2007). Torture survivors may be singled out for specific protection, but it is very hard indeed to qualify for that protection.

Perpetrators in Faraway Places

A different set of issues emerges when it comes to the identification of perpetrators. All too often innocence has to be taken on faith; guilt, by comparison, is more politically determined (see Arendt 1973, 87). There has only ever been one successful prosecution for torture in British legal history. Faryadi Zardad, an Afghan warlord, was convicted in the United Kingdom for crimes committed in Afghanistan in the 1990s. Given the British track record in its wars of counterinsurgency, as well as some of its domestic policing practices, this conviction might seem slightly surprising. The allegations of British abuse in Iraq since the 2003 invasion have not resulted in a single prosecution for torture, despite the Ministry of Defence agreeing to pay millions of pounds in compensation for the ill-treatment of detainees. As a crime under English domestic law, acts that could be charged as torture can also be charged under other crimes, such as assault. This is a common feature of criminal law, where prosecutors have to choose what is felt to be the most appropriate charge. However, the particular stigma associated with torture raises the costs for placing any individual or event within its framework. The very abhorrence of torture ironically can make it harder to prosecute. There can always be a sense, that "real" torture is something that happens elsewhere.[6] In contrast, Zardad's acts in Afghanistan the 1990s had to be squeezed into the framework of torture, as this was one of the few crimes over which English law could claim universal jurisdiction. Unlike for the British soldiers in Iraq, charges of assault, or other similar crimes, were simply not available. There is therefore a structural disposition to seeing torture as a crime committed in distant places by little-known people.

A similar situation exists in the United States, where, according to US law, the crime of torture applies only to acts committed outside the United States.[7] Inside the United States, other charges have to be used. The crime of torture is simply not applicable to acts committed on US soil. The Torture Victims Protection Act of 1991 also gives individuals the right to sue foreign governments for complicity in torture, waiving the principle of state immunity. Yet, at the same time, the US courts have also effectively ruled that US officials have immunity from civil litigation over torture if it implicates issues of national security. In the autumn of 2002, for example, the US courts dismissed a case brought by a Canadian citizen, Mohammed Arar, alleging US complicity in his torture in Syria.[8] In the same month as Arar's case was rejected, the US Second Circuit Court of Appeals upheld a judgment for $19 million, against Emmanuel "Toto" Constant, the former leader of FRAPH (Revolutionary Front for the Advancement and Progress of Haiti), for his part in torture, extrajudicial killing, and crimes against humanity in Haiti in the early 1990s.

The prosecution of individual perpetrators of torture requires making an imaginative leap that someone can be capable of what is widely seen as one of the very worst things that one person can do to another. All too often this is a leap too far. It seems to be very difficult for a person from the United Kingdom or the United States to imagine that a British or an American soldier could be guilty of such an act. In contrast, it seems relatively easy to imagine that someone from a faraway place can be. If one makes torture a monstrous crime, one needs monsters, and monsters who torture seem to live elsewhere.

Evidence of Torture

The legal notion of torture prioritizes individual suffering and cruelty. Yet, given the ways in which this suffering is defined and assessed, we need to ask whether we have adequate devices through which it can be grasped. Are legal processes demanding something that cannot be given? We live in a world that prioritizes the ability to measure and calculate, yet torture remains beyond uniform evaluation.

Torture is not the only serious crime or human rights abuse about which it is difficult to produce evidence. Two other obvious examples are rape and genocide. In the United Kingdom, as elsewhere, the success rate for rape prosecutions is very low when compared to success rates for other serious crimes. In England and Wales, it hovers around 6 percent (Rees 2010). Notions of consent, as currently interpreted by the courts, can create a large evidential burden for prosecutors. Police officers, lawyers, and juries hang onto a sense of "real rape," involving an unsuspecting woman being attacked by a stranger, outdoors, at night, using weapons, and leaving physical injuries (Estrich 1986; Temkin and Krahe 2008). As with torture, all too often the sexual assaults encountered by the legal process fail to match this stereotype and therefore charges are not successful. Unlike rape, however, proof of torture requires a consideration of the level of pain and suffering experienced by the victim.

Genocide has also proved remarkably difficult to prosecute. At the time of writing, for example, there has been no successful prosecution for genocide at the International Criminal Tribunal for the Former Yugoslavia (ICTY). As Richard Wilson argues, proving genocide in modern tribunals has faced at least two evidential stumbling blocks, which are largely the result of how genocide is defined in law (2011). At the International Criminal Tribunal for Rwanda, prosecutions were nearly sent off course on whether the victims could be said to constitute a "stable or permanent group." At the ICTY it has been very difficult, if not impossible, to produce the required evidence of a special intent to destroy a national ethnic racial or religious group.

Although torture is associated with a very different form of intention than the crime of genocide, the broader implication is that a partial move toward intent in human rights definitions of torture does not offer an easy way past evidential barriers. Even relatively "mundane" prosecutions around murder can face difficulties proving intent. These problems are amplified in immigration and asylum cases where in nearly all claims the perpetrator is absent, making proof even more difficult. In politically charged criminal prosecutions for torture, proving intentions can become especially difficult, as it means providing persuasive evidence that the accused was deliberately responsible for a crime that is widely seen as among the worst that one human can do to another.

The problems involved in the recognition of torture survivors and perpetrators raise the question as to whether the very ways in which torture is understood are to blame. As Alan Badiou has argued, when harms in the abstract are placed on a pedestal, as among the very worst things that anyone can do or that can happen to a person, there is always a danger that they become impossible to recognize in concrete events (2001, 62–63). If a particular form of cruelty and suffering is unique, unrivaled, or incomparable, it can also become immeasurable. By singling out torture for particular disapprobation, the obstacles to entry may become more difficult.

For the people concerned, the cost of raising the specter of torture in legal claims may be too high. By aiming for torture, a prosecution can fall short. It is important to remember that torture can be recognized in many other ways. The law does not exhaust the options. Clinicians, activists, welfare officers, and next-door neighbors can all offer their own types of recognition with very different forms of proof. There may be good psychological and political reasons why a survivor or the survivor's lawyer might want to have a claim of torture legally recognized. Legal recognition might be important for some survivors as a form of ethical acknowledgment of the wrongs they suffered. Politically, the naming of torture can be important in a situation where states claim impunity.

However, on a purely practical level, individuals seeking legal redress might have more success claiming seemingly lesser harms, with less of an ethical and a political load.

Law has provided the wider abhorrence of torture with the hope of clarity and enforcement. On its own, the ethical objection to cruelty and suffering risks becoming a vague aspiration with no hope of application. The turn to law seemingly offers the possibility of precision and political clout. However, the move from a broad ethical injunction to a legal category creates important limits for individuals seeking recognition, as it keeps short-circuiting in a maze of evidentiary and conceptual requirements. Legal arguments can take us further and further away from the suffering that lies at the heart of the moral objection to torture. Legal recognition can also require forms of evidence that are simply beyond the reach of most survivors. As such, the moral and the legal can sit uneasily beside each other (Meckled-Garcia and Çali 2006). There is a double bind here: Risk the compromises of law or the potential irrelevance of self-righteousness (Kennedy 2009). The choice is between the freedom of indignation or the restraint of legality.

Torture with a Capital *T*

Just because something is hard to establish does not mean that we should not try to do so. There is an indirect relationship between things of value and the techniques we have for measuring them. Objects can have importance even though we have difficulty proving they exist. Torture has a core that does not seem able to be reducible to empirical observations, but we might nevertheless want to retain it as a category. The prohibition of torture can serve as a broad political and ethical principle that helps knit together a range of key prohibitions. As philosopher Jeremy Waldron puts it, the ban on torture expresses a "determination to sever the link between law and brutality, between law and terror, and between law and the enterprise of trying to break a person's will" (2005, 1727). Over the last ten years, the issue of torture has brought together a set of otherwise disparate concerns, such as access to lawyers, detention without trial, immigration regulations, and accountability of the security services, among other things. Shouting about torture makes people sit up and listen when they might otherwise not. Keeping the notion at the heart of the political process serves as a useful reminder of the need to avoid deliberately inflicting undue suffering.

It is useful here to make a distinction between *Torture* and *torture*. Torture with a capital *T* refers to torture in the abstract, as a general principle; torture with a lowercase *t* refers to the individual act. The category of torture, in the lowercase, might create obstacles for victims of cruelty and violence as they seek restitution and protection. However, Torture can serve as an important ethical and political category. A muffled cheer for abstract principles may be a counterintuitive conclusion for an anthropologist to come to, given the general propensity among anthropologists in general to critique abstractions. Abstract principles can of course have their disadvantages, in that they efface the particularity of any situation (see, for example, Merry 2011). Abstractions can gloss over the specific causes and consequences of historically located political struggles. A focus on torture as a specific harm can risk bracketing it from the wider spectrum of violence of which it is a part and implicitly legitimizing other forms of coercion (Parry 2010). Equally important, as an abstract principle, Torture, with a capital *T*, produces a rather limited vision of the future. It is about the absence of violence rather than carrying any positive content. It offers what Badiou has called a "right to non-evil"; namely, the right to not be killed, mistreated, or tortured, and the right to protection from abusive interference (2001, 9). It has little positive space for any vision of the good life, creating at best minimalist ethical vision.

However, there is no reason why the broad principles around the legal prohibition of torture should not be thought of as a starting point rather than an end in itself. As such, abstractions, however negative in content, can also make new ways of thinking possible (Asad 2004). Although talk of torture can break down when it comes to specific individuals, it is on most solid ground when the talk is about access to lawyers, the training of security staff, and the laws of evidence, and it is to these issues that debates often return. The allegations about abuse by British troops in Iraq or complicity of British security forces, turned into judicial inquiries that could not allocate individual guilt but could only make broad recommendations for new standards and procedures. In the United States, the incidents in Abu Ghraib and Guantanamo also produced inquiry after inquiry.[9] Despite the detour through notions of trauma and intention, the eighteenth-century origins of the campaign to prohibit torture, as an issue of due process, still resonate.

Notes

Introduction

1. *Mohamed, R (on the application of) v Secretary of State for Foreign & Commonwealth Affairs* [2010] EWCA Civ 65 [23].

2. *Mohamed, R (on the application of) v Secretary of State for Foreign & Commonwealth Affairs* [2008] EWHC 2048 (Admin), [2009] 1 WLR 2579 [147].

3. *Mohamed, R (on the application of) v Secretary of State for Foreign & Commonwealth Affairs* [2010] EWCA Civ 65 [296].

4. *Mohamed, R (on the application of) v Secretary of State for Foreign & Commonwealth Affairs* [2010] EWCA Civ 65.

5. Hansard, HC Deb 6 July 2010, col 153.

6. Hansard, HC Deb 16 Nov 2010, col 723.

7. The editor of the *Daily Mirror*, Piers Morgan, lost his job because of the incident. He would later become a judge on the television show *America's Got Talent* and host of *Piers Morgan Tonight* on CNN.

8. See, for example, "Declaration of Binyam Mohamed," http://www.reprieve.org.uk/static/downloads/Exhibit_B_2009_04_30_BM_declaration_preservation_evidence.pdf (accessed 20 January 2011).

9. See, for example, Barrett (2001a; 2001b), Evans (2002), Evans and Morgan (1998), Greenberg (2006), Nagan and Atkins (2001), Novak (2006), Parry (2005), Rodley (1987), Seidman (2005), Sivakumaran (2005), Sussman (2005), Tindale (1996).

10. See, for example, Novak (2006), Parry (2005), Rodley (1987), Seidman (2005).

11. See, for example, Elshtain (2004), Ignatieff (2005), Luban (2006), Shue (2004), Steinhoff (2006), Sussman (2005).

12. The prohibition on torture is expressed in Article 5 of the Universal Declaration of Human Rights (1948), Article 7 of the International Covenant on Civil and Political Rights (1966), Article 3 of the European Convention for the Protection of Human Rights and Fundamental Freedoms (1950), Article 5 of the African Charter on Human and Peoples' Rights (1981), Article 5 of the American Convention on Human Rights (1969), Article 99 of the Geneva Conventions dealing with the Protection of Prisoners' of War (1949), and the UN Convention Against Torture and Other Cruel, Inhuman or Degrading Treatment or Punishment (1984).

13. See, for example, Amnesty International (2008a), Human Rights Watch (1998), US Department of State (2003).

14. English and Scottish law are distinct, with their own traditions, legislation and case law. However, in one of the few exceptions, immigration tribunals are British in jurisdiction, as immigration law has not been devolved. Throughout the rest of the book, I refer to English law and courts, when referring to the specific body of English law, and British law and courts when referring to law that applies across Great Britain.

15. *A & Ors v Secretary of State for the Home Department* [2004] EWCA Civ 1123, [2005] 1 WLR 414.

16. *A & Ors v Secretary of State for the Home Department* [2006] 1 All ER 575, 19 BHRC 441, [2006] UKHRR 225, [2006] HRLR 6, [2006] 2 AC 221, [2005] UKHL 71, [2005] 3 WLR 1249.

17. *A & Ors v Secretary of State for the Home Department* [2006] 1 All ER 575, 19 BHRC 441, [2006] UKHRR 225, [2006] HRLR 6, [2006] 2 AC 221, [2005] UKHL 71, [2005] 3 WLR 1249.

18. Hansard, HC Deb 2 Aug 1893, vol 15, col 1101–65.

19. For an account that sees prohibition of torture and human rights in general as part of a process of revealing universal moral principles, see Lauren (2003).

Chapter 1

1. See, for example, letter from Harold MacMichael, high commissioner for Palestine, to Malcolm McDonald, secretary of state for the colonies, 22 September 1939, National Archives (NA) WO/32/4562.

2. See, for example, letter from Jamal Hussein to the president of the Permanent Mandates Commission of the League of Nations, 12 June 1939, NA WO/32/4562.

3. Memorandum from the National Council for Civil Liberties to Howard League for Penal Reform, 6 April 1938; letter from the League for the Rights of Man, Affiliate of the National Council for Civil Liberties, Tel Aviv, to high commissioner for Palestine, 28 December 1938, Middle East Centre, St Anthony's College, University of Oxford (MEC) GB 165–0161 Jerusalem and the East Mission (JEM) Box 55, File 5.

4. Letter from Under Secretary of State J. Phillip, Colonial Office, no date, NA CO 733/413/3.

5. Opening statement of Gerard Elias, counsel to the Baha Mousa inquiry, Monday, 13 July 2009, p 20.

6. Compensation claims (Iraq): Written ministerial statement by the Rt Hon Des Browne, MP, Secretary of State for Defence. Hansard, HC Deb 27 March 2008, vol 474, col 14WS.

7. The Mousa inquiry started in December 2008 and was headed by the Right Honourable Sir William Gage, a retired Court of Appeal judge. His terms of reference were "to investigate and report on the circumstances surrounding the death of Baha Mousa and the treatment of those detained with him, taking account of the investigations which have already taken place, in particular where responsibility lay for approving the practice of conditioning detainees by any members of the 1st Battalion, the Queen's Lancashire Regiment in Iraq in 2003, and to make recommendations" (Gage 2008).

8. Note from C. Parkinson, Berlin, 10 June 1939, NA CO 733/413/3.

9. Telegram from Sir N. Henderson, British ambassador in Berlin, 14 June 1939, NA CO 733/413/3.

10. Allegations of Ill-Treatment of Arabs by British Crown Forces in Palestine, translated from the Arabic by Frances Newton, sent to Bishop of Jerusalem and League of Nations, 19 July 1939, MEC GB 165–0161 JEM Box 55, File 5.

[11] Telegram from Arab Women's Committee to the prime minister, 16 May 1939, NA CO 733/413/3.

11. Letter from archdeacon of Jerusalem to the chief secretary of the high commissioner for Palestine, 2 June 1936, MEC GB 165–1061 JEM, Box 61, File 1.

12. Memorandum from the National Council for Civil Liberties to Howard League for Penal Reform, 6 April 1938, MEC GB 165–0161 JEM Box 55, File 5.

13. Letter from the League for the Rights of Man, affiliate of the National Council for Civil Liberties, Tel Aviv, to high commissioner for Palestine, 28 December 1938, MEC GB 165–0161 JEM Box 55, File 5.

14. Textual comparison of the International Bill of Rights (prepared by the Secretariat), the United Kingdom Draft Bill of Rights, United States Proposals, 12 June 1947, E/CN.4/AC.1/11. The documents from the drafting process of the Universal Declaration are available from the Dag Hammarskjöld Library and the Library of the UN Office in Geneva (DHLUN), http://www.un.org/Depts/dhl/udhr/.

15. Commission on Human Rights, Drafting Committee on an International Bill of Human Rights, First Session, Report of the Drafting Committee to the Commission on Human Rights, 1 July 1947, E/CN.4.21.

16. Commission on Human Rights, Drafting Committee, First Session, Preliminary Record of the Third Meeting, 13 June 1947, E/CN.4/AC.1/SR.3.

17. Commission on Human Rights, Drafting Committee, International Bill of Rights, First Session, Summary Record of the Sixteenth Meeting, 3 July 1947, E/CN.4/AC.1/SR.16.

18. Collation of the Comments of Governments on the Draft International Declaration on Human Rights, Draft International Covenant on Human Rights and the Question of Implementation, 1 May 1948, E/CN.4/85.

19. Report of the Drafting Committee to the Commission on Human Rights, 21 May 1948, E/CN.4/95.

20. Commission on Human Rights, Second Session, Summary Record of Thirty-Seventh Meeting, 13 December 1947, E/CN.4/SR.37.

21. Commission on Human Rights, Drafting Committee, Second Session, Summary Record of the Thirtieth Meeting, 20 May 1948, E/CN.4/AC.1//SR.30.

22. Compilations of Amendments to the Draft Declaration of Human Rights Submitted to the Third Committee before 4 p.m. 6 October, in Chronological Order, 6 October 1948, A/C.3/230.

23. Commission on Human Rights, Drafting Committee, Second Session, Twenty-Third Meeting, 10 May 1948, E/CN.4/AC.1/SR.23.

24. Commission on Human Rights, Drafting Committee, Second Session, Twenty-Third Meeting, 10 May 1948, E/CN.4/AC.1/SR.23.

25. Report of the Third Session of the Commission on Human Rights, 28 June 1948, E/800.

26. Draft International Declaration of Rights Submitted by Working Group Drafting Committee (Preamble and Articles 1–6), 16 June 1947, E/CN.4/AC.1/W.1; Commission on Human Rights, Third Session, Observations of Governments on the Draft International Declaration on Human Rights, the Draft International Covenant on Human Rights, and Methods of Application, Communication Received from the French Government, 6 May 1948, E/CN.4/82/Add.8.

27. European Commission of Human Rights, 1956, Preparatory Work on Article 3 of the European Convention on Human Rights, Travaux Preparatoires, p 2.

28. European Commission of Human Rights, 1956, Preparatory Work on Article 3 of the European Convention on Human Rights, Travaux Preparatoires, p 5.

29. European Commission of Human Rights, 1956, Preparatory Work on Article 3 of the European Convention on Human Rights, Travaux Preparatoires, pp 9 and 12.

30. European Commission of Human Rights, 1956, Preparatory Work on Article 3 of the European Convention on Human Rights, Travaux Preparatoires, p 13.

31. Convention (III) Relative to the Treatment of Prisoners of War, Geneva, 12 August 1949, Part 1, Article 3.

32. Barbara Castle uses the word *torture* once in her House of Commons speech of 16 December 1959. Hansard, HC Deb 16 June 1959, vol 607, col 248–38.

33. Letter to governor from T. F. C. Bewes, secretary African Missionary Society, dated 28 January 1953, NA CO 822/471.

34. General Report of the Mission of the International Committee of the Red Cross to Kenya—February 20–April 19 1957, NA CO 822/1258.

35. Hansard, HC Deb 26 January 1954, vol 522, col 1610–22. See also Rubin (2005).

36. *Greece v United Kingdom* (1958–59), Collection of Decisions of the European Commission on Human Rights (CD).

37. Corporal punishment in Cyprus, NA FO 371/123926.

38. Minutes of Gen 47 Cabinet Committee Meeting, 18 October 1971, cited in the opening statement of Gerard Elias, counsel to the Baha Mousa inquiry (BMI), Monday, 13 July 2009, p 59.

39. Note dated 8 Nov 1971 from the prime minister, Edward Heath, to Sir Burke Trend, the cabinet secretary, (BMI), Monday, 13 July 2009, p 106.

40. Seamas O Tuathail, 1971, They Came in the Morning, pamphlet (on file with author).

41. Denis Faul and Raymond Murray, no date, British Army and Special Branch RUC Brutalities, pamphlet (on file with author); Campaign for Social Justice in Northern Ireland, 1971, Northern Ireland—The Mailed Fist: A Record of Army & Police Brutality, from 9 August –9 November 1971, pamphlet (on file with author).

42. Minutes of Gen 77 Cabinet Committee Meeting 9 February 1972, (BMI), Monday, 13 July 2009, p 177.

43. Indeed a civil action was later taken in Lurgan County Court against the RUC chief constable, which resulted in an award of £300 (US$480) for wrongful arrest and assault. Damages were also awarded a few months later to nine internees and seven former internees. Two army privates were fined £25 (US$40) after they pled guilty to assault and causing actual bodily harm.

44. Hansard, HC Deb 2 March 1972, vol 832, col 743–49.

45. The mandate was expanded to refer to all of Article 5 of the UDHR, rather than specifically to torture.

46. Interview with Stefanie Grant, 18 January 2010.

47. *Greek Case* (1969) CD 186.

48. United Nations General Assembly Resolution 3452 (XXX), 9 December 1975, Declaration on the Protection of All Persons from Being Subjected to

Torture and Other Cruel, Inhuman or Degrading Treatment or Punishment, Article 1.1.

49. United Nations General Assembly Resolution 3452 (XXX), 9 December 1975, Declaration on the Protection of All Persons from Being Subjected to Torture and Other Cruel, Inhuman or Degrading Treatment or Punishment, Article 1.2.

50. *Ireland v United Kingdom* (1972) CD.

51. *Ireland v United Kingdom* (1972) CD 154. The distinction also implicitly reproduced the findings of the European Commission of Human Rights in the *Greek Case.*

52. Interview with Stefanie Grant, London, 19 January 2010.

53. *Ireland v United Kingdom* (1976), Decisions and Reports of the European Commission of Human Rights (DR) 786.

54. *Ireland v United Kingdom* (1976) DR 786

55. *Ireland v United Kingdom* (1976) DR 794.

56. *Ireland v United Kingdom* [1978] 2 EHRR 25, [1978] ECHR 1, 2 EHRR 25 (1978) 2 EHRR 25, (1980) 2 EHRR 25, para 167.

57. Interview with Nigel Rodley, 28 September 2009.

58. United Nations General Assembly Resolution 3452 (XXX), 9 December 1975, Declaration on the Protection of All Persons from Being Subjected to Torture and Other Cruel, Inhuman or Degrading Treatment or Punishment, Article 1.2.

59. While at the Foreign Office, Fitzmaurice had argued strongly against international intervention in domestic human rights matters (Simpson 2001, 315). In a later dissenting opinion for the European Court of Human Rights, Fitzmaurice would argue that the birching of a schoolboy on the Isle of Man was not degrading under Article 3. He partly based his argument on the claim that he was caned as a boy and "cannot remember that any boy felt degraded or debased" (*Tyrer v United Kingdom* 2 EHRR 1, [1978] ECHR 2, (1980) 2 EHRR 1, [1978] 2 EHRR 1, (1978) 2 EHRR 1, separate opinion of Judge Sir Gerald Fitzmaurice, para 12).

60. *Ireland v United Kingdom* [1978] 2 EHRR 25, [1978] ECHR 1, 2 EHRR 25, (1978) 2 EHRR 25, (1980) 2 EHRR 25, separate opinion of Judge Sir Gerald Fitzmaurice, para 12.

61. *Ireland v United Kingdom* [1978] 2 EHRR 25, [1978] ECHR 1, 2 EHRR 25, (1978) 2 EHRR 25, (1980) 2 EHRR 25, separate opinion of Judge Sir Gerald Fitzmaurice, para 22.

62. Article 1 of the UN Convention Against Torture defines torture as "any act by which severe pain or suffering, whether physical or mental, is intentionally inflicted on a person for such purposes as obtaining from him or a third person information or a confession, punishing him for an act he or a third person has committed or is suspected of having committed, or intimidating or coercing him or a third person, or for any reason based on discrimination of any kind, when such pain or suffering is inflicted by or at the instigation of or with the consent or acquiescence of a public official or other person acting in an official capacity. It does not include pain or suffering arising only from, inherent in or incidental to lawful sanctions."

63. Interview with Nigel Rodley, 28 September 2009.

64. UN Convention Against Torture and Other Cruel, Inhuman or Degrading Treatment or Punishment (1986), Article 16.

65. Criminal Justice Act 1988, para 134.

66. Hansard, HC Deb 16 June 1988, vol 135, col 619–33.

67. Memo to Linda Duffield from Michael Wood, chief legal adviser to the Foreign & Commonwealth Office, dated 13 March 2003. Available at http://www.craigmurray.org.uk/documents/Wood.pdf (accessed 12 March 2010).

68. Memo to Alberto Gonzalez, counsel to the president from Jay Bybee, assistant attorney general, U.S. Department of Justice's Office of Legal Counsel, 1 August 2002.

Chapter 2

1. Torture survivors are granted protection under the Foreign Affairs Reform and Restructuring Act 1998. Cases for civil damages can be made under the Torture Victim Protection Act of 1991 (TVPA) Pub. L. N. 102–256, 106 Sat. 73 (1992). The TVPA is used along with the Alien Tort Claims Act 1789. The TVPA applies to torture victims and victims of extrajudicial killings. In practice the TVPA has mainly been used to file claims against states designated by the US government as supporters of terrorism.

2. The Human Rights Act 1998, in conjunction with the jurisprudence of the European Court of Human Rights, promises protection to those tortured for non–Refugee Convention reasons, to those persecuted by non-state actors, and perhaps most important, unlike the Refugee Convention, provides absolute protection, that cannot be derogated for any reason.

3. In particular, it has had an agreement with the Medical Foundation for the Care of Victims of Torture that places all cases that have been accepted for assessment by the Medical Foundation on hold and accepts that torture victims should not be placed in immigration detention (UKBA 2009).

4. *Horvath v Secretary of State for the Home Department* [2000] 3 WLR 379, [2000] Imm AR 552, [2000] UKHL 37, [2001] 1 AC 489, [2000] INLR 239, [2000] 3 All ER 577, [2001] AC 489. The Home Office initially tried to argue that claims under the Human Rights Act should be proved "beyond reasonable doubt," but the courts ruled that refugee and human rights claims should have the same standard as refugee claims. *Kacaj (Article 3, Standard of Proof, Non-State Actors) Albania* [2001] UKIAT 18, [2001] INLR 354, [2002] Imm AR 213, [2001] UKIAT 01TH0634, [2001] UKIAT 00018. In immigration cases, Article 3 claims before the European Court of Human Rights are decided on the standard of "beyond reasonable doubt." However, where a person has been in detention and comes out with injuries, the burden of proof is reversed and the state must show that the injuries did not result from ill-treatment (*Tomasi v France* [1993] 15 EHRR 1, [1992] ECHR 53, (1993) 15 EHRR 1, 15 EHRR 1).

5. *FS and Others (Iran–Christian Converts) Iran* [2004] UKIAT 00303, [2004] UKIAT 303 [187].

6. In England and Wales by the Legal Services Commission and in Scotland by the Scottish Legal Aid Board (SLAB).

7. For a general discussion on the political commitments of lawyers, see Sarat and Scheingold (1998).

8. UN Convention Relating to the Status of Refugees, 1951, Article 1A(2).

9. In *Soering v United Kingdom* 11 EHRR 439, [1989] ECHR 14038/88, [1989] ECHR 14, [1989] 11 EHRR 439, (1989) 11 EHRR 439, the European Court of Human Rights ruled that the principle of non-refoulement was inherent within Article 3 of the European Convention, building on the UN Convention Against Torture 1984.

10. *Chahal v United Kingdom* [1996] ECHR 54, 23 EHRR 413, (1997) 23 EHRR 413, 1 BHRC 405, (1996) 23 EHRR 413.

11. *Chahal v United Kingdom* [1996] ECHR 54, 23 EHRR 413, 1997) 23 EHRR 413, 1 BHRC 405, (1996) 23 EHRR 413.

12. Separate laws were passed for Scotland and Northern Ireland.

13. *FS and Others (Iran–Christian Converts) Iran* [2004] UKIAT 00303, [2004] UKIAT 303, [145]. See also *SF (Article 3–Prison Conditions) Iran* [2002] UKIAT 00973, [2002] UKIAT 973 [15].

14. *SF (Article 3–Prison Conditions) Iran* [2002] UKIAT 00973, [2002] UKIAT 973; *FT (Fair Trial–Adultery) Iran* [2002] UKIAT 7576, [2002] UKIAT 07576; *HA (Article 3–Refugee–Adultery–Punishment) Iran* [2003] UKIAT 95, [2003] UKIAT 00095; *BE (Military Service–Punishment–Landmines) Iran* [2004] UKIAT 00183, [2004] UKIAT 183; *RM and BB (Homosexuals) Iran* [2005] UKIAT 00117, [2005] UKAIT 00117, [2005] UKIAT 117.

15. *FS and Others (Iran–Christian Converts) Iran* [2004] UKIAT 00303, [2004] UKIAT 303 [169]; *SF (Article 3–Prison Conditions) Iran* [2002] UKIAT 00973, [2002] UKIAT 973 [11].

16. *RT (Medical Reports–Causation of Scarring) Sri Lanka* [2008] UKAIT 00009, [2008] UKAIT 9 [7].

17. The UK Border Agency statistics suggest that Iranian cases are fairly average in terms of their refusal rates at the initial claim and appeal stages. In 2008, 21 percent of all asylum and immigration appeals involving Iranians were allowed, compared to the overall average of 23 percent. This of course cannot be adjusted for the details and nature of the claim (Home Office 2009).

18. Under the Surendran Guidelines, see *MNM (Surendran Guidelines for Adjudicators) Kenya* [2000] INLR 576, [2000] UKIAT 5, [2000] UKIAT 00TH02423, [2000] UKIAT 00005.

19. There are repeated calls from lawyers for the tribunal to produce statistics of the refusal rates of specific judges and hearing centers. However, unlike in the United States and Canada, the British court system refuses to produce those statistics. Such an analysis might be able to show that it is easier to win cases before some judges than before others, and if accompanied by some kind of qualitative analysis might be able to show that particular types of cases are easier to win than others. However, it would not add certainty to individual cases, as statistics would demonstrate general trends rather than ironclad rules.

20. Interview with lawyer, 10 July 2009.

21. The origins of this common informal assumption can be found in a US Supreme Court decision: *I.N.S. v Cardoza-Fonseca*, 67 U.S. 407 (1987), 453.

22. Asylum and Immigration Tribunal Procedure Rules, SJ 230/205 r 51(1)0.

23. *Karanakaran v Secretary of State for the Home Department* [2000] Imm AR 271, [2000] INLR 122, [2000] 3 All ER 449, [2000] EWCA Civ 11 [477–479].

24. *Karanakaran v Secretary of State for the Home Department* [2000] Imm AR 271, [2000] INLR 122, [2000] 3 All ER 449, [2000] EWCA Civ 11.

25. *HF (Algeria) v Secretary of State for the Home Department* [2007] EWCA Civ 445, [25].

26. *MM (DRC–Plausibility) Democratic Republic of Congo* [2005] UKIAT 00019, [2005] UKAIT 00019, [2005] UKIAT 19 [16]

27. *MM (DRC–Plausibility) Democratic Republic of Congo* [2005] UKIAT 00019, [2005] UKAIT 00019, [2005] UKIAT 19 [15].

28. I am indebted to Robert Thomas for this point.

29. *SM (Section 8: Judge's Process) Iran* [2005] UKAIT 00116.

30. Indeed, judges are expressly told that demeanor is an unreliable way to assess credibility. *MM (DRC–Plausibility) Democratic Republic of Congo* [2005] UKIAT 00019, [2005] UKAIT 00019, [2005] UKIAT 19.

31. For more on the issues raised by credibility assessments, see Beard and Noll (2009), Kagan (2003), Millbank (2009), Thomas (2006).

32. See, for example, *MS (Iran) v Secretary of State for the Home Department* [2007] EWCA Civ 271; *Y v Secretary of State for the Home Department* [2006] EWCA Civ 1223.

33. *A v Secretary of State for the Home Department (Pakistan)* [2002] UKIAT 439, 2002 Imm AR 318, [2002] INLR 345, [2002] UKIAT 00439, [2002] Imm AR 318 [31].

34. See, for example, *Kesharvaz v Secretary of State for the Home Department* (unreported 16 September 2009) (AIT); *Mohammed v Secretary of State for the Home Department* (unreported 10 July 2008) (AIT); *Ali v Secretary of State for the Home Department* (unreported 13 December 2006) (AIT).

35. Immigration Rules (1994 HC 395) r 339K.

36. *HE (DRC–Credibility and Psychiatric Reports) Democratic Republic of Congo* [2005] Imm AR 119, [2004] UKIAT 321, [2004] UKIAT 00321 [16].

37. Interview with lawyer, 24 August 2009.

38. *Slimani (Content of Adjudicator Determination) Algeria* [2001] UKIAT 9, [2001] UKIAT 00009, [2001] UKIAT 01TH00092 [17].

39. The case law says that a judge can dismiss a psychiatric diagnosis when making negative credibility findings but must give reasons for doing so. *BN (Psychiatric Evidence–Discrepancies) Albania* [2010] UKUT 279 (IAC).

40. See, for example, *Isa v Secretary of State for the Home Department* (unreported 17 April 2008) (AIT); *Kiesa v Secretary of State for the Home Department* (unreported 30 June 2005) (AIT); *Bashir v Secretary of State for the Home Department* (unreported 27 April 2007) (AIT).

41. *A v Secretary of State for the Home Department (Turkey)* [2003] UKIAT 61, [2003] UKIAT 00061 [15].

42. Under Section 7 of the Human Rights Act 1998, a person can bring a claim concerning the rights and protections in the European Convention on Human Rights in conjunction with other claims or as a freestanding claim.

43. Personal communication with Graham Virgo, 28 October 2010; personal communication with Richard Hermer QC, 28 October 2010.

44. Personal communication with Michael Crystal QC, 1 November 2010.

45. *Jones v Ministry of Interior for the Kingdom of Saudi Arabia & Ors* [2006] 2 WLR 1424, [2007] 1 All ER 113, [2007] 1 AC 270, [2006] UKHL 26.

46. Interview with judge, 8 October 2009.

Chapter 3

1. Memorandum for Alberto R. Gonzales, counsel to the president Re Standards of Conduct for Interrogation under 18 U.S.C. §§ 2340–2340A, pp 6–7.

2. *Ireland v United Kingdom*, App no 5310/71 (ECtHR, 18 January 1978), para 167.

3. Such reports became particularly important following a series of cases in the 1990s that ruled that Sri Lankan Tamils could be at risk simply for having scars if they were picked up by the army. *SN (Scarring–Bribes–LTTE–Reprisals) Sri Lanka* [2003] UKIAT 00150, [2003] UKIAT 150. The cases hinged on the issue

of whether Sri Lankan Tamils were at risk from the military simply because they had observable scars that could indicate they had been involved in armed conflict or were victims of torture.

4. Names and details of both the client and the doctor have been changed to protect anonymity.

5. Interview with Yoav Landau-Pope, 28 November 2008.

6. Interview with Michael Peel, 22 October 2008.

7. As one doctor pointed out to me, a great deal of medical research is carried out without randomized controlled trials, which in many cases would simply be unethical. As he said, "We treat children with anaphylactic shock with adrenalin. There might be better drugs for doing this, but which parent is going to take the risk and let you test this out?"

8. *RT (Medical Reports–Causation of Scarring) Sri Lanka* [2008] UKAIT 00009.

9. *RT (Medical Reports–Causation of Scarring) Sri Lanka* [2008] 00009 [42].

10. For a similar technique used by Forensic Medical Examiners with rape survivors, see Rees (no date).

11. Interview with doctor, 4 October 2008.

12. *RT (Medical Reports—Causation of Scarring) Sri Lanka* [2008] UKAIT 00009.

13. Interview with doctor, 10 November 2008.

14. Interview with psychologist, 18 November 2008.

15. Interview with therapist, 1 June 2010.

16. Some differences exist, however, between PTSD as set out in the ICD-10 (the most recent version of the ICD) and the DSM-IV. Unlike the DSM-IV, ICD-10 requires no emotional reaction to the initial stressor and requires no symptoms of avoidance and detachment. The ICD-10 also requires that symptoms arise within six months, rather than the one month of the DSM-IV. There is a debate about whether these differences are clinically significant, but they can result in differences in diagnosis. See Peters, Slade, and Andrews (1999); Peters et al. (2006); Andrews, Slade, and Peters (1999).

17. The Home Office and many judges have argued that only psychiatrists can diagnose PTSD, a claim disputed by many other doctors and psychologists.

18. Leigh Neal, Notes for Assessing Psychiatric Injury in Asylum Seekers, no date, on file with author.

19. Stuart Turner, A General Response to a Report by Dr. Leigh Anthony Neal, 2002, on file with author.

20. Interview with psychiatrist, 10 November 2008.

21. In an attempt to respond to some of the criticisms of the diagnosis of PTSD, it has been suggested that a new disorder, known as complex-PTSD, should be included in the DSM-V, due in 2012. Straightforward PTSD, it is argued, works best as a diagnosis for those who have been exposed to a single traumatic event, such as an earthquake or a plane crash. However, many people, whether they are victims of domestic violence or are tortured prisoners, are exposed to repeated and prolonged traumas, which develop into "an insidious, progressive form of post-traumatic stress disorder that evades and erodes the personality" (Herman 2001, 86). Even complex-PTSD, though, does not enable us to talk specifically about torture as a form of trauma. Instead, it narrows down the scope one degree.

22. Interview with psychologist, 14 November 2008.

23. Interview with Yoav Landau-Pope, 28 November 2008.

24. Interview with doctor, 12 March 2009.

25. Interview with psychiatrist, 10 November 2008.

26. Personal communication with doctor, 24 November 2010.

27. *HY (Medical Evidence) Turkey* [2004] UKIAT 00048.

28. Interview with doctor, 4 September 2008.

29. Personal communication with doctor, 24 November 2010.

30. *HE (DRC–Credibility and Psychiatric Reports) DRC* [2004] UKIAT 00321, [17].

31. *HE (DRC–Credibility and Psychiatric Reports) DRC* [2004] UKIAT 00321, [20].

32. As Elizabeth Davis has argued, a concern with the implications of lying has been particularly important in the history of psychiatry (2010).

33. Interview with doctor, 12 March 2009.

34. For examination of the sense of duplicitousness felt by UNHCR workers, see Sandvik (2009).

35. One result of this is that if a client does not know how a particular injury was sustained, it can be difficult to give an opinion on causation. There is a reliance on survivors being able to pinpoint particular blows and their resulting injuries—for example, when scars that can be examined were not necessarily the result of the blows felt to be most significant at the point of their infliction.

36. Interview with doctor, 12 March 2009.

37. *SN (Medical and Corroborative Evidence–Credibility–Article 3) Kenya* [2004] UKIAT 00053 [7].

38. Interview with doctor, 17 November 2008. Interestingly, in contrast, the Dutch anti-torture movement, following the recommendation of the Istanbul Protocol, has decided that photographs can be a powerful form of evidence (Park and Oomen 2010).

39. Interview with doctor, 17 November 2008.

Chapter 4

1. *Fernandez v Government of Singapore* HL 1971 ([1971] 1 WLR 987, [1971] 2 All ER 691).

2. *Ullah, R (on the Application of) v Special Adjudicator* [2004] INLR 381, [2004] 3 All ER 785, [2004] 2 AC 323, [2004] UKHL 26, [2004] UKHRR 995, [2004] 3 WLR 23 [24]. Similarly, the European Court of Human Rights has ruled that the key question is whether "substantial grounds have been shown for believing in the existence of a real risk of treatment contrary to Article 3 of the European Convention on Human Rights." *Soering v United Kingdom* 11 EHRR 439, [1989] ECHR 14038/88, [1989] ECHR 14, [1989] 11 EHRR 439, (1989) 11 EHRR 439, para 91.

3. Pseudonyms were used in the cases to reduce the risk of any future retribution against the accused and their families.

4. *U v Secretary of State for the Home Department* [2007] UKSIAC 32/2005 [9].

5. *U v Secretary of State for the Home Department* [2007] UKSIAC 32/2005 [6].

6. *U v Secretary of State for the Home Department* [2007] UKSIAC 32/2005 [10].

7. Most details of this case are taken from *BB v Secretary of State for the Home Department* [2007] UKSIAC/29/2005..

8. In 2004, the United States requested the extradition of Abu-Hamza for his role in trying to set up a "terrorist training camp" in Oregon.

9. United Nations Security Council Resolution 1276 (1999).

10. *BB v Secretary of State for the Home Department* [2005] UKSIAC 39/2005; *U v Secretary of State for the Home Department* [2007] UKSIAC 32/2005.

11. There is only one vague mention of risk in the 1992 UNHCR *Handbook on Procedures and Criteria for Determining Refugee Status Under the 1951 Convention and the 1967 Protocol Relating to the Status of Refugees*. The first mention of risk in refugee determinations in British case law is in *Bugdaycay v Secretary of State for the Home Department* [1987] AC 514, [1986] UKHL 3, [1987] 1 All ER 940. The first sustained analysis of the meanings of risk came the following year in *Sivakumuran, R (on the application of) v Secretary of State for the Home Department* [1988] AC 958, [1987] UKHL 1, [1988] 1 All ER 193, [1988] Imm AR 147, [1988] 2 WLR 92.

12. As Sheila Jasanoff has argued elsewhere, formal risk analysis is often used by governmental agencies once their decisions are subjected to judicial scrutiny (1990, 66).

13. *Youssef v Secretary of State for the Home Department* [2004] EWHC 1884 (QB) [14].

14. *Youssef v Secretary of State for the Home Department* [2004] EWHC 1884 (QB) [14].

15. Interview with Home Office lawyer, 19 October 2009.

16. *Saadi v Italy* (2009) 49 EHRR 30, [2008] INLR 621, 49 EHRR 30, [2008] ECHR 179, para 32.

17. *Saadi v Italy* (2009) 49 EHRR 30, [2008] INLR 621, 49 EHRR 30, [2008] ECHR 179, para 52.

18. *Saadi v Italy* (2009) 49 EHRR 30, [2008] INLR 621, 49 EHRR 30, [2008] ECHR 179, para 55.

19. *Saadi v Italy* (2009) 49 EHRR 30, [2008] INLR 621, 49 EHRR 30, [2008] ECHR 179.

20. *Chahal v United Kingdom* [1996] ECHR 54, 23 EHRR 413, (1997) 23 EHRR 413, 1 BHRC 405, (1996) 23 EHRR 413.

21. *Saadi v Italy* (2009) 49 EHRR 30, [2008] INLR 621, 49 EHRR 30, [2008] ECHR 179, para 122.

22. Observations of the governments of Lithuania, Portugal, Slovakia, and the United Kingdom intervening in the application of *Saadi v Italy*, para 18.

23. *Saadi v Italy* (2009) 49 EHRR 30, [2008] INLR 621, 49 EHRR 30, [2008] ECHR 179, para 139.

24. *Saadi v Italy* (2009) 49 EHRR 30, [2008] INLR 621, 49 EHRR 30, [2008] ECHR 179, concurring opinion of Judge Zupančič, para 2.

25. *Saadi v Italy* (2009) 49 EHRR 30, [2008] INLR 621, 49 EHRR 30, [2008] ECHR 179, para 147.

26. *Saadi v Italy* (2009) 49 EHRR 30, [2008] INLR 621, 49 EHRR 30, [2008] ECHR 179, para 149.

27. In the case of *Chahal*, the United Kingdom had sought to rely on assurances of the Indian government that Chahal would not be ill-treated on return. However, the European Court of Human Rights found that although the assurances were made in good faith, large parts of the security forces in Punjab remained "recalcitrant," and the assurances could therefore not be relied upon.

28. *Youssef v Secretary of State for the Home Department* [2004] EWHC 1884 (QB) [4].

29. *Youssef v Secretary of State for the Home Department* [2004] EWHC 1884 (QB) [14].

30. *Youssef v Secretary of State for the Home Department* [2004] EWHC 1884 (QB) [18].

31. *Youssef v Secretary of State for the Home Department* [2004] EWHC 1884 (QB) [52].

32. Letter from Prime Minister Tony Blair to President Abdelaziz Bouteflika, 11 July 2006; letter from President Abdelaziz Bouteflika to Prime Minister Tony Blair, 11 July 2006.

33. Hansard, House of Lords (HL) Deb 4 Dec 2007, vol 696, col WA 181.

34. Memorandum of Understanding between the Government of the United Kingdom of Great Britain and Northern Ireland and the Government of the Hashemite Kingdom of Jordan Regulating the Provision of Undertakings in Respect of Specified Persons Prior to Deportation, signed 10 August 2005; Memorandum of Understanding between the General People's Committee for Foreign Liaison and International Cooperation of the Great Socialist People's Libyan Arab Jamahiriya and the Foreign and Commonwealth Office of the United Kingdom of Great Britain and Northern Ireland Concerning the Provision of Assurances in Respect of Persons Subject to Deportation, signed 18 October 2005; Memorandum of Understanding between the Government of the United Kingdom of Great Britain and Northern Ireland and the Government of the Lebanese Republic Concerning the Provision of Assurances in Respect of Persons Subject to Deportation, signed 23 December 2005; Memorandum of Understanding between the Government of the United Kingdom of Great Britain and Northern Ireland and the Government of the Federal Democratic Republic of Ethiopia Concerning the Provision of Assurances in Respect of Persons Subject to Deportation, signed 12 December 2008.

35. Interview with Home Office lawyer, 19 October 2009.

36. *Omar Othman v Secretary of State for the Home Department* [2007] UKSIAC 15/2005 [179].

37. Witness statement of Julia A. Hall, no date (on file with author).

38. See also the decision of the ECtHR: *Mamatkulov and Askarov v Turkey* 18 BHRC 203, [2005] ECHR 64, (2005) 41 EHRR 25, 41 EHRR 25.

39. These include the decision that the National Health Service had a duty of care to provide treatment to failed asylum seekers (*A, R (on the application of) v West Middlesex University Hospital NHS Trust* [2008] ACD 50, [2008] EWHC 855 (Admin), [2008] HRLR 29, (2008) 11 CCL Rep 358).

40. *U v Secretary of State for the Home Department* [2007] UKSIAC 32/2005 [13]; *BB v Secretary of State for the Home Department* [2006] UKSIAC 39/2005 [14].

41. *BB v Secretary of State for the Home Department* [2006] UKSIAC 39/2005 [15].

42. *BB v Secretary of State for the Home Department* [2006] UKSIAC 39/2005 [16].

43. *BB v Secretary of State for the Home Department* [2006] UKSIAC 39/2005 [9].

44. *BB v Secretary of State for the Home Department* [2006] UKSIAC 39/2005 [9].

45. *BB v Secretary of State for the Home Department* [2006] UKSIAC 39/2005 [11].

46. *Y, BB and U v Secretary of State for the Home Department* [2007] UKSIAC 32/ 36/39/2005 [10].

47. *Y v Secretary of State for the Home Department* [2006] UKSIAC 36/2004.

48. *Y v Secretary of State for the Home Department* [2006] UKSIAC 36/2004 [181].

49. *Y v Secretary of State for the Home Department* [2006] UKSIAC 36/2004 [201].

50. *U v Secretary of State for the Home Department* [2007] UKSIAC 32/2005 [17].

51. *U v Secretary of State for the Home Department* [2007] UKSIAC 32/2005 [18].

52. *U v Secretary of State for the Home Department* [2007] UKSIAC 32/2005 [19].

53. *BB v Secretary of State for the Home Department* [2006] UKSIAC 39/2005 [8].

54. *Y, BB and U v Secretary of State for the Home Department* [2007] UKSIAC 32/36/39/2005.

55. *Y, BB and U v Secretary of State for the Home Department* [2007] UKSIAC 32/36/39/2005 [9].

56. *Y v Secretary of State for the Home Department* [2006] UKSIAC 36/2004 [205].

57. See, for example, UN Committee Against Torture, CAT/C/41/D/316/2007.

58. *Vilvarajah & Ors v United Kingdom* (1992) 14 EHRR 248, (1991) 14 EHRR 60, (1991) 14 EHRR 248, [1991] ECHR 47, 14 EHRR 248 [111].

59. *Saadi v Italy* (2009) 49 EHRR 30, [2008] INLR 621, 49 EHRR 30, [2008] ECHR 179, para 142.

60. *Karanakaran v Secretary of State for the Home Department* [2000] Imm AR 271, [2000] INLR 122, [2000] 3 All ER 449, [2000] EWCA Civ 11 [47].

61. *Horvath v Secretary of State for the Home Department* [2000] Imm AR 205, [1999] EWCA Civ 3026, [2000] INLR 15.

62. Cited, for example, in *Demirkaya v Secretary of State for the Home Department* [1999] INLR 441, [1999] EWCA Civ 1654, [1999] Imm AR 498 [15].

63. *Karanakaran v Secretary of State for the Home Department* [2000] Imm AR 271, [2000] INLR 122, [2000] 3 All ER 449, [2000] EWCA Civ 11 [82].

64. *Karanakaran v Secretary of State for the Home Department* [2000] Imm AR 271, [2000] INLR 122, [2000] 3 All ER 449, [2000] EWCA Civ 11 [63].

65. *Y, BB and U v Secretary of State for the Home Department* [2007] UKSIAC 32/36/39/2005 [9].

66. *Y, BB and U v Secretary of State for the Home Department* [2007] UKSIAC 32/36/39/2005 [12].

67. *BB v Secretary of State for the Home Department* [2006] UKSIAC 39/2005 [8].

68. *BB v Secretary of State for the Home Department* [2006] UKSIAC 39/2005 [10].

69. The hierarchy of expertise applied here is not universal, see, in contrast, for example, *LP (LTTE area–Tamils–Colombo–risk?) Sri Lanka* [2007] 76, [2007] UKIAT 00076, [2007] UKAIT 00076.

70. *U v Secretary of State for the Home Department* [2007] UKSIAC 32/2005 [35].

71. *U v Secretary of State for the Home Department* [2007] UKSIAC 32/2005 [35].

72. *U v Secretary of State for the Home Department* [2007] UKSIAC 32/2005 [34].

73. *U v Secretary of State for the Home Department* [2007] UKSIAC 32/2005 [31].

74. *Y, BB and U v Secretary of State for the Home Department* [2007] UKSIAC 32/36/39/2005 [22].

75. *BB v Secretary of State for the Home Department* [2006] UKSIAC 39/2005 [6].

76. *BB v Secretary of State for the Home Department* [2006] UKSIAC 39/2005 [18].

77. *BB v Secretary of State for the Home Department* [2006] UKSIAC 39/2005 [18].

78. *BB v Secretary of State for the Home Department* [2006] UKSIAC 39/2005 [21].

79. *BB v Secretary of State for the Home Department* [2006] UKSIAC 39/2005 [17].

80. *U v Secretary of State for the Home Department* [2007] UKSIAC 32/2005 [37].

81. *BB v Secretary of State for the Home Department* [2006] UKSIAC 39/2005 [9].

82. *Y, BB and U v Secretary of State for the Home Department* [2007] UKSIAC 32/36/39/2005 [22].

83. *MT (Algeria) & Ors v Secretary of State for the Home Department* [2008] 2 All ER 786, [2007] UKHRR 1267, [2007] EWCA Civ 808, [2008] 2 WLR 159, [2007] HRLR 41, [2008] QB 533.

84. *MT (Algeria) & Ors v Secretary of State for the Home Department* [2008] 2 All ER 786, [2007] UKHRR 1267, [2007] EWCA Civ 808, [2008] 2 WLR 159, [2007] HRLR 41, [2008] QB 533 [97].

85. For separate, undisclosed reasons, the case was sent back to the SIAC by the Court of Appeal to hear more evidence. The SIAC rejected the new claim and an appeal is expected at the time of writing (*Y, BB and U v Secretary of State for the Home Department* [2007] UKSIAC 32/36/39/2005).

86. *RB (Algeria) v Secretary of State for the Home Department* [2009] UKHL 10, [2009] 2 WLR 512.

87. There are obvious parallels here with Walter Benjamin's distinction between messianic and homogeneous empty time (1992).

88. Ironically, the lawyers who negotiated some of the diplomatic assurances on the British side told me privately that they were uncertain as to the continuity of the assurances. Elections in Lebanon and changes in the Algerian regime might mean they had to be renegotiated. Interview with Home Office lawyer, 19 October 2009. Civil and armed uprisings in North Africa in early 2011 have since completely changed the political picture.

89. *DD and AS v Secretary of State for the Home Department* [2007] UKSIAC 42/2005 [11].

90. *DD and AS v Secretary of State for the Home Department* [2007] UKSIAC 42/50/2005 [339].

91. *DD and AS v Secretary of State for the Home Department* [2007] UKSIAC 42/50/2005 [345].

92. *DD and AS v Secretary of State for the Home Department* [2007] UKSIAC 42/50/2005 [346].

93. *DD and AS v Secretary of State for the Home Department* [2007] UKSIAC 42/50/2005 [348].

94. *Omar Othman v Secretary of State for the Home Department* [2007] UKSIAC 15/2005 [356].

95. Interview with Hugh Southey, 28 July 2010.

Chapter 5

1. *R. v Zardad* [2004] Royal Courts of Justice (unreported case), Prosecution Opening Note, p 1.

2. *Filartiga v Pena-Irala*, 630 F.2d 876, 878 (2d Cir. 1980).

3. *Ireland v United Kingdom* [1978] 2 EHRR 25, [1978] ECHR 1, 2 EHRR 25 2 EHRR 25, (1980) 2 EHRR 25, para 167.

4. At the time of writing in late 2010 it is unclear whether allegations of complicity by MI5 and MI6 officers in torture will lead to criminal prosecutions.

5. In the United States, the Leiber Code of 1863, often seen as the first real codification of the customary laws of war, stressed that "military necessity does not admit of cruelty . . . nor of torture to extort confessions" (General Orders No. 100, Instructions for the Government of Armies of the United States in the Field, 24 April 1863).

6. Geneva Convention 1, Article 50; Geneva Convention II, Article 51; Geneva Convention III, Article 130; Geneva Convention IV, Article 147.

7. Statute of the International Tribunal for the Prosecution of Persons Responsible for Serious Violations of International Humanitarian Law Committed in the Territory of the Former Yugoslavia since 1991 (1993).

8. The Rome Statute of the International Criminal Court (1998) Articles 7 and 8.

9. UN Convention Against Torture 1984, Article 4 and Article 5.2.

10. See, for example, Concluding Observations of the Committee Against Torture, Australia, 22 May 2008, CAT/C/AUS/CO/3, para 8.

11. Criminal Justice Act 1988 § 134.

12. Criminal Justice Act 1988 § 134.1.

13. The UN Convention Against Torture 1984 requires that torture is inflicted "for such purposes as obtaining from him or a third person information or a confession, punishing him for an act he or a third person has committed or is suspected of having committed, or intimidating or coercing him or a third person, or for any reason based on discrimination of any kind" (Article 1).

14. United Nations Convention Against Torture, 1984, Article 1.

15. Criminal Justice Act 1988 § 134.5.

16. UN Committee Against Torture, Conclusions and Recommendations of the Committee against Torture, United Kingdom of Great Britain and Northern Ireland, Crown Dependencies and Overseas Territories, 10 Dec 2004, CAT/C/CR/33/3, para 4(a)(ii).

17. Geneva Conventions Act, 1957, § 1(1).

18. British law provides for universal jurisdiction over the crimes of torture, hostage taking, participating in the slave trade, offenses against United Nations personnel, piracy, and grave breaches of the 1949 Geneva Conventions and its first additional Protocol. For a discussion of these issues, see JCHR (2009).

19. *Commissioner of Police for the Metropolis and Others, Ex Parte Pinochet* [2000] 1 AC 147, [1999] 2 All ER 97, [1999] UKHL 17, [1999] 2 WLR 827.

20. Interview with investigating police officers, 4 March 2010 and 30 March 2010.

21. Goldsmith, however, was not present for the rest of the trial.

22. *R. v Zardad* [2005] (unreported case), prosecution opening note, p 5 (on file with author).

23. *R. v Zardad*, court transcript, 9 June 2005, p 103.

24. *R. v Zardad*, court transcript, 12 June 2005, pp 20–27.

25. *R. v Zardad*, court transcript, 13 July 2005, p 20.

26. *R. v Zardad*, court transcript, 4 July 2005, p 6.

27. *R. v Zardad*, court transcript, 4 July 2005, p 15.

28. Interview with James Lewis, 5 March 2010.

29. *R. v Zardad*, court transcript, 11 July 2005, p 30.

30. *R. v Zardad*, court transcript, 12 July 2005, p 40.

31. *R. v Zardad*, court transcript, 5 July 2005, p 53.

32. *R. v Zardad* [2005] Royal Courts of Justice (unreported case).

33. *R. v Zardad*, court transcript, 12 July 2005, pp 39–40.

34. *R. v Zardad*, court transcript, 11 July 2005, p 94.

35. *R. v Zardad*, court transcript, 11 July 2005, p 121.

36. Interview with James O'Keeffe and Sara Alessandrini, 24 February 2010.

37. Interview with Paul Taylor, 1 March 2010.

38. *R. v Zardad*, court transcript, sentencing, pp 3–4.

39. Witness statement of Colonel Jorge Emanuel Mendonca, to Baha Mousa Inquiry, no date, p 48. Available at http://www.bahamousainquiry.org/ (accessed 22 January 2011).

40. Most details of the investigation are taken from evidence presented in a case against the Ministry of Defence, alleging that the investigation of the death of Baha Mousa was inadequate: *Al Skeini & Ors, R (on the application of) v Secretary of State for Defence* [2007] Inquest LR 168, [2007] 3 All ER 685, [2008] AC 153, [2008] 1 AC 153, [2007] UKHRR 955, [2007] HRLR 31, [2007] 3 WLR 33, 22 BHRC 518, [2007] UKHL 26.

41. Witness statement of Ian Rowland Hill to Baha Mousa Inquiry, 22 May 2009, p 4. Available at http://www.bahamousainquiry.org/ (accessed 21 January 2011).

42. The "Guildford Four" were convicted in 1976 for involvement in a series of bombing attacks across England. They were released on appeal in 1989, after the judge ruled that the investigating police officers had fabricated much of their evidence. Three British police officers were charged over the incident, but none was convicted.

43. *R. v Payne,* court-martial transcript, 19 September 2006, pp 33–36.

44. International Criminal Court Act 2001, § 51(1).

45. International Criminal Court Act 2001 (Elements of Crimes) Regulations, Article 8(2)(a)(iii)-1.

46. *R. v Payne,* court-martial transcript, 21 September 2006, p 81.

47. *R. v Payne,* court-martial transcript, 7 September 2006, p 4.

48. *R. v Payne,* court-martial transcript, 7 September 2006, p 6.

49. *R. v Payne,* court-martial transcript, 8 January 2007, pp 72–71.

50. *R. v Payne,* court-martial transcript, 20 September 2006, p 9.

51. *R. v Payne,* court-martial transcript, 19 September 2006, p 118.

52. *R. v Payne,* court-martial transcript, 13 February 2007, p 12.

53. *R. v Payne,* court-martial transcript, 22 September 2006, p 42.

54. *R. v Payne,* court-martial transcript, 21 September 2006, pp 22–25.

55. *R. v Payne,* court-martial transcript, 22 September 2006, p 81.

56. *R. v Payne,* court-martial transcript, 22 September 2006, p 83.

57. *R. v Payne,* court-martial transcript, 21 September 2006, pp 12–13.

58. *R. v Payne* court-martial transcript, 8 January 2007, p 16.

59. Two of the accused were acquitted after a full trial.

60. *R. v Payne,* court-martial transcript, 13 February 2007, p 6.

61. *R. v Payne,* court-martial transcript, 13 February 2007, pp 18–12.

62. *Al Skeini & Ors, R (on the application of) v Secretary of State for Defence* [2007] Inquest LR 168, [2007] 3 All ER 685, [2008] AC 153, [2008] 1 AC 153, [2007] UKHRR 955, [2007] HRLR 31, [2007] 3 WLR 33, 22 BHRC 518, [2007] UKHL 26.

63. Hansard, HC 27 March 2008, col 13 WS.

64. *R. v Payne,* court-martial transcript, 22 September 2006, p 94.

65. *R. v Zardad,* court transcript, 9 June 2005, p 2.

66. *R. v Zardad,* court transcript, 11 June 2005, p 84.

67. *R. v Zardad,* court transcript, 8 June 2005, p 17.

68. Interview with Paul Taylor, 1 March 2010.

69. Interview with Paul Taylor, 1 March 2010.

70. This has since been replaced by the Armed Forces Act 2006.

71. Personal communication with military lawyer, 27 July 2010.

72. International Criminal Court Act 2001 (Elements of Crimes) Regulations, Article 8(2)(a)(iii)-1.

73. Personal communication with military lawyer, 20 May 2010.

74. *A & Ors v Secretary of State for the Home Department* [2006] 1 All ER 575, 19 BHRC 441, [2006] UKHRR 225, [2006] HRLR 6, [2006] 2 AC 221, [2005] UKHL 71, [2005] 3 WLR 1249 [53], [97].

75. Personal communication with military lawyer, 27 July 2010.

76. For a discussion of the role of character in judgments about responsibility, see Lacey (2007) and Tadros (2005).

77. *R. v Zardad*, court transcript, 12 July 2005, pp 39–40.

78. *R. v Zardad*, court transcript, 13 July 2005, p 35.

79. *R. v Zardad*, court transcript, 9 June 2005, p 6.

80. *R. v Zardad*, court transcript, 9 June 2005, p 5.

81. *R. v Zardad*, court transcript, 12 July 2005, p 16.

82. *R. v Payne*, court-martial transcript, 16 November 2006, p 180.

83. *R. v Payne*, court-martial transcript, 23 November 2006, pp 89–92.

84. *R. v Payne*, court-martial transcript, 23 September 2006, p 4.

85. *R. v Zardad*, court transcript, 9 June 2005, p 6.

86. Interview with police officer, 30 March 2010.

87. Court transcript, 6 July 2005, p 33.

88. Interview with prosecutor, 4 March 2010.

89. Interview with prosecutor, 30 March 2010.

90. Personal communication with military lawyer, 27 July 2010.

91. US *federal Extraterritorial Torture Statute*, 18 USC § 2340A.

92. International criminal law does not require the involvement of a public official. It is only the Criminal Justice Act 1988, with its origins in human rights law, that does so.

93. Such as General Mile Mrkšić of the Yugoslav National Army, and Dragan Nikolić, the commander of the Sušica Detention Camp.

94. *Prosecutor v Dragoljub Kunarac, Radomir Kovac and Zoran Vukovic (Appeal)*, International Criminal Tribunal for the former Yugoslavia, 12 June 2002 IT-96–23& IT-96–23/1-A, para 150. See also Burchard (2008).

95. I am indebted to Richard Wilson for this point.

Chapter 6

1. On the relationship between NGOs and the UN system more broadly, see Keck and Sikkink (1998) and Merry (2006a).

2. AR v Secretary of State for the Home Department [2004] UKSIAC 3/2002 [7].

3. Anti-terrorism, Crime and Security Act 2001, Part 4, § 21.

4. Anti-terrorism, Crime and Security Act 2001, Part 4, § 23.

5. In order to do so, the British government had also announced that they were derogating from Article 5 of the European Convention on Human Rights, which guarantees the right to liberty. Although their detention was being reviewed by a tribunal (SIAC), much of the evidence was secret and not revealed to the detainees or their lawyers.

6. In addition to visiting Belmarsh Prison, the delegation visited Highdown Prison, where other people detained under ATCSA were also being held.

7. CPT/Inf (2003) 18, para 12. Committee for the Prevention of Torture and Inhuman or Degrading Treatment or Punishment paper reports are available at http://www.cpt.coe.int/en/ (accessed 20 Jan 2011).

8. CPT/Inf (2003) 18, paras 15 and 17.

9. CPT/Inf (2003) 18.

10. CPT/Inf (2003) 18, para 27.

11. CPT/Inf (2003) 18, para 17.

12. CPT/Inf (2003) 18, para 16.

13. *P v Secretary of State for the Home Department* [2004] UKSIAC 20/2002 [2].

14. CPT/Inf (2005) 11, para fn. 7.

15. CPT/Inf (2005) 11, para 24.

16. CPT/Inf (2005) 11, para 7.

17. CPT/Inf (2005) 11, para 19.

18. *A & Ors v Secretary of State for the Home Department* [2006] 1 All ER 575, 19 BHRC 441, [2006] UKHRR 225, [2006] HRLR 6, [2006] 2 AC 221, [2005] UKHL 71, [2005] 3 WLR 1249.

19. CPT/Inf (2005) 10, para 15.

20. A new unit was apparently also refurbished, but the detainees refused to be moved there. CPT/Inf (2005) 10, para 42. Similar recommendations were made by HM Chief Inspector of Prisons (HMIP 2003).

21. CPT/Inf (2005) 10, para 81.

22. CPT/Inf (2005) 10, para 70.

23. Along with its formal sessions, the CAT establishes two parallel mechanisms. The first is an optional system of complaints, known as communications, by private individuals about specific incidences of torture. Despite constant requests by the Committee Against Torture, the United Kingdom has not opted into the individual complaints system. The second is a "confidential inquiry" by one of the CAT members. Committee members have only used this process in three cases (Brazil, Egypt, and Turkey).

24. UN Convention Against Torture and Other Cruel, Inhuman or Degrading Treatment or Punishment 1984, Article 19.

25. Members are elected every four years by the states that have ratified the CAT. Members are nominated by their states, but once they sit on the committee they are supposed to act independently. The practice has been to have two South American, two African, three European, one North American, one Eastern European, and one Chinese member. Of the ten members in 2008, two worked in NGOs, three as diplomats, three in law schools, and two as judges.

26. The Council of Europe, which predates the European Union and has a wider membership, is also the body that created the European Convention on Human Rights.

27. For a comprehensive analysis of the CPT, see Evans and Morgan (1998).

28. European Convention for the Prevention of Torture and Inhuman or Degrading Treatment or Punishment 1987, Article 1.

29. The CPT must give some notification of its visit, but it does not have to inform in advance the visited state of every detention facility it would like to visit. About twenty countries are visited each year, for periods varying from a few days to a few weeks, and delegations vary in size from four to twelve people, depending on whether it is a periodic or an ad hoc visit.

30. With the exception of Russia and, during the 1990s, Turkey.

31. The CPT draws on the European Convention on Human Rights, the case law of the European Court for Human Rights, the International Covenant on Civil and Political Rights, the UN Convention Against Torture, European Penitentiary Rules, and UN Minimum Standards for the Treatment of Prisoners. See CPT (2002).

32. Optional Protocol to the Convention Against Torture and Other Cruel, Inhuman or Degrading Treatment or Punishment, 2002, Article 1.

33. Interview with Silvia Casale, 3 July 2009.

34. CAT/C/67/Add.2

35. He then went on to set out developments in asylum procedure, conditions in prison, and the outlawing of female genital mutilation, before handing over to an official of the Ministry of Defence. In the light of the revelations from Abu Ghraib, he described the training given to British military personnel and the rules that govern their conduct.

36. CAT/C/SR.624, para 23.

37. CAT/C/SR.624, para 27.

38. CAT/C/CR/33/3, paras 4(a) and 5 (b).

39. Criminal Justice Act 1988 § 134.5.

40. CAT/C/CR/33/3, para 4(d).

41. CAT/C/CR/33/3, paras 4(e) and 5(h).

42. CAT/C/CR/33/3, para 5.

43. Interview with Andreas Mavromatis, 4 May 2007, Geneva.

44. CAT/C/USA/CO/2 para 24.

45. CAT/C/GBR/CO/4/Add 1, para 5.

46. CAT/C/GBR/CO/4/Add 1, paras 21, 33, 49–74.

47. Interview with civil servant, Ministry of Justice, 9 July 2009.

48. Interview with civil servant, 24 June 2009.

49. Interview with Adam Ingram, former Armed Forces minister, 22 September 2009.

50. Interview with Silvia Casale, 3 July 2009.

51. Interview with civil servant, Ministry of Justice, 20 November 2008.

52. Interview with Home Office legal adviser, 19 October 2009.

53. Interview with Lord Carlile, 22 July 2008.

54. Interview with Phil Wheatley, chief executive of NOMS, 20 October 2009.

55. Interview with Benjamin Ward, 10 July 2009.

56. Interview with Silvia Casale, 3 July 2009.

57. Interview with Phil Wheatley, chief executive of NOMS, 20 October 2009.

58. Interview with Eric Metcalf, 4 July 2009.

59. Interview with Silvia Casale, 3 July 2009.

60. Interview with Murray Hunt, legal adviser to the JCHR, 8 July 2009.

61. For a nonimmigration case, see, for example, *Napier, Re Petition for Judicial Review* 2005 1 SC 229, [2005] 1 Prison LR 176, [2004] UKHRR 881, 2004 GWD 14–316, 2004 SLT 555, [2004] ScotCS 100, 2004 SCLR 558. However, the European Court of Human Rights is increasingly referring to the CPT reports as authoritative pieces of evidence about the situation on the ground and they are therefore likely to feed back into domestic case law. For more on the use of CPT recommendations in ECtHR judgments, see Murdoch (2006, 46–51).

62. For a rare example, see *AQ v Secretary of State for the Home Department* [2004] UKSIAC 15/2002.

63. *Jones v Ministry of Interior for the Kingdom of Saudi Arabia & Ors* [2006] 2 WLR 1424, [2007] 1 All ER 113, [2007] 1 AC 270, [2006] UKHL 26 [5].

64. *A & Ors v Secretary of State for the Home Department* [2006] 1 All ER 575, 19 BHRC 441, [2006] UKHRR 225, [2006] HRLR 6, [2006] 2 AC 221, [2005] UKHL 71, [2005] 3 WLR 1249.

65. *A & Ors v Secretary of State for the Home Department* [2005] 2 AC 68, [2004] UKHL 56, [2005] 2 WLR 87.

Conclusion

1. In contrast to empathy ("I feel your pain"), there is no claim to try to stand in the other's shoes (Wilson and Brown 2008).

2. In 1969, the European Commission of Human Rights argued that some prisoners "may tolerate . . . a certain roughness of treatment." The commission was implicitly saying that whether an act counted as torture depended on the subjective expectations of the victim. *Greek Case* (1969) Collection of Decisions of the European Commission of Human Rights (CD).

3. *Selmouni v. France* [1999] ECHR 66, 29 EHRR 403, (2000) 29 EHRR 403, 7 BHRC 1, para 100. The ICTY has taken a similar approach, arguing that there is no absolute threshold of pain or suffering, and the necessary level of severity needs to be assessed in reference to each individual case. For a detailed analysis, see Burchard (2008).

4. *A & Ors v. Secretary of State for the Home Department* [2006] 1 All ER 575, 19 BHRC 441, [2006] UKHRR 225, [2006] HRLR 6, [2006] 2 AC 221, [2005] UKHL 71, [2005] 3 WLR 1249, [126].

5. It is arguable that this is a good thing, as it makes it harder for states to try to play with the line between acceptable and unacceptable levels of suffering. Ambiguity can be constructive.

6. There are obvious comparisons with the prosecution of rape. See Estrich (1986).

7. US *Federal Extraterritorial Torture Statute*, 18 USC § 2340A.

8. See the account of Arar's lawyer, David Cole (2010).

9. These inquiries have resulted in the Taguba report, the ICRC Report on Abu Ghraib, the Schlesinger Report, the Fay/Jones report, the Church Report, the Schmidt Report, the Armed Committee Report, and the ICRC report on Guantanamo.

Bibliography

Aitken, Robert. 2008. *The Aitken Report: An Investigation into Cases of Deliberate Abuse and Unlawful Killing in Iraq in 2003 and 2004*. London: Ministry of Defence.

Allodi, Federico. 1991. "Assessment and Treatment of Torture Victims: A Critical Review." *Journal of Nervous and Mental Disease* 179: 4–11.

Amnesty International. 1968. *Situation in Greece*. London: Amnesty International.

———. 1972. *Report of an Enquiry into Allegations of Ill-Treatment in Northern Ireland*. London: Amnesty International.

———. 1973. *Report on Torture*. London: Gerald Duckworth and Co.

———. 1974. *Workshop on Human Rights: Report and Recommendations of Danish Medical Group*. London: Amnesty International.

———. 1976. *Amnesty International, A Chronology: 1961–1976*. London: Amnesty International.

———. 1977. *Evidence of Torture: Studies by Amnesty International Danish Medical Group*. London: Amnesty International.

———. 2007. "United Kingdom Court Martial Acquittals: Many Questions Remain Unanswered and Further Action Required to Ensure Justice, Press Release, 15 March 2007." http://212.78.226.15/news/news-releases?page=66 (accessed 14 January 2011).

———. 2008a. *Israel and the Occupied Territories (OPT): Briefing to the Committee Against Torture*. London: Amnesty International.

———. 2008b. *United Kingdom: Briefing to the Human Rights Committee*. London: Amnesty International.

Anderson, David. 2005. *Histories of the Hanged: The Dirty War in Kenya and the End of Empire*. New York: W. W. Norton.

Anderson, Paul. 2011. "Selling from the Heart: Ordinary Ethics among Muslim Traders in Aleppo." PhD diss., University of Edinburgh.

Anderson, Warwick. 1992. "The Reasoning of the Strongest: The Polemics of Skill and Science in Medical Diagnosis." *Social Studies of Science* 22: 653–84.

Andrews, Gavin, Tim Slade, and Lorna Peters. 1999. "Classification in Psychiatry: ICD-10 Versus DSM-IV." *British Journal of Psychiatry* 174: 3–5.

Antze, Paul, and Michael Lambek, eds. 1996. *Tense Past: Cultural Essays in Trauma and Memory*. London: Routledge.

Arendt, Hannah. 1973. *On Revolution*. London: Pelican.

Asad, Talal. 2003. *Formations of the Secular: Christianity, Islam, Modernity*. Stanford, Calif.: Stanford University Press.

———. 2004. "Where Are the Margins of the State?" In *Anthropology and the Margins of the State*, edited by Veena Das and Deborah Poole, 279–88. Sante Fe, N.Mex.: School of American Research Press.

Badiou, Alan. 2001. *Ethics: An Essay on the Understanding of Evil.* Translated by Peter Hallward. London: Verso.

Bank, Roland. 2000. "Country-Oriented Procedures under the Convention Against Torture: Towards a New Dynamism." In *The Future of UN Human Rights Treaty Monitoring,* edited by Philip Alston and James Crawford, 145–74. Cambridge: Cambridge University Press.

Barnes, John. 2004. "Expert Evidence: The Judicial Perception in Asylum and Human Rights Appeals." *International Journal of Refugee Law* 16: 349–57.

Barrett, Justine. 2001a. "The Prohibition of Torture under International Law— Part 1: The Institutional Organization." *International Journal of Human Rights* 5: 1–36.

———. 2001b. "The Prohibition of Torture under International Law—Part 2: The Normative Content." *International Journal of Human Rights* 5: 1–29.

Barry, John, and Phillip Jacobsen. 1971. "Brutality? What the Army Is Accused of." *Sunday Times,* 22 August.

Basoglu, Metin. 2006. "Rehabilitation of Traumatised Refugees and Survivors of Torture." *British Medical Journal* 333: 1230–31.

Bass, Gary. 2000. *Stay the Hand of Vengeance: The Politics of War Crimes Tribunals.* Princeton, N.J.: Princeton University Press.

Bayefsky, Anne. 2001. *The UN Human Rights Treaty System: Universality at the Crossroads.* Ardsley, N.Y.: Transnational Publishers.

Beard, Jennifer, and Gregor Noll. 2009. "Parrhesia and Credibility: The Sovereignty of Refugee Status Determination." *Social and Legal Studies* 18: 455–77.

Beccaria, Cesare. 1778. *An Essay on Crimes and Punishments.* Edinburgh: Alexander Donaldson.

Beck, Ulrich. 1992. *Risk Society: Towards a New Modernity.* London: Sage.

———. 2002. "The Terrorist Threat: World Risk Society Revisited." *Theory, Culture & Society* 19: 39–55.

Beeston, Richard, and James Bone. 2007. "Hostage Fears Over Troops Seized by Iran." *The Times,* 24 March.

Benedict, Ruth. 2006. *The Chrysanthemum and the Sword.* New York: Mariner Books.

Benjamin, Walter. 1992. *Illuminations.* Translated by Harry Zohn. New York: Fontana.

Bennett, Jamie. 2005. "Interview with Silvia Casale." *Prison Service Journal* 161: 1–8.

Berlant, Lauren. 2003. "The Subject of True Feeling: Pain, Privacy and Politics." In *Left Legalism / Left Critique,* edited by Wendy Brown and Janet Halley, 105–33. Durham, N.C.: Duke University Press.

Berman, Nathaniel. 2004. "Privileging Combat? Contemporary Conflict and the Legal Construction of War." *Columbia Journal of Transnational Law* 43: 1–71.

Bishop, Patrick. 2004. "Ordinary, Decent Soldiers Doing a Good Job in a Dangerous Place." *Daily Telegraph,* 5 May.

Blackstone, William. 1829. *Commentaries on the Laws of England: Book IV.* London: Sweet.

Bloch, Maurice. 1977. "The Past in the Present and the Past." *Man* 12: 278–92.

Bonafe, Beatrice I. 2007. "Finding a Proper Role for Command Responsibility." *Journal of International Criminal Justice* 5: 599–618.

Bowen, Roderic. 1966. *Report on Procedures for the Arrest, Interrogation and Detention of Suspected Terrorists in Aden 14 November 1966.* Command paper (3165) presented to parliament by the Secretary of State for Foreign Affairs.

Bracha, H. Stefan, and Kentaro Hayashi. 2008. "Torture, Culture, War Zone Exposure, and Posttraumatic Stress Disorder: Criterion A's Bracket Creep." *Archives of General Psychiatry* 65: 115–16.

British Psychological Society. 2010. *Guidelines on Memory and the Law: Recommendations from the Scientific Study of Human Memory*. Leicester: British Psychological Society.

Brown, Wendy. 1995. *States of Injury: Power and Freedom in Late Modernity*. Princeton, N.J.: Princeton University Press.

Buch, Lotte. 2010. "Uncanny Affect Relations, Enduring Absence and the Ordinary in Families of Detainees in the Occupied Palestinian Territory." PhD diss., Institute of Anthropology, University of Copenhagen.

Burchard, Christoph. 2008. "Torture in the Jurisprudence of the Ad Hoc Tribunals: A Critical Assessment." *Journal of International Criminal Justice* 6: 159–82.

Burgers, J. Herman, and Hans Danelius. 1988. *The United Nations Convention Against Torture: A Handbook on the Convention Against Torture and Other Cruel, Inhuman or Degrading Treatment or Punishment*. The Hague: Martinus Nijhoff.

C. de C. Williams, Amanda, and Kristine Amris. 2007. "Pain from Torture." *Pain* 133: 5–8.

Çali, Basak, and Alice Wyss. 2009. "Why Do Democracies Comply with Human Rights Judgments? A Comparative Analysis of the UK, Ireland and Germany." Unpublished working paper.

Campbell, Duncan. 2005. "Watchdog Backs Expulsion of Radicals." *Guardian*, 15 August.

Candea, Matei. 2010. "'I Fell in Love with Carlos the Meerkat': Engagement and Detachment in Human–Animal Relations." *American Ethnologist* 37: 241–48.

Castel, Robert. 1991. "From Dangerousness to Risk." In *The Foucault Effect: Studies in Governmentality*, edited by Graham Burchell, Colin Gordon, and Peter Miller, 281–98. Chicago: University of Chicago Press.

Cavanagh, Thomas. 1998. *Torture and the Eucharist: Theology, Politics and the Body of Christ*. Oxford: Wiley-Blackwell.

Cavell, Stanley. 1987. *Disowning Knowledge in Six Plays of Shakespeare*. Cambridge: Cambridge University Press.

Charlton, J. Edmond, ed. 2005. *Core Curriculum for Professional Education in Pain*. Seattle, Wash.: IASP Press.

Clark, Ann Marie. 2001. *Diplomacy of Conscience: Amnesty International and Changing Human Rights Norms*. Princeton, N.J.: Princeton University Press.

Clarke, Charles. 2005. "Speech Made by Charles Clarke, UK Home Secretary to the European Parliament (Strasbourg), September 7, 2005." http://press.home office.gov.uk/Speeches/speeches-archive/sp-euro-parliament-1005 (accessed 12 June 2008).

Clarke, Kamari Maxine. 2009. *Fictions of Justice: The International Criminal Court and the Challenge of Legal Pluralism in Sub-Saharan Africa*. Cambridge: Cambridge University Press.

Cobain, Ian. 2010. "David Cameron Announces Torture Inquiry: Prime Minister Says the Inquiry, Chaired by Sir Peter Gibson, Will Remove the 'Stain' on Britain's Reputation." *The Guardian*, 6 July.

Cohen, Juliet. 2001. "Errors of Recall and Credibility: Can Omissions and Discrepancies in Successive Statements Reasonably Be Said to Undermine Credibility of Testimony?" *Medico-Legal Journal* 69: 25–34.

Cohen, Stanley. 2000. *States of Denial: Knowing About Atrocities and Suffering*. Cambridge: Polity.

COIS. 2009. "Country of Origin Information Report—Iran 17 March 2009." http://rds.homeoffice.gov.uk/rds/pdfs09/iran-170309.doc (accessed 1 December 2010).

Cole, David. 2010. "Getting Away with Torture." *New York Review of Books*, 14 January.

Commissioners for the Investigation of Alleged Cases of Torture in the Madras Presidency. 1855. *Report of the Commissioners for the Investigation of Alleged Cases of Torture in the Madras Presidency.* Madras: Fort St. George Gazette Press.

Compton, Edmund. 1971. *Report of the Enquiry into Allegations Against the Security Forces of Physical Brutality in Northern Ireland Arising out of the Events of the 9th August, 1971.* Command Paper (4823) presented to parliament by the Secretary of State for the Home Department.

Condron, Stephanie. 2007. "Mendonca Quits Army over Inquiry 'Injustice.'" *Daily Telegraph*, 1 June.

CPT. 2002. *The CPT Standards: "Substantive" Sections of the CPT's General Reports.* Strasbourg: Council of Europe.

———. 2006. *Fifteenth Annual General Report.* Strasbourg: Council of Europe.

Crawford, James. 2000. "The UN Human Rights Treaty System: A System in Crisis?" In *The Future of UN Human Rights Treaty Monitoring*, edited by Philip Alston and James Crawford, 1–12. Cambridge: Cambridge University Press.

Crossland, Zoe. 2009. "Of Clues and Signs: The Dead Body and Its Evidential Traces." *American Anthropologist* 111: 69–80.

Cryer, Robert. 2005. *Prosecuting International Crimes: Selectivity and the International Criminal Law Regime.* Cambridge: Cambridge University Press.

Daily Mail. 2007. "A 'Witch-hunt' That Cost £20m." *Daily Mail*, 14 March.

Dalyell, Tam. 1994. "Obituary: Sir Edmund Compton." *The Independent*, 14 March.

Danielsen, Lis, Tonny Karlsmark, and Henrik Klem Thomsen. 1997. "Diagnosis of Skin Lesions Following Electrical Torture." *Romanian Journal of Legal Medicine* 5: 15–20.

Das, Veena. 1997. *Critical Events: An Anthropological Perspective on Contemporary India.* New Delhi: Oxford University Press.

———. 2007. "Commentary: Trauma and Testimony: Between Law and Discipline." *Ethos* 35: 330–35.

Daston, Lorraine. 1995. "The Moral Economy of Science." *Osiris* 10: 2–24.

Daston, Lorraine, and Peter Galison. 2008. *Objectivity.* New York: Zone Books.

Davis, Elizabeth. 2010. "The Anti-Social Profile: Deception and Intimacy in Greek Psychiatry." *Cultural Anthropology* 25: 130–64.

Dodier, Nicolas. 1997. "Clinical Practice and Procedures in Occupational Medicine: A Study of the Framing of Individuals." In *Difference in Medicine: Unravelling Practice, Techniques and Bodies*, edited by Marc Berg and Annemarie Mol, 53–85. Durham, N.C.: Duke University Press.

Dubois, Page. 1991. *Torture and Truth.* London: Routledge.

Edwards, Alice. 2006. "The 'Feminizing' of Torture Under International Human Rights Law." *Leiden Journal of International Law* 19: 349–91.

Eggleston, Richard. 1978. *Evidence, Proof and Probability.* London: Weidenfeld and Nicolson.

Eitinger, Leo, and Weisaeth, Lars. 1998. "Torture: History, Treatment and Medical Complicity." In *Caring for Victims of Torture*, edited by James Jaranson and Michael Popkin, 3–14. Washington, D.C.: American Psychiatric Press.

Elshtain, Jean Bethke. 2004. "Reflections of the Problem of 'Dirty Hand.'" In *Torture: A Collection*, edited by Sanford Levinson, 80–83. New York: Oxford University Press.

Empson, Rebecca, ed. 2006. *Time, Causality and Prophecy in the Mongolian Cultural Region*. Kent: Global Oriental / University of Hawaii Press.

Estrich, Susan. 1986. "Rape." *Yale Law Journal* 95: 1087–118.

Evans, Malcolm. 2002. "Getting to Grips with Torture." *International Comparative Law Quarterly* 51: 365–83.

Evans, Malcolm, and Rod Morgan. 1998. *Preventing Torture: A Study of the European Convention for the Prevention of Torture and Inhuman or Degrading Treatment or Punishment*. Oxford: Oxford University Press.

Evans-Pritchard, E. E. 1976. *Witchcraft, Oracles and Magic Among the Azande*. Oxford: Clarendon.

Ewald, François. 1991. "Insurance and Risk." In *The Foucault Effect: Studies in Governmentality*, edited by Graham Burchell, Colin Gordan, and Peter Miller, 197–210. London: Harvester Wheatsheaf.

Fassin. Didier. 2005. "Compassion and Repression: The Moral Economy of Immigration Policies in France." *Cultural Anthropology* 20: 363–87.

———. 2007. "Humanitarianism as Politics of Life." *Public Culture* 19: 499–520.

———. 2010. "Critique of Humanitarian Reason." Lecture given at Princeton University, Institute for Advanced Study, 17 February.

Fassin, Didier, and Estelle d'Halluin. 2005. "The Truth from the Body: Medical Certificates as Ultimate Evidence for Asylum Seekers." *American Anthropologist* 107: 597–608.

———. 2007. "Critical Evidence: The Politics of Trauma in French Asylum Policies." *Ethos* 35: 300–329.

Fassin, Didier, and Richard Rechtman. 2009. *The Empire of Trauma: An Inquiry into the Condition of Victimhood*. Princeton, N.J.: Princeton University Press.

Fisk, Robert. 2004. "'They Laughed at Him and Kicked Him More': Who Killed Baha Mousa?" *The Independent*, 15 December.

Ford, Richard T. 1999. "Law's Territory (A History of Jurisdiction)." *Michigan Law Review* 97: 843–930.

Foucault, Michel. 1989. *The Birth of the Clinic: An Archaeology of Medical Perception*. Translated by A. M. Sheridan. London: Routledge.

Franck, Thomas M. 1998. *Fairness in International Law and Institutions*. Oxford: Oxford University Press.

Fumerton, Richard, and Ken Kress. 2001. "Causation and the Law: Preemption, Lawful Sufficiency, and Causal Sufficiency." *Law and Contemporary Problems* 64: 101–22.

Gage, William. 2008. "Chairman's Opening Statement: 15 October 2008. The Baha Mousa Public Inquiry." http://www.bahamousainquiry.org/linkedfiles/baha_mousa/key_documents/prelimstatement.pdf (accessed 1 December 2010).

Gardiner, Gerald. 1972. *Minority Report of the Report of the Committee of Privy Counsellors Appointed to Consider Authorised Procedures for the Interrogation of Persons Suspected of Terrorism*. Command paper (4901) presented to parliament by the prime minister.

Gell, Alfred. 1992. *The Anthropology of Time: Cultural Constructions of Temporal Maps and Images*. Oxford: Berg.

Genefke, Inge. 2008. "Action Against Torture." *New Letters* 74: 69–82.

Goldfeld, Anne, Richard Mollica, Barbara Pesavento, and Stephen Faraone. 1988. "The Physical and Psychological Sequelae of Torture: Symptomatology and Diagnosis." *Journal of the American Medical Association* 259: 2725–29.

Good, Anthony. 2007. *Anthropology and Expertise in the Asylum Courts.* London: Routledge.

———. 2009. "The Taking and Making of Asylum Claims: Credibility Assessments in the British Asylum Courts." Unpublished paper.

Greenberg, Karen. 2006. "The Rule of Law Finds Its Golem: Judicial Torture Then and Now." In *The Torture Debate in America,* edited by Karen Greenberg, 1–10. Cambridge: Cambridge University Press.

Hacking, Ian. 1975. *The Emergence of Probability: A Philosophical Study of Early Ideas About Probability, Induction and Statistical Inference.* Cambridge: Cambridge University Press.

———. 1990. *The Taming of Chance.* Cambridge: Cambridge University Press.

Hafner-Burton, Emilie M. 2008. "Sticks and Stones: Naming and Shaming the Human Rights Enforcement Problem." *International Organization* 62: 689–716.

Hall, Ryan, and Richard Hall. 2007. "Detection of Malingered PTSD: An Overview of Clinical, Psychometric, and Physiological Assessment—Where Do We Stand?" *Journal of Forensic Science* 52: 717–25.

Hammarberg, Thomas. 2006. "Viewpoint: 'Torture Can Never, Ever Be Accepted,' Council of Europe Commissioner on Human Rights, June 27." http://www.coe.int/t/commissioner/Viewpoints/060626_en.asp (accessed 1 December 2010).

Haskell, Thomas. 2000. *Objectivity Is Not Neutrality: Explanatory Schemes in History.* Baltimore: Johns Hopkins University Press.

Hastrup, Kirsten. 2003. "Violence, Suffering and Human Rights: Anthropological Reflection." *Anthropological Theory* 3: 309–23.

Hathaway, James. 1991. *The Law of Refugee Status.* London: Butterworths.

Hathaway, Oona A. 2002. "Do Human Rights Treaties Make a Difference?" *Yale Law Journal* 111: 1935–2042.

Helfer, Laurence R., and Anne-Marie Slaughter. 1997. "Toward a Theory of Effective Supranational Adjudication." *Yale Law Journal* 107: 273–328.

Herman, Judith Lewis. 2001. *Trauma and Recovery: From Domestic Abuse to Political Terror.* London: Pandora.

Hirsh, David. 2003. *Law Against Genocide.* London: Glass House Press.

HMIP. 2003. *Report on a Full Announced Inspection of HM Prison Belmarsh 26 May–4 June 2003 by HM Chief Inspector of Prisons.* London: HMIP.

Home Office. 2006. "Press Release, The New Asylum Model: Swifter Decisions—Faster Removals, 18 January 2006." http://press.homeoffice.gov.uk/press-releases/new-asylum-model-swifter-decisio (accessed 1 November 2009).

———. 2009. *Home Office Statistical Bulletin—Control of Immigration: Statistics, United Kingdom 2008.* London: HMSO.

Honneth, Axel. 1996. *The Struggle for Recognition: The Moral Grammar of Social Conflicts.* Cambridge: Polity

Horowitz, Allan V. 2002. *Creating Mental Illness.* Chicago: Chicago University Press.

House of Commons Home Affairs Select Committee. 2004. *Asylum Applications.* Second Report of the Session 2003/4. London: HMSO.

Howe, Leopold. 1981. "The Social Determination of Knowledge: Maurice Bloch and Balinese Time." *Man* 16: 220–34.

Hughes, Matthew. 2009. "The Banality of Brutality: British Armed Forces and the Repression of the Arab Revolt in Palestine, 1936–39." *English Historical Review* 124: 314–54.

Human Rights Watch. 1998. *Israel's Record of Occupation: Violations of Civil and Political Rights.* New York: Human Rights Watch.

———. 2006. *Dangerous Ambivalence: UK Policy on Torture Since 9/11.* New York: Human Rights Watch.

———. 2008. "US: First Verdict for Overseas Torture—Decision in Trial of Ex-Liberian President's Son Significant for Justice, Press Release October 30 2008." http://www.hrw.org/en/news/2008/10/30/us-first-verdict-overseas-torture (accessed 23 November 2010).

Hunt, Lynn. 2004. "The 19th Century Body and the Origins of Human Rights." *Diogenes* 51: 41–56.

IAC. 2008. *Fit for Purpose Yet? The Independent Asylum Commission's Interim Findings.* London: Independent Asylum Commission.

Ignatieff, Michael. 2005. "Moral Prohibition at a Price." In *Torture: Does It Make Us Safer? Is It Ever OK?* edited by Kenneth Roth and Minky Worden, 18–27. New York: New Press.

Innes, Martin. 2003. *Investigating Murder: Detective Work and the Police Response to Criminal Homicide.* Oxford: Oxford University Press.

IRCT. 2009. *Medical Physical Examination of Alleged Torture Victims: A Practical Guide to the Istanbul Protocol–For Medical Doctors.* Copenhagen: International Rehabilitation Council for Torture Victims.

Jaranson, James. 1995. "Government-Sanctioned Torture: Status of the Rehabilitation Movement." *Transcultural Psychiatric Research Review* 32: 253–86.

———. 1998. "The Science and Politics of Rehabilitating Torture Survivors: An Overview." In *Caring for Victims of Torture*, edited by James Jaranson and Michael Popkin, 14–40. Washington, D.C.: American Psychiatric Press.

Jasanoff, Sheila. 1990. "American Exceptionalism and the Political Acknowledgment of Risk." *Daedalus* 119: 61–81.

———. 1997. *Science at the Bar: Law, Science and Technology in America.* Cambridge, Mass.: Harvard University Press.

JCHR. 2006. *The UN Convention Against Torture (UNCAT). Nineteenth Report of the Session 2005–6, Joint Committee on Human Rights.* London: HMSO.

———. 2009. *Closing the Impunity Gap: UK Law on Genocide and Related Crimes: Twenty-Fourth Report of the Session 2008–09.* London: HMSO.

Jones, Richard. 2003. "Wound and Injury Awareness Amongst Students and Doctors." *Journal of Clinical Forensic Medicine* 10: 231–34

Juhler, Marianne, and Peter Vesti. 1989. "Torture: Diagnosis and Rehabilitation." *Medicine and War* 5: 69–79.

Kagan, Michael. 2003. "Is Truth in the Eye of the Beholder? Objective Credibility Assessment in Refugee Status Determination." *Georgetown Immigration Law Journal* 17: 367–81.

Keck, Margaret, and Kathryn Sikkink. 1998. *Activists Beyond Borders: Advocacy Networks in International Politics.* Ithaca, N.Y.: Cornell University Press.

Keenan, Thomas. 2004. "Mobilizing Shame." *South Atlantic Quarterly* 103: 435–49.

Kennedy, David. 2002. "The International Human Rights Movement: Part of the Problem?" *Harvard Human Rights Journal* 15: 101–25.

———. 2004. *The Dark Side of Virtue: Reassessing International Humanitarianism.* Princeton, N.J.: Princeton University Press.

————. 2006. *Of War and Law.* Princeton, N.J.: Princeton University Press.

————. 2009. *The Rights of Spring: A Memoir of Innocence Abroad.* Princeton, N.J.: Princeton University Press.

Knight, Frank. 2009. *Risk, Uncertainty and Profit.* Mineola, N.Y.: Dover Publications.

Koselleck, Reinhart. 2004. *Futures Past: On the Semantics of Historical Time.* New York: Columbia University Press.

Koskenniemi, Martti. 2002. "Between Impunity and Show Trials." *Max Planck Yearbook of United Nations Law* 6: 1–35.

Kroll, Jerome. 2003. "Posttraumatic Symptoms and the Complexity of Responses to Trauma." *Journal of the American Medical Association* 290: 667–70.

Kumar, Sharad, O. Tandon, and R. Mathur. 2002. "Pain Measurement: A Formidable Task." *Indian Journal of Physiology Pharmacology* 46: 396–406.

Kurasawa, Fuyuki. 2007. *The Work of Global Justice: Human Rights as Practices.* Cambridge: Cambridge University Press.

Lacey, Nicola. 2007. "Space, Time and Function: Intersecting Principles of Responsibility Across the Terrain of Criminal Justice." *Criminal Law and Philosophy* 1: 233–50.

————. 2009. "Historicising Criminalisation: Conceptual and Empirical Issues." *Modern Law Review* 72: 936–60.

Langbein, John. 2006. *Torture and the Law of Proof: Europe and England in the Ancien Régime.* Chicago: University of Chicago Press.

Latour, Bruno. 2004. "Scientific Objects and Legal Objectivity." In *Law, Anthropology, and the Constitution of the Social: Making Persons and Things,* edited by Alain Pottage and Martha Mundy, 73–114. Cambridge: Cambridge University Press.

————. 2009. *The Making of Law: An Ethnography of the Conseil d'État.* Translated by Marina Brilam and Alain Pottage. Cambridge: Polity.

Lauren, Paul. 2003. *The Evolution of International Human Rights: Visions Seen.* Philadelphia: University of Pennsylvania Press.

Lauterpacht, Hersh. 1945. *An International Bill of Rights.* New York: Columbia University Press.

Law, John, and Annemarie Mol, eds. 2002. *Complexities: Social Studies of Knowledge Practices.* Durham, N.C.: Duke University Press.

Levinson, Stanford. 2004. "Contemplating Torture." In *Torture: A Collection,* edited by Stanford Levinson, 23–43. Oxford: Oxford University Press.

Lewis, William Draper. 1945. "The Statement of Essential Human Rights by Representatives of the Principal Cultures of the World." *Proceedings of the American Philosophical Society* 89: 489–94.

Li, Tania Murray. 2007. *The Will to Improve: Governmentality, Development and the Practice of Politics.* Durham, N.C.: Duke University Press.

Liberty. 2006. "Independent Reviewer Calls to Renew Prevention of Terrorism Act 2005, Press Release, February 2." http://www.liberty-human-rights.org.uk/media/press/2006/independent-reviewer-calls-to-renew-prevention-of-terrorism-act-2005.php (accessed 13 October, 2010).

————. 2008. "Press Release: Independent Inquiry Announced into the Circumstances Surrounding the Death of Baha Mousa, 14 May 2008." http://www.liberty-human-rights.org.uk/media/press/2008/independent-inquiry-announced-into-the-circumstances-surrounding-the-death.php (accessed 1 December 2010).

Luban, David. 2006. "Liberalism, Torture and the Ticking Bomb." In *The Torture Debate in America*, edited by Karen Greenberg, 35–83. New York: Cambridge University Press.

Luhrmann, Tanya. 2001. *Of Two Minds: The Growing Disorder in American Psychiatry*. New York: Knopf.

Lyotard, Jean-François. 1989. *The Differend: Phrases in Dispute*. Minneapolis: University of Minnesota Press.

Maklin, Audrey. 2007. "Truth or Consequences: Credibility Determinations in the Refugee Context International." In *Refugee Law and Policy: A Comparative and International Approach*, edited by Karen Musalo, Jennifer Moore, and Richard A. Boswell, 1103–09. Durham, N.C.: Carolina Academic Press.

Makua, Mutua. 2001. "Savages, Victims, and Saviours: The Metaphor of Human Rights." *Harvard International Law Journal* 42: 201–45.

Marsella, Anthony, Matthew Friedman, and E. Huland Spain. 1992. "A Selective Review of the Literature on Ethnocultural Aspects of PTSD." *PTSD Research Quarterly* 2: 1–7.

McBarnett, Doreen. 1983. *Conviction: Law, the State and the Construction of Justice*. London: Macmillan.

McCain, John. "Statement of Senator John McCain Amendment on Army Field Manual, 25 July 2005." http://mccain.senate.gov/ (accessed 12 October 2007).

McGlynn, Clare. 2009. "Rape, Torture and European Convention on Human Rights." *International and Comparative Law Quarterly* 58: 565–95.

McIvor, Ronan J., and Stuart W. Turner. 1995. "Assessment and Treatment Approaches for Survivors of Torture." *British Journal of Psychiatry* 166: 705–11.

Meckled-Garcia, Saladin, and Başak Çali, eds. 2006. *The Legalization of Human Rights: Multidisciplinary Perspectives on Human Rights and Human Rights Law*. London: Routledge.

Meierhenrich, Jens. 2006. "Conspiracy in International Law." *Annual Review of Law and Social Science* 2: 341–57.

Merry, Sally Engle. 2006a. *Human Rights and Gender Violence*. Chicago: University of Chicago Press.

———. 2006b. "Transnational Human Rights and Local Activism: Mapping the Middle." *American Anthropologist* 108: 38–51.

———. 2011. "Measuring the World: Indicators, Human Rights and Global Governance." *Current Anthropology* 52.

Millbank, Jenni. 2009. "The Ring of Truth: A Case Study of Credibility Assessment in Particular Social Group Refugee Determinations." *International Journal of Refugee Law* 21: 1–33.

Ministry of Defence. 2004. "Iraq Abuse Courts-Martial—Latest Information." http://webarchive.nationalarchives.gov.uk/+/http://www.operations.mod.uk/telic/newsItem_id=3141.htm (accessed 23 June 2008).

———. 2007. "Press Release. General Dannatt Speaks after Close of Cpl. Payne Court Martial, 30 April 2007." http://webarchive.nationalarchives.gov.uk/+/http://www.mod.uk/DefenceInternet/DefenceNews/DefencePolicyAndBusiness/GeneralDannattSpeaksAfterCloseOfCplPayneCourtMartial.htm (accessed 1 December 2010).

———. 2008. "MOD Releases Report into Abuse of Iraqi Civilians, Press Release, 25 January." http://webarchive.nationalarchives.gov.uk/+/http://

www.mod.uk/defenceinternet/defencenews/defencepolicyandbusiness/mod
releasesreportintoabuseofiraqicivilians.htm (accessed 1 December 2010).

Mitchell, Sandra. 2010. *Unsimple Truths: Science, Complexity and Policy*. Chicago:
University of Chicago Press.

Mollica, Richard, and Yael Caspi-Yavin. 1992. "Overview: The Assessment and
Diagnosis of Torture Events and Symptoms." In *Torture and Its Consequences:
Current Treatment Approaches*, edited by Metin Basoglu, 38–55. Cambridge:
Cambridge University Press.

Morris, Steven. 2000. "Afghan Warlord Goes to Ground in Suburbia." *Guardian*,
28 July.

Morsink, Johannes. 1999. *The Universal Declaration of Human Rights: Origins, Drafting and Intent*. Philadelphia: University of Pennsylvania Press.

Moyn, Samuel. 2006. "Empathy in History, Empathizing with Humanity." *History
and Theory* 45: 397–415.

———. 2007. "On the Genealogy of Morals." *The Nation*, 16 April.

———. 2010. *Last Utopia: Human Rights in History*. Cambridge, Mass.: Harvard
University Press.

Murdoch, Jim. 2006. *The Treatment of Prisoners: European Standards*. Strasbourg:
Council of Europe.

Nagan, Winston, and Lucie Atkins. 2001. "The International Law of Torture:
From Universal Proscription to Effective Application and Enforcement." *Harvard Human Rights Journal* 14: 87–121

National Audit Office. 2004. *Improving the Speed and Quality of Asylum Decisions*.
London: HMSO.

Naughton, Philippe, and Sean O'Neil. 2010. "Johnson Rails Against Media and
Tories Over 'Baseless' Torture Claims." *The Times*, 12 February.

Normand, Roger, and Sarah Zaidi. 2008. *Human Rights at the UN: The Political
History of Universal Justice*. Bloomington: Indiana University Press.

Norris, Jacob. 2008. "Repression and Rebellion: Britain's Response to the Arab
Revolt in Palestine of 1936–39." *Journal of Imperial and Commonwealth History*
36: 25–45.

Novak, Manfred. 2006. "What Practices Constitute Torture? US and UN Standards." *Human Rights Quarterly* 28: 809–41.

OHCHR. 2004. *Istanbul Protocol: Manual on the Effective Investigation and Documentation of Torture and Other Cruel, Inhuman or Degrading Treatment or Punishment*.
Geneva: OHCHR.

O'Malley, Pat. 2003. "Governable Catastrophes: A Comment on Bougen." *Economy and Society* 32: 275.

OPICC. 2010. *Prosecutorial Strategy, 2009–2012*. The Hague: International Criminal Court.

Park, Rebeka, and Janus Oomen. 2010. "Context, Evidence and Attitude: The
Case for Photography in Medical Examinations of Asylum Seekers in the
Netherlands." *Social Science and Medicine* 71: 228–35.

Parker, Hubert. 1972. *Report of the Committee of Privy Counsellors Appointed to Consider Authorised Procedures for the Interrogation of Persons Suspected of Terrorism*.
Command paper (4901) presented to parliament by the prime minister.

Parry, John. 2005. "Just for Fun: Understanding Torture and Understanding
Abu Ghraib." *Journal of National Security Law and Policy* 1: 252–84.

———. 2010. *Understanding Torture: Law, Violence and Political Identity*. Ann
Arbor: University of Michigan Press.

Penketh, Anne. 2006. "Howells in Row Over 'No-Torture' Memos." *The Independent*, 6 February.

Perrin, Colin. 2004. "Breath from Nowhere: The Silent 'Foundation' of Human Rights." *Social and Legal Studies* 13: 133–51.

Peters, Edward. 1996. *Torture.* Philadelphia: University of Pennsylvania Press.

Peters, Lorna, Cathy Issakidis, Tim Slade, and Gavin Andrews. 2006. "Gender Differences in the Prevalence of DSM-IV and ICD-10 PTSD." *Psychological Medicine* 36: 81–89.

Peters, Lorna, Tim Slade, and Gavin Andrews. 1999. "A Comparison of ICD-10 and DSM-IV Criteria for Post-Traumatic Stress Disorder." *Journal of Traumatic Stress* 12: 335–43.

Piers, Gerhart, and Milton Singer. 1972. *Shame and Guilt: A Psychoanalytic and Cultural Study.* London: W. W. Norton.

Plotkin, Mariano Ben. 2001. *Freud on the Pampas: The Emergence and Development of a Psychoanalytic Culture in Argentina, 1910–1983.* Stanford, Calif.: Stanford University Press.

Porter, Theodore. 1995. *Trust in Numbers: The Pursuit of Objectivity in Science and Public Life.* Princeton, N.J.: Princeton University Press.

Povinelli, Elizabeth. 2002. *The Cunning of Recognition: Indigenous Alterities and the Making of Australian Multiculturalism.* Durham, N.C.: Duke University Press.

Power, Jonathan. 2001. *Like Water on a Stone: The Story of Amnesty International.* London: Allen Lane.

Power, Michael. 2007. *Organized Uncertainty: Designing a World of Risk Management.* Oxford: Oxford University Press.

Pupavac, Vanessa. 2008. "Refugee Advocacy, Traumatic Representations and Political Disenchantment." *Government and Opposition,* 43: 270–92.

Quiroga, Jose, and James Jaranson. 2005. *Politically-Motivated Torture and Its Survivors: A Desk Study Review of the Literature.* Copenhagen: Rehabilitation and Research Centre for Torture Victims.

Ramji-Nogales, Jaya, Andrew Schoenholtz, and Phillip Schrag, eds. 2009. *Refugee Roulette: Disparities in Asylum Adjudication and Proposals for Reform.* New York: New York University Press.

Rasiah, Nathan. 2009. "The Court Martial of Corporal Payne and Others and the Future Landscape of International Criminal Justice." *Journal of International Criminal Justice* 7: 177–99.

RAWA. No date. "Some Reports of Crimes Committed by Zardad in Afghanistan." http://www.rawa.org/zardad-5.htm (accessed 24 November 2009).

Raymont, Sean. 2006. "SAS Soldier Quits Army in Disgust at 'Illegal' American Tactics in Iraq." *Daily Telegraph,* 12 March.

Rees, Gethin. 2010. "'It Is Not for Me to Say Whether Consent Was Given or Not': Forensic Medical Examiners' Construction of 'Neutral Reports' in Rape Cases." *Social and Legal Studies* 19: 371–86.

———. No date. "Morphology Is a Witness Which Doesn't Lie": Diagnosis by Similarity Relation and Analogical Inference in Clinical Forensic Medicine." Unpublished paper.

Reid, John. 2006. "Speech by John Reid, UK Home Secretary, to DEMOS, 9 August 2006." http://press.homeoffice.gov.uk/Speeches/sp-hs-DEMOS-090806 (accessed 16 March 2009).

Rejali, Darius. 2009. *Torture and Democracy.* Princeton, N.J.: Princeton University Press.

Risse, Thomas, Stephen Ropp, and Kathryn Sikkink. 1999. *The Power of Human Rights: International Norms and Domestic Change.* Cambridge: Cambridge University Press.

Robben, Antonius. 2005. *Political Violence and Trauma in Argentina*. Philadelphia: University of Pennsylvania Press.

Rodley, Nigel. 1987. *The Treatment of Prisoners Under International Law.* Oxford: Clarendon Press.

Rojas, John-Paul Ford. 2010. "'Mercy Killing' Mother Is Jailed for Life." *The Independent*, 20 January.

Rorty, Richard. 1993. "Human Rights, Rationality, and Sentimentality." In *On Human Rights: The Oxford Amnesty Lectures 1993*, edited by Stephen Shute and Susan Hurley, 111–33. New York: Basic Books.

Roth, Kenneth. 2004. "Defending Economic, Social and Cultural Rights: Problems Faced by an International Human Rights Organization." *Human Rights Quarterly* 26: 63–73.

Rubin, Gerry. 2005. "Courts Martial from Bad Nenndorf (1948) to Osnabrück (2005)." *RUSI Journal* 150: 52–53.

Sandvik, Kristin Bergtora. 2009. "The Physicality of Legal Consciousness: Suffering and the Production of Credibility in Refugee Resettlement." In *Humanitarianism and Suffering: The Mobilization of Empathy*, edited by Richard Ashby Wilson and Richard Brown, 233–44. New York: Cambridge University Press.

Sarat, Austin, and Stuart Scheingold, eds. 1998. *Cause Lawyering: Political Commitments and Professional Responsibilities*. Oxford: Oxford University Press.

Scarry, Elaine. 1988. *The Body in Pain: The Making and the Unmaking of the World*. Oxford: Oxford University Press.

SCFA. 2008. *Human Rights: Ninth Report of the Session 2007/8, Select Committee on Foreign Affairs*. London: HMSO.

Sedley, Stephen. 2002. "Asylum: Can the Judiciary Maintain Its Independence?" Paper presented at the International Association of Refuge Law Judges, Wellington, New Zealand, October 11–12.

Seidman, Louis Michael. 2005. "Torture's Truth." *University of Chicago Law Review* 72: 881–918.

Seltzer, Abigail, Alex Sklan, and Nimisha Patel. 2006. "Treating Torture Survivors—There Is No 'Quick Fix'—Response to Metin Basoglu, 2006: Rehabilitation of Traumatised Refugees and Survivors of Torture." *British Medical Journal* 333: 1230–31.

Seton, Craig. 1978. "Irish Government Justifies Pursuit of Case by Claiming Use of Torture Now Outlawed in Ulster." *The Times*, 19 January.

Shklar, Judith. 1984. *Ordinary Vices*. Cambridge, Mass.: Harvard University Press.

Shue, Henry. 2004. "Torture." In *Torture: A Collection*, edited by Stanford Levinson, 47–60. New York: Oxford University Press.

Sikkink, Kathryn. 1993. "Human Rights, Principled Issue-Networks, and Sovereignty in Latin America." *International Organization* 47: 411–41.

Simpson, A. W. Brian. 2001. *Human Rights and the End of Empire: Britain and the Genesis of the European Convention*. Oxford: Oxford University Press.

Simpson, Gerry. 2007a. "The Death of Baha Mousa." *Melbourne Journal of International Law* 8: 340–55.

———. 2007b. *Law, War and Crime*. Cambridge: Polity.

Sivakumaran, Sandesh. 2005. "Torture in International Human Rights and International Humanitarian Law: The Actor and the Ad Hoc Tribunals." *Leiden Journal of International Law* 18: 541–56.

Smith, Ellie. 2004. *Right First Time? Home Office Interviewing and Reasons for Refusal Letters*. London: Medical Foundation for the Care of Victims of Torture.

Steinhoff, Uwe. 2006. "Torture: The Case for Dirty Harry against Alan Dershowitz." *Journal of Applied Philosophy* 23: 337–53.

Summerfield, Derek. 1999. "A Critique of Seven Assumptions behind Psychological Trauma Programmes in War-Affected Areas." *Social Science and Medicine* 48: 1449–62.

Sunday Times, 1971. "Catholics Force Inquiry into Ulster Brutality." *The Sunday Times*, 22 August.

Sussman, David. 2005. "Defining Torture." *Case Western Reserve Journal of International Law* 37: 225–30;

Tadros, Victor. 2005. *Criminal Responsibility.* Oxford: Oxford University Press.

Taussig, Michael. 1999. *Defacement: Public Secrecy and the Labor of the Negative.* Stanford, Calif.: Stanford University Press.

Temkin, Jennifer, and Barbara Krahe. 2008. *Sexual Assault and the Justice Gap: A Question of Attitude.* Oxford: Hart.

Thomas, Robert. 2006. "Assessing the Credibility of Asylum Claims: EU and UK Approaches Examined." *European Journal of Migration and Law* 8: 79–96.

———. 2008. "Consistency in Asylum Adjudication: Country Guidance and the Asylum Process in the United Kingdom." *International Journal of Refugee Law* 20: 489–532.

———. 2009. "Refugee Roulette: A UK Perspective." In *Refugee Roulette: Disparities in Asylum Adjudication and Proposals for Reform,* edited by Jaya Ramji-Nogales, Andrew Schoenholtz, and Philip Schrag, 164–86. New York: New York University Press.

Ticktin, Miriam. 2006a. "Medical Humanitarianism in and Beyond France: Breaking Down or Patrolling Borders?" In *Medicine at the Border: Disease, Globalization and Security, 1850 to the Present,* edited by Alison Brashford, 117–35. New York: Palgrave.

———. 2006b. "Where Ethics and Politics Meet: The Violence of Humanitarianism in France." *American Ethnologist* 33: 33–49.

Timerman, Jacobo. 1981. *Prisoner without a Name, Cell without a Number.* New York: Knopf.

Timmermans, Stefan, and Marc Berg. 2003. *The Gold Standard: The Challenge of Evidence-Based Medicine and the Standardization of Health Care.* Philadelphia: Temple University Press.

Times. 2007. "Case Collapses against British Soldiers on Trial for War Crimes Against Iraqis." *The Times,* 15 February.

———. 2008. "Anthony Jennings." *The Times,* 30 January.

Tindale, Christopher. 1996. "The Logic of Torture: A Critical Examination." *Social Theory and Practice* 22: 349–74.

Townsend, Mark. 2005. "'Concerns' over Iraq Abuse Trial." *Guardian,* 16 October.

Turner, Stuart, and Caroline Gorst-Unsworth. 1990. "Psychological Sequelae of Torture: A Descriptive Model." *Journal of Psychiatry* 157: 475–80.

Turner, Victor. 1975. *Revelation and Divination in Ndembu Ritual.* Ithaca, N.Y.: Cornell University Press.

UKBA. No date. "Guidance on 'Considering Human Right Claims.. http:// www.ukba.homeoffice.gov.uk/sitecontent/documents/policyandlaw/asylum processguidance/consideringanddecidingtheclaim/guidance/considering hrclaims.pdf?view=Binary (accessed 1 November 2009).

———. 2009. "API/May 2006 (Re-Branded Jan 2009). The Medical Foundation for the Care of Victims of Torture." http://www.ukba.homeoffice.gov.uk/ sitecontent/documents/policyand law/asylumpol icyinstructions/apis/medi calfoundation.pdf?view=Binary (accessed 1 November 2010).

UNHCR. 1992. *Handbook on Procedures and Criteria for Determining Refugee Status Under the 1951 Convention and the 1967 Protocol Relating to the Status of Refugees.* Geneva: UNHCR.

———. 1998. *Note on Burden and Standard of Proof in Refugee Claims.* Geneva: UNHCR.

———. 2005. *Quality Initiative Project: Second Report to the Minister.* London: UNHCR.

———. 2006. "Note on Diplomatic Assurances and International Refugee Protection. Protection Operations and Legal Advice Section, Division of International Protection Services, Geneva." http://www.unhcr.se/Pdf/protect/Diplomatic_assurances_Int_Ref_protection.pdf (accessed 1 October 2010).

US Department of State. 2003. "Country Reports on Human Rights Practices: Israel and the Occupied Territories." http://www.state.gov/g/drl/rls/hrrpt/2003/27929.htm (accessed 1 October 2009).

———. 2006. "Country Reports on Human Rights Practices: Libya." http://www.state.gov/g/drl/rls/hrrpt/2005/61694.htm (accessed 13 September 2009).

———. 2008. "Country Report on Human Rights Practices: Iran." http://www.state.gov/g/drl/rls/hrrpt/2008/nea/119115.htm (accessed 1 October 2009).

Van Velsen, Cleo, Caroline Gorst-Unsworth, and Stuart Turner. 1996. "Survivors of Torture and Organized Violence: Demography and Diagnosis." *Journal of Traumatic Stress* 9: 181–93.

Veitch, Scott. 2007. *Law and Irresponsibility: On the Legitimation of Human Suffering.* London: Routledge-Cavendish.

Virgo, Graham. 2001. "Characterisation, Choice of Law and Human Rights." In *Torture as Tort: Comparative Perspectives on the Development of Transnational Human Rights Litigation,* edited by Craig Scott, 245–52. Oxford: Hart.

Voltaire. 1764. *A Treatise on Religious Toleration. Occasioned by the Execution of the Unfortunate John Calas; Unjustly Condemned and Broken Upon the Wheel at Toulouse, for the Supposed Murder of His Own Son.* Translated by Emilius Eloisa. London: Becket and P. A. de Hondt.

Wachman, Alan M. 2001. "Does the Diplomacy of Shame Promote Human Rights in China?" *Third World Quarterly* 22: 257–81.

Waldron, Jeremy. 2005. "Torture and Positive Law: Jurisprudence for the Whitehouse." *Columbia Law Review* 105: 1681–750.

Walker, Christopher. 1978. "Strasbourg Court Clears UK of Torture." *The Times,* 19 January.

Walker, Peter, and Martin Wainwright. 2010. "Edlington Brothers Jailed for Torture of Two Boys." *Guardian,* 22 January.

Wenzel, Thomas. 2002. "Forensic Evaluation of Sequels to Torture." *Current Opinion in Psychiatry* 15: 611–15.

Williams, Andrew. 2007. "Human Rights and Law: Between Sufferance and Insufferability." *Law Quarterly Review* 123:132–57.

Williams, Bernard. 2008. *Shame and Necessity.* Berkeley: University of California Press.

Wilson, Richard A. 1996. "Representing Human Rights Violations: Social Contexts and Subjectivities." In *Human Rights, Culture and Context: Anthropological Perspectives,* edited by Richard A. Wilson, 111–33. London: Pluto.

———. 2011. *Writing History in International Criminal Trials.* New York: Cambridge University Press.

Wilson, Richard A., and Richard Brown. 2008. "Introduction." In *Humanitarianism and Suffering: The Mobilization of Empathy,* edited by Richard A. Wilson and Richard Brown, 1–30. New York: Cambridge University Press.

Wright, Richard. 1987. "Causation, Responsibility, Risk, Probability, Naked Statistics and Proof: Pruning the Bramble Bush by Clarifying the Concepts." *Iowa Law Review* 73: 1001–77.

Young, Allan. 1993. "A Description of How Ideology Shapes Knowledge of a Mental Disorder (Post Traumatic Stress Disorder)." In *Knowledge, Power and Practice: The Anthropology of Medicine and Everyday Life,* edited by Shirley Lindenbaum and Margaret Lock, 108–28. Berkeley: University of California Press.

———. 1995. *Harmony of Illusions: Inventing Posttraumatic Stress Disorder.* Princeton, N.J.: Princeton University Press.

Zaloom, Caitlin. 2009. "How to Read the Future: The Yield Curve, Affect, and Financial Prediction." *Public Culture* 21: 245–68.

Zizek, Slavoj. 2004. *Iraq: The Borrowed Kettle.* London: Verso.

Index

Acknowledgments

Words cannot possibly begin to express my gratitude to all those people whose help went into the writing of this book. The research and writing were made possible by the generous support of an ESRC Research Fellowship. Colleagues in Social Anthropology at the University of Edinburgh genially covered for me during my absence. Many people who are engaged in the important struggle against torture and other forms of ill-treatment also gave generously of their valuable time. They include Leanne MacMillan, David Rhys Jones, Norma McKinnon, Syd Bolton, Erica Robb, Simon Carruth, Alison Kelly, Keith Best, Elise Marshall, Kathleen Van De Vijver, Juliet Cohen, Ben Newton-Mold, John O'Donnell, James O'Keeffe, Sara Alesandrini, Aspals, Joe Bryce, Therese Rytter, Ronnie Graham, Stephanie David, Alexandra Pomeon O'Neil, Mervat Rishmawi, Helen Bamber, Lucy Kralj, Lesley Anne Mulholland, and Gregory McGowan. Many of the people who helped me throughout this project will have to remain anonymous, but I am grateful nevertheless. A large part of this research was made possible by the access offered by the Medical Foundation for the Care of Victims of Torture. Staff members at the Medical Foundation were exceedingly generous with their time. I feel privileged that they were willing to share their experiences with me, in the middle of their often difficult but extremely important work. The Medical Foundation in no way endorses my conclusions in this book. As this book went to press, the Medical Foundation (apart from the medicolegal service) changed its name to *Freedom from Torture*.

The writing of this book has gone through various stages. Audiences at SOAS, CNRS in Paris, LSE, Cambridge, Oxford, Philadelphia, Onati, Glasgow, Ljubljana, New Orleans, the RCT in Copenhagen, Kent, Edinburgh, the Max Planck Institute in Halle, and UCL have all provided useful feedback. The following people have all provided constructive criticism at various stages of the writing process: Tony Good, Cormac Mac Amlaigh, Mike Adler, Jane Cowan, Matthew Engelke, Basak Çali, Michelle Burgis, Stephanie Grant, Richard Wilson, Susie Sanders, Sharon Cowan, Nigel Rodley, Birgit Muller, Kathleen Van De Vijver,

Kristin Sandvik, Monique Nuijten, Andrew Jefferson, Gerhard Anders, Kamari Clarke, David Rhys Jones, Laëtitia Atlani-Duault, Joe Bryce, Leanne MacMillan, Sharika Thiranagama, Rebecca Wallace, Robert Thomas, Lori Allen, Juliet Cohen, Norma McKinnon, Alison Scott, Steffen Jensen, Nigel Eltringham, Henrik Ronsbo, Geth Rees, Peter Loizos, Richard Baxstrom, Ian Harper, Janet Carsten, Rebecca Marsland, and the Tuesday lunchtime reading group. Jonathan Spencer, Marie Dembour, and the anonymous reviewer at the University of Pennsylvania Press deserve particular thanks for reading the entire draft manuscript. Veena Das, Michael Silverstein, Elizabeth Povinelli, Darius Rejali, John Joyce, Julia Eckert, Kit Davis, Marina Kurkchiyan, Susan Coutin, Justin Richland, Sally Merry, and Sam Moyn have all engaged in conversations with me at various times, knowingly or unknowingly, that have helped me develop my own thinking. Susie Sanders provided invaluable help as the book was going to press. Needless to say, all errors and omissions are my own responsibility. At the University of Pennsylvania Press, Julia Rose Roberts and Erica Ginsburg have been forever helpful, and Peter Agree is the editor for whom every author hopes.

Above all, I must thank Faye and Matilda, for their love, support, and patience.

www.ingramcontent.com/pod-product-compliance
Lightning Source LLC
Chambersburg PA
CBHW020349270326
41926CB00007B/360